The Government
and Politics of
France

JOHN S. AMBLER
RICE UNIVERSITY

with

LAWRENCE SCHEINMAN
UNIVERSITY OF MICHIGAN

HOUGHTON MIFFLIN COMPANY · BOSTON

NEW YORK · ATLANTA · GENEVA, ILLINOIS · DALLAS · PALO ALTO

COPYRIGHT ACKNOWLEDGMENTS

To Harper & Row for excerpts from Bayeux Speech — June 16, 1946 by Charles de Gaulle, translated by Roy C. Macridis in DE GAULLE: IMPLACABLE ALLY (pp. 41, 42–3), edited by Roy C. Macridis. Copyright © 1966 by Roy C. Macridis. Reprinted by permission of Harper & Row, Publishers, Inc.

To Criterion Books and Berger-Levrault for excerpts from THE EDGE OF THE SWORD by Charles de Gaulle. English translation Copyright © by Criterion Books, Inc., and Faber and Faber, Ltd. By permission of Criterion Books and of Berger-Levrault.

PRINTED IN THE U.S.A.

Library of Congress Catalog Card Number: 71–159263
ISBN: 0–395–12532–4

TO MY PARENTS

CONTENTS

ACKNOWLEDGMENTS

In few countries is politics as dramatic, as paradoxical, as full of surprises as in France. I was first introduced to the fascinations of French politics as a Fulbright student in Bordeaux, where I shared the admiration which students at the Institut d'Etudes Politiques had for their black-gowned professors, including Maurice Duverger and Jacques Ellul. This book owes much to that Bordeaux experience, as well as to the able instruction in comparative government which I received from Professors Leslie Lipson and Eric Bellquist at the University of California. Portions of this book were written during one of several subsequent visits to France. At this time, in 1969, I was again under the auspices of the Fulbright program, shortly before that valuable program was drastically curtailed in a government economy drive.

I am indebted to my collaborator and friend, Lawrence Scheinman, who wrote the chapter on French foreign policy and whose expertise in that field far exceeds my own. Mark Kesselman read the entire manuscript and offered invaluable suggestions for improving it. He cannot be blamed for passages where limited space and the author's stubbornness precluded the acceptance of his advice. Dayton McKean also read the whole manuscript and saved me from a number of errors of fact and interpretation. Whatever clarity can be claimed for the style of exposition is to be credited largely to Mrs. Shirley Quinn, who edited the manuscript with care and intelligence. Finally, there would have been no book had my wife, Joyce, not been willing to carry groceries and to coax two small children up the six flights of stairs to our Paris apartment.

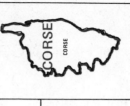

CORSE

CORSE

DEPARTMENTS AND REGIONS OF

FRANCE

——— Departmental Boundaries

▬▬▬ Regional Boundaries

Departments of the Paris Region

VAL D'OISE

SEINE-ST-DENIS

YVELINES

HAUTS-DE-SEINE

PARIS

VAL-DE-MARNE

ESSONE

CHRONOLOGY OF EVENTS

1789   Fall of the Bastille

1792   Creation of the First Republic

1793–94 Reign of Terror

1795   Directorate begins

1799   Coup d'état of 18 brumaire. Napoleon becomes First Consul

1804   Empire is proclaimed

1814   Abdication of Napoleon. Bourbon Monarchy restored

1815   Napoleon's Hundred Days

1830   Revolution fells Bourbon Monarchy. July Monarchy begins

1848   Revolution fells July Monarchy. Second Republic created

1851   Coup d'état by Louis Napoleon

1852   Second Empire proclaimed

1870   Louis Napoleon surrenders. Government of National Defense

1875   Constitutional Laws of Third Republic voted

1897–99 Dreyfus Affair

1905   Separation of Church and State

1917   Clemenceau government wields extensive wartime powers

1936   Popular Front wins parliamentary majority

1937   Popular Front government led by Léon Blum falls

1940   Pétain government signs armistice with Germany, then is voted full powers

1944   General de Gaulle returns to Paris as head of Provisional Government

1946   De Gaulle resigns

1947   Communist ministers leave the government

1954   Indochinese War ends. Algerian War begins

1957   Common Market Treaty ratified

1958   May 13: Revolt of French settlers in Algiers wins Army support

         General de Gaulle becomes Prime Minister (June), then President (December)

         September: Constitution of Fifth Republic approved by referendum

1960   French settlers' revolt in Algeria fails

1961   Army revolt in Algeria fails

1962   April: Michel Debré replaced by Georges Pompidou as Prime Minister

         July: Algeria becomes independent

         October: Constitutional amendment providing for direct popular election of President approved by referendum

         November: Gaullist majority elected in National Assembly elections

1965   General de Gaulle re-elected President

1966   Withdrawal of French forces from NATO

1967   Gaullists retain narrow majority in National Assembly elections

1968   May: Massive student demonstrations and general strike

         June: Gaullists win large majority in National Assembly elections

         July: Maurice Couve de Murville named Prime Minister

1969   April: De Gaulle's proposals for reform of Senate and regional government defeated in referendum. De Gaulle resigns

         June: Georges Pompidou elected President. Jacques Chaban-Delmas named Prime Minister

1

The French
Political Tradition

At a time when a strong Gaullist majority lends an apparent stability and order to the French political scene, the student of politics must bear in mind that since the Revolution of 1789, French constitutions have enjoyed an average longevity of only twelve years. When in May 1958, plagued with crumbling authority at home and raging rebellion in Algeria, the French National Assembly recalled that historic but near-forgotten figure, Charles de Gaulle, to power, his mandate was to draw up France's fifteenth formal constitution since 1789. It remains to be seen whether Gaullist France will achieve for the Fifth Republic that sense of political legitimacy and that constitutional consensus which have eluded Frenchmen for nearly two centuries. A brief examination of the nature and causes of France's broken political tradition will help to throw the present Gaullist search for stability into perspective.[1]

From the Revolution to the Third Republic

Alexis de Tocqueville in his classic *The Old Regime and the French Revolution* was perhaps the first to note that in centralizing French political institutions, the Revolution and the Napoleonic empire had only continued a process launched under the Old Regime. Indeed, in a figurative sense one might view French history since the reign of Clovis the Salien Frank in the sixth century as a search for national unity — first in physical and political terms and then in social terms.

[1] One of the best general histories of modern France is Gordon Wright's *France in Modern Times* (Chicago: Rand McNally, 1960). See also Alfred Cobban, *A History of Modern France,* 2 vols. (Baltimore: Penguin, 1957 and 1961).

With the exception of certain border areas in the North and the East, most of the territory of modern France has been French since the Middle Ages. Like England, and unlike Germany and Italy, France was a state before she became a nation. The spread from Paris of the French kingdom, the development of a common language, then the creation of a centralized administration (under Louis XIV in the seventeenth century) helped gradually to bind the French together with a common sense of national identity. Whatever their quarrels may be, Frenchmen agree today, as they have for centuries, that they are French. As a cursory glance at the problems of emerging nations in the twentieth century will show, such an old and abiding sense of nationhood is of no mean importance.

In the eighteenth century, though France's territorial unity had long since been assured, her social and political unity was gravely threatened from several quarters. With the death in 1715 of Louis XIV, the Sun King, there ascended to the throne an infant, Louis XV, who even in maturity had few of his great-grandfather's many talents. His successor, Louis XVI, was equally incompetent to restore the authority of a monarchy whose moral base of divine right was rapidly being eroded by the pungent critiques of such Enlightenment philosophers as Voltaire and Rousseau. More importantly, the leaders of the effete noble aristocracy, which had been shorn by Louis XIV of most of their economic and political power but not of their tax exemptions and feudal privileges, chose this moment of monarchical weakness to demand that the army officer corps and the upper ranks of government service purge all representatives of the rising middle class. This action added to the growing resentment of the middle class over the barriers which limited its access to social status and political power.

When the Estates General was called together in 1789 for the first time since 1614, largely at the behest of the clergy and the nobility who hoped to impose new restraints on the king, the Third Estate (the commoners) seized the opportunity to demand abolition of all feudal privileges. Temporary economic depression fired the revolutionary fervor of those numerous Parisian shopkeepers, craftsmen, and journeymen who composed the mob which drew the Revolution further and further to the Left. The king was sent to the guillotine in 1793, to be followed by wave after wave of new-found traitors, until a frightened bourgeoisie finally managed to tame the mobs and turn the country from mobocracy to dictatorship under the Directorate.

To the world the Revolution portrayed itself as the bearer of such lofty ideals as liberty, equality, and fraternity. A deeper look, however, would reveal it as an aggressive and near-totalitarian nationalist movement, bent upon destroying both internal and external enemies in a gigantic crusade — in Rousseau's words — to "force man to be free." Here, in the wars waged by the Revolution against foreign powers eager to crush it, are to be seen the origins of that frightful phenomenon of modern times — total war.

To be sure, French revolutionaries could not be expected to behave like their American predecessors, whose primary intention had been to preserve an already democratic society. In France, where men were not "born free," as Alexis de Tocqueville said of Americans, and where the Revolution had many enemies from within, the task of radical reconstruction seemed to require a powerful central government, willing at times to sacrifice freedom in the interests of equality.[2]

The ambiguity of the message of the Revolution allowed one of its heroic generals, Napoleon Bonaparte, to return from battle, swallow up his civilian masters, and proclaim himself a loyal bearer of the revolutionary tradition. Indeed, though he left pitifully little power to legislative bodies, and though he declared himself emperor, did he not consult the popular will through plebiscites? Did his armies not carry the message of equality to foreign lands? Did he not open government careers to merit, at least until his flirtation with nobility in his last years as emperor? Clearly the nationalist fervor of his regime, its insistence on national unity, and the mystic and plebiscitary oneness with the masses which Napoleon claimed — all of these find roots in the Revolution. Napoleon himself might well have seen no irony in those gold pieces coined from 1804 to 1808 which bear on one face the inscription "Napoléon Empereur" and on the reverse "République Française." Despite its commitment to freedom and equality, the Revolution had laid down no clear and agreed-upon political institutions around which all might rally; even a Napoleon could claim to be its standard bearer and turn the doctrine of popular sovereignty to the service of a new kind of dictatorship.

Though the Napoleonic empire was short-lived, the thoroughgoing legal and administrative reforms enacted by the Corsican — the Napoleonic Code, the centralized prefecture system, the Council of State — survived him to become permanent features of the French state, whether organized as monarchy, empire, or republic. When Louis XVIII was maneuvered onto the throne in 1814 with the assent of France's conquerors, it was not a question of turning the clock back to 1789. Rather, it was announced that although the king was to exercise all executive power, his legislative proposals would become law only with the approval of the Chamber of Peers and the Chamber of Deputies,

[2] On the contrasting styles of revolution, see Samuel Huntington, *Political Order in Changing Societies* (New Haven: Yale University Press, 1968), Ch. 2.

the Peers being hereditary and the Deputies elected by a restricted corps of wealthy taxpayers. Such gifts of the Revolution as abolition of feudal privileges, equality before the law, and religious freedom were to be preserved in a *constitutional* monarchy.

For those aristocratic *émigrés* who swarmed back into France from exile, having "learned nothing and forgotten nothing," as Talleyrand described them, any compromise with the Revolution was unthinkable. Through their demands for compensation for confiscated property, for high posts in government and the army, and for the delegation of wide powers and privileges to the church (now viewed as a bulwark of social conservatism), the old nobility contributed mightily to the discrediting and demise of the Restoration. The rigid and incompetent Charles X, who succeeded to the throne in 1824, failed to recognize the dangers inherent in his unpopularity until street revolts in Paris in 1830 forced his abdication and ushered in the "Bourgeois Monarchy" under the crown of Louis Philippe, the Duke of Orleans.

Louis Philippe adopted the tricolor flag of the Revolution, extended the electorate slightly, replaced the hereditary upper chamber with an appointed one, and gave the bourgeoisie a definitive victory over the old nobility. As a usurper placed on the throne by a small group of kingmakers, this bourgeois king was able to claim neither the sanctifying support of tradition and lineage, nor the democratic legitimacy of popular election. Government by the wealthy proved no more stable than government by the bluebloods. The depression of 1846–1847 and Louis Philippe's refusal to part with an unpopular ministry led to the Parisian riots of February 1848 which quickly toppled the wobbly monarchy.

With restoration of the Bourbons quite out of the question, the leaders of the opposition to Louis Philippe created a republic. In a brief period of hope and social harmony, a symbolic worker was taken into the provisional government; a national workshop scheme was launched to absorb the numerous unemployed; and election by universal suffrage was announced. But harmony soon gave way to a new and bitter class hatred, and the elections of April 1848 produced a conservative majority in the National Assembly and a government which voted to abandon the expensive and inefficient national workshop. The Parisian working class, by then of far greater size and strength than in 1789 and determined not to be cheated out of the fruits of yet another revolution, swarmed into the streets, built the traditional street barricades of revolution, then died by the thousands as army regulars moved in on them with artillery. Out of these tragic June days emerged on the one hand a permanently alienated urban working class and on the other a bourgeoisie even more nervous about democracy and more willing to embrace Mother Church as a buttress to social stability.

In the presidential election of December 1848, Louis Napoleon, Napoleon's nephew, was elected by a landslide, and in the legislative elections of the spring of 1849, the monarchists won a clear majority. This was a republic almost without republicans, and France's only experiment with a presidential system before 1958 proved short-lived. President Louis Napoleon clashed repeatedly with the National Assembly, principally over his right to run for re-election. Less than four years after its creation, the Second Republic died in the coup of December 1851, prepared by Louis Napoleon himself, who soon thereafter emerged as emperor of France.

Legitimists, Orleanists, and republicans in turn had failed to provide France with a stable institutional framework for political life. The majority of Frenchmen — peasantry and middle class alike — clearly was not displeased when Louis Napoleon produced the Second Empire as a solution to the long quest for political order and stability. In the name of order, the press was tightly censored and political opponents arrested and exiled by the thousands. The plebiscite was re-instituted to support the emperor's claim to popular support. The Legislative Body, chosen by universal male suffrage in elections tightly controlled by government officials, was composed principally of official government candidates, who obediently accepted the minor role assigned to them.

In the decade of the "Liberal Empire" from 1860 to 1870, with the church disgruntled over Napoleon's encouragement to Italian nationalists and industrialists discontented with his low tariff policy, the empire moved toward parliamentary government of the type which had been evolving from 1815 to 1851. Napoleon decreed that beginning in 1870, the Legislative Body was to be empowered to overthrow any cabinet which did not have its support. The parliamentary empire was stillborn, however, for the sudden French defeat in the Franco-Prussian War of 1870 produced an equally sudden collapse of France's last flirtation with the Bonapartes — a regime built upon a legend of military glory could hardly survive such a humiliating military defeat.

The Third Republic

The elections of 1871, the first after the collapse of the Second Empire, produced a parliament dominated by monarchists. It seemed clear that genuine republicans were still in the minority in France, as, in all probability, they always had been outside Paris. However, by 1876 republicans had gained a majority in the Chamber of Deputies and by 1879 had captured the Senate, indicating that a majority of the town councils of France, which made up most of the electoral college which elected the Senate, had now been converted. In the 1870's,

France at last turned republican. The reasons for that conversion are revealing.

With a solid majority of monarchists in control of the first postwar parliament, France would have crowned a new king had it not been for the rivalry of three pretenders, two Orleanist and one Bourbon. As Adolphe Thiers, the first President of the Republic put it, there was not room on the throne for three backsides. Compromise proved impossible when the Bourbon candidate, the Count of Chambord, refused to reign under the tricolor flag, insisting instead upon the white flag of his ancestors.

The Republic gradually emerged as the only possible compromise solution, "the regime which divides us least." Aware, as Thiers said, that "the republic will be conservative or it won't be at all," republican leaders succeeded in squelching the Jacobins (radicals) among them and calming those conservative peasants and bourgeois who feared that republicanism meant social revolution. Thiers could point out that he himself had helped to establish the Third Republic by putting down the uprising of the Paris Commune in 1871, at a cost of some 20,000 dead and thousands more imprisoned.

In fact, the Third Republic proved anything but revolutionary, once such political reforms as universal suffrage, freedom of speech, and separation of church and state had been assured. The spirit of the Third Republic is best exemplified by the Radical Party, which played a dominant role in French politics for most of the years from 1899 to 1940. Like the small-town merchants and artisans who were so numerous in its electoral clientele, the Radical Party espoused an individualistic creed which denounced concentrated power in any form — be it in the church, in big business, or in the state. "Resistance to authority rather than practical reform is their watchword," said Alain, the foremost philosopher of radicalism.

Aware that their lower middle-class supporters, like most Frenchmen, "wore their hearts on the Left and their pocketbooks on the Right," the Radicals tended to talk like revolutionaries, but to act in social and economic policy matters like conservatives. Many a coalition government under the Third Republic fell because the Radicals sided with the Socialists on the church-state issue and in defense of "revolutionary principles," only to desert to the Right when welfare state measures were proposed. So long as the urban working class remained too weak to threaten the social order, so long as a fundamentally conservative society feared change more than stagnation, the Radical philosophy of the noninterventionist state thrived.

The piecemeal, compromise constitution of the Third Republic, dating from 1875, admirably suited the Radical ideal of a strong legislature and weak executive. The constitution provided for a bicameral legislature composed of the Chamber of Deputies elected directly by universal suffrage, and the Senate, elected indirectly by an electoral college in which rural areas were overrepresented. It also provided for a president, elected by both houses of the legislature and armed with the power of dissolution; in practice, the first presidential attempt to dissolve the Chamber of Deputies — by President (and Marshal) Mac-Mahon in 1877 — was so unpopular and resulted in the election of an Assembly so contrary to the President's hopes, that the power of dissolution quickly atrophied and was never used again. As the President of France came to resemble the King of England more than the President of the United States, executive leadership was left to a series of coalition cabinets with a life expectancy of little over six months.

The primary reason for this rapid rise and fall of cabinets was the shifting, multiparty system found in the popularly elected Chamber of Deputies, where stable majorities capable of supporting stable governments were not easily concocted. In the wide political spectrum from monarchists on the Right to Socialists (then Communists after 1920) on the Left, some eight to ten parties were usually represented, with no single party ever commanding an absolute majority. To complicate matters further, apart from the Communists and Socialists, most parties were too faction-ridden to guarantee solid support for any cabinet. Party discipline often broke down when the career advantages of the deputy or the vested interests of his constituents were at stake. The contrasting examples of Switzerland and the Scandinavian countries show that multi-party systems do not always produce unstable governments. Coupled with the individualism, the bitter political rivalries, and the uncompromising outlook of the French political world, however, French multipartyism produced instability in government personnel and immobility in government policy. The National Assembly was admirably well equipped — and often disposed — to overthrow governments, but quite unsuited to solving policy problems. In the frequent policy vacuums, the civil service could act, but not so vigorously as to effect major reforms. As the saying went, "France was not governed, but administered." One can imagine the problems of a new and inexpert minister attempting to establish his authority when both he and his subordinates knew from the beginning that his days were already numbered.

However ineffectively the French political machine seemed to function at times, it seemed at last that a minimal political consensus had been achieved around "Marianne," the Third Republic. Depression and political scandal in the 1930's, and, finally, World War II, revealed the shallowness of that consensus. Economic crisis heightened class hatreds and generally undermined French confidence in parliamentary institutions which seemed more deadlocked and immobile than ever. A growing Communist Party, in the service of the Communist International, and a swelling horde of antirepublican leagues — most authoritarian and a few genuinely fascist — fought each other with such violence that the famous French "nation of patriots" seemed in full disintegration. The Radicals, Socialists, and Communists joined forces temporarily in 1936 to elect a popular front majority, but succeeded primarily in demonstrating their lack of agreement regarding economic policies with which to fight the depression. Radical politicians shivered with those good bourgeois of the Right when the Communist Party displayed the flag of the future Soviet France, complete with hammer and sickle, at a victory celebration and when Communist Party leader Maurice Thorez later explained that workers had taken good care of the plants during sit-in strikes because they knew that "the factories would soon be the property of the workers, anyway."[3] Such radical polarization of political beliefs quite naturally threatened a republic which had always depended for its survival upon the support of moderate and practical men of the Center, whatever their party labels.

When France finally succumbed before the onslaught of Hitler's panzer divisions in June 1940, after a bewildering six-week blitzkrieg, the defeat was first of all a *military* defeat, attributable to the defense-minded strategy of a French army which was by habit always a war behind in its thinking. German stuka bombers and tank formations were aided mightily, however, by France's loss of solidarity and resiliency. With French Communists openly obstructing the war effort after Hitler and Stalin became temporary allies in the Molotov-Ribbentrop Pact of 1939, and with numerous French authoritarians secretly attracted to the thought that Hitler would smash both the Communists and the Republic, another "sacred union" between parties of the Left and of the Right, such as emerged in 1914, was out of the question.

Bewildered and disillusioned with parliamentary government, French politicians and citizens alike turned eagerly to Marshal Philippe Pétain, the "victor of Verdun" in World War I and who in World War II had supported the commander in chief, Maxime Weygand, in his refusal to carry on a war which both felt was already lost. Approaching senility at age eighty-four, he was vested with full powers on July 10, 1940, by a National Assembly vote of 569 to 80. Pétain was determined to protect French interests as well as possible and to restore such traditional, prerevolutionary values as social hierarchy, religion,

---

[3] Alexander Werth, *The Twilight of France, 1933–1940* (New York: Howard Fertig, 1966 [original: 1942]), pp. 99–100.

and paternalism. "The French school of tomorrow will teach respect not only for the human person, but also for family, society, country," wrote Pétain in the summer of 1940. "It will no longer make any claims of neutrality. Life is not neutral: it consists of vigorously taking sides. There is no neutrality possible between the true and the false, between good and evil, between health and sickness, between order and disorder, between France and anti-France."[4] With that intolerance for ambiguity so typical of the authoritarian personality, Pétain called a halt to liberalism and parliamentarianism and announced the replacement of "Liberty, Equality, Fraternity," the motto of the Revolution, with "Work, Family, Country."

Pétain's regime, which made its headquarters in the resort town of Vichy in central France, clearly belonged to the old, authoritarian, and fundamentally antirepublican strain ever present in the French political tradition. It was by no means fascist, if one takes fascism to be a type of totalitarianism. Pétain's intent was to establish order and stability under the church and the traditional elites, not to throw up a new elite class in command of a mass party, nor to stir up the frenzy of fascism's permanent revolution. Those few genuine French fascists who initially came to Vichy were quickly disillusioned and took refuge in Paris, in the German-occupied section of France.

But Vichy failed to remedy many of the ills of the Republic. Within the court of the aging Pétain there developed the same pattern of factionalism, intrigue, and rapid turnover of personnel which had plagued the Third Republic.[5] Outside Vichy, the country was torn, in what at times approached civil war, between those who remained loyal to the Marshal, and those — ever more numerous — who looked to Charles de Gaulle for national salvation. After November 1942, when the Allies invaded North Africa and the Germans occupied all of France, Vichy lost most of the limited independence which it had enjoyed up to that point.

Had General Weygand been correct in June 1940 when he predicted that England's neck would be wrung within six weeks, his decision and that of Pétain would have appeared much more noble in the perspective of history. In fact, that brash young brigadier general, Charles de Gaulle, was the better prophet (as he had been once before — in promoting tank warfare in the 1930's) when he fled to London to organize continued resistance. Allied with the British, he was forced

[4] From a message to the nation entitled "L'Education National," published in *Revue des deux mondes*, August 15, 1940, pp. 249–253. The quotation is found on p. 250.

[5] Alfred Cobban, "France," in Arnold and Veronica Toynbee, eds., *Hitler's Europe* (London: Oxford University Press, 1954), pp. 341–344.

to send his small Free French army into fratricidal battles against Vichy troops in Senegal and Syria before the defection of the French army in North Africa finally gave him an army which commanded respect. His political skills, coupled with the talents of his collaborators, gradually gave de Gaulle control not only over French Africa, but also over the internal French resistance, in which the Communist Party played a key role. Despite Franklin Roosevelt's fears of de Gaulle's dictatorial pretensions, there was no doubt who would be head of liberated France after the Germans were driven from Paris in August, 1944. The more serious question was whether or not the unity of *La France Résistante* would prove lasting.

The Fourth Republic

In a referendum held in October 1945, the French voters by an overwhelming majority of 18,600,000 to 700,000 decided to leave the Third Republic in its grave. In a climate of hope born of the Resistance, the National Assembly, dominated by a coalition of the big three, the Communists, the Socialists, and the new Christian Democratic Party entitled the Popular Republican Movement (MRP), set about drafting a constitution for the Fourth Republic. With the anti-republican Right discredited and almost destroyed by the Vichy experiment, it seemed as if effective democratic government might at last be possible.[6]

The mood of optimism was short-lived. De Gaulle resigned as Prime Minister in early 1946 after clashing repeatedly with the parties. The Popular Republicans then quarrelled bitterly with their coalition partners over a draft constitution proposed by the Communists, which granted the Assembly almost unlimited powers. When the MRP lost that battle in the Assembly, it carried the day before the electorate, which rejected a proposed constitution for the first time in French history. A second draft was satisfactory to the MRP but drew vigorous fire from de Gaulle, who felt that a stronger executive was essential. It was adopted in October 1946 by a narrow margin of 9 million votes to 8 million — a third of the disillusioned electorate stayed home.

The new constitution, launched so inauspiciously, was not strikingly

---

[6] The best overall description and analysis of politics in the Fourth Republic is Philip Williams' *Crisis and Compromise: Politics in the Fourth Republic* (New York: Doubleday Anchor, 1966). See also Duncan MacRae, *Parliament, Parties and Society in France, 1946–1958* (New York: St. Martin's Press, 1967); Jacques Fauvet, *La IVe République* (Paris: Fayard, 1959); and Georgette Elgey, *La République des Illusions, 1945–1951* and *La République des Contradictions, 1951–1954* (Paris: Fayard, 1965 and 1968).

different from its predecessor. The first draft, written largely by the Communists and the Socialists, would have abolished the Senate on the grounds that it had acted during the Third Republic as a conservative and undemocratic check upon the power of the lower house. The Senate was restored in the final version, and again its members were elected indirectly, for six-year terms, by an electoral college composed primarily of representatives of municipal and departmental councils. Recalling the Senate's frequent obstruction of reform measures under the Third Republic, however, the drafters deprived it of the right of legislative initiative and empowered the lower house to override Senate amendments. The lower house was purposefully renamed the National Assembly, a term previously used to designate the entire two-house parliament.

In accordance with the wishes of the three dominant parties, the National Assembly was to be elected from multi-member districts, averaging five deputies per district. Election was by proportional representation, with voters casting their ballots for a party list of candidates. From 1945 to 1947 the Assembly was often little more than the place for registering decisions already taken by the Communists, Socialists, and Popular Republicans. Gradually, however, after the Communist Party went into permanent opposition in May 1947, and as party control among Popular Republicans began to weaken, the familiar pattern of shifting coalition politics reappeared.

None of the constitutional devices introduced to guarantee governmental stability was of much use, as the absence of stable parliamentary majorities and the tendency of deputies to revert to old habits produced a turnover in cabinets averaging a new one every six months. The prime minister (as opposed to the president under the Third Republic) had the power to dissolve the Assembly when his cabinet was the second to be overthrown by absolute majority vote within eighteen months. In practice, prime ministers were hesitant to antagonize the Assembly and thereby jeopardize their chances of being accepted for leadership on a future occasion; hence the power of dissolution was used only once. On that occasion, in December 1955, the ensuing election produced an Assembly so hampered by Communists on the Left and Poujadists (composed primarily of disgruntled small businessmen) on the Right, that it was almost incapable of governing. Other constitutional innovations, such as the investiture of the prime minister alone, leaving him free to form his own cabinet, and the delay of twenty-four hours between the posing of a vote of confidence and the vote upon it, had little importance in practice. A politician eager to become prime minister found it advantageous to promise the parties their share of ministries before the vote of investiture, no matter what the constitution said, and a prime minister fearful of displeasing a jealous Assembly, asked for "informal" rather than formal votes of confidence.

To the credit of the oft-maligned Fourth Republic, it must be said that it prevented a powerful French Communist Party from taking over in the troubled postwar years; it did not prevent (if it did not produce) a period of unprecedented prosperity beginning in the early 1950's; it dared take France into the European Common Market through the Treaty of Rome of 1957; and it supported the vigorous Prime Minister Pierre Mendès-France long enough in 1954–1955 to end the Indochinese war and set Tunisia and Morocco on the road to independence. On the negative side of the balance sheet, one must note that again, as in the Third Republic which was so overwhelmingly rejected by the voters in 1945, political legitimacy, stability, and effectiveness seemed beyond reach. Throughout the Fourth Republic, the Communist Party, with the support of over a quarter of the French electorate, worked for the destruction of parliamentary democracy. On the Right, the Gaullist Rally of the French People (RPF), until it split in 1953, worked long and hard to prove the unworkability of the 1946 constitution. When Gaullist obstructionists were reduced in number in the National Assembly from 120 elected in 1951 to 22 chosen in the election of 1956, they were replaced by a belligerent team of Poujadists, who were equally hostile to *"le système."* Defense of the Fourth Republic was left to the Socialists, the Popular Republicans, and to an increasing number of Radicals and Independents. Within this potential "Third Force," deep disagreement over economic policy, over the church-school issue, and over colonial policy made stable majorities virtually impossible to organize.

In no area of public policy was the resulting immobility of the Fourth Republic more dangerous than in that of colonial affairs. The Algerian war, like the Indochinese war before it, was allowed to grow and to continue without much attention to French goals in the area. The French army, resentful of politicians who often condemned it or treated it as a corps of mercenaries and scornful of a government which seemed unable to govern, filled the policy vacuum in Algeria with a policy of its own.[7] When the National Assembly considered investing as prime minister Pierre Pflimlin, a man whose loyalty to French Algeria was in doubt, the army came to the support of a revolt launched by European settlers in Algiers on May 13, 1958, and demanded the formation of a "Government of Public Safety" in Paris.

---

[7] The causes of French military intervention in politics are explored in J. S. Ambler, *Soldiers Against the State* (New York: Doubleday Anchor, 1968).

The government, unable to control either the army or the police and aware of public apathy over the plight of an unloved Republic, finally accepted General de Gaulle as the only possible savior-assassin of the regime. On June 1, 1958, by a vote of 329 to 224, the Assembly accepted Charles de Gaulle as prime minister. The following day it empowered him to supervise the drafting of a new constitution. Again, as in July 1940, the Republic's doubtful legitimacy and authority proved fatal in time of crisis.

The Origins of French Political Instability

For nearly two centuries, political power in France has shifted back and forth between the two poles of legislative supremacy and executive dominance. Though the regicides of 1793 determined that the Assembly should rule in republican France, they and succeeding French legislators frequently have been too quarrelsome, too deeply divided among themselves to provide effective government. When governmental stalemate eroded the prestige of the Assembly and allowed problems to grow into crises, there was usually a Man on Horseback waiting in the wings, eager to take power. In 1795, in 1851, in 1940, and in 1958, impotent assembly government gave way to strong executive leadership as growing numbers of discontented citizens complained that France could no longer see herself in the broken mirror of her Assembly. But authoritarian government dominated by a strong executive has proved no more stable than assembly government once the crisis is past. Since vigorous governmental action usually creates grievances among some portion of the population, there are always those who are ready to join any movement to "restore the Republic."

The quarrel over constitutional questions has been a real and important one in modern France. The French have been unable to achieve a lasting constitutional settlement whereby the executive is allowed to lead and to act, but within controls set by the legislature. For most of her modern history, France has been a nation without a political consensus, and the constitutional quarrel has been symptomatic of more fundamental schisms within French society.

Certain causes of political instability in France — the individualism of her citizenry, their *incivisme,* and their ambivalence toward authority, for example — will be reserved for discussion in a later chapter. The lack of French political consensus, however, is the result of particular features of France's modern history and hence deserves attention here. Those who dismiss the French as a people by nature incapable of stable government had best look more carefully at the seventeenth century, when France remained a model of political order, while across the Channel the British were fighting a civil war, executing one king and deposing another, and even for a time enduring a military dictatorship.

When the commercial, then the industrial revolutions put an end to the relative stability of medieval society, European governments had either to adjust to newly emerging social forces or ultimately to be destroyed by them. Despite a period of political troubles in the seventeenth century, the British managed to extend the base of political power from the feudal nobility to the new middle class and finally to the entire citizenry — all without destroying such institutions as the monarchy, Parliament, and the common law. Why were the French less fortunate? Why did the middle class resort to violent revolution, and why did the Revolution settle nothing?

The beginnings of an answer are to be found in Alexis de Tocqueville's analysis of class relations in pre-Revolutionary France. While in England the nobility provided leadership in public affairs, their French counterparts were reduced by Louis XIV (who viewed them as rivals to royal power) to a class of privileged parasites, with neither social utility nor a sense of social responsibility. The implicit bargain imposed by Louis XIV was one which gave the king and his chosen ministers a preponderance of political power and the nobility a guaranty of its privileged status. Clearly this was a bargain which precluded major reforms in the social order. Paying little or no taxes, doing virtually no useful work, status conscious to the extreme, and intent upon exploiting to the full their feudal rights over peasants, the French nobility aroused deepening hatred among commoners. The growing middle class was particularly embittered when the small flow of bourgeois into high positions of state and into the titled nobility was halted in the half century before the Revolution.[8] It is not surprising, therefore, that when the Old Regime opened its gates a hair to let in moderate reformers, the mobs came charging in, trampling into the dust monarchy, nobility, and church.

Once the fortress had been taken and the spell of tradition broken, the revolutionaries soon found themselves too badly divided to create a stable new order. Was the Revolution complete when legal and political equality had been achieved, as the bourgeoisie contended, or did its fulfillment require equality of property as well, as leaders of the growing (and alienated) working class began to argue, particularly after 1848? Did the Revolution mean strong government (as the Jacobins contended) or weak government (as the Radical Party later pre-

---

[8] On the impact of the eighteenth century feudal reaction on the middle class, see Elinor G. Barber, *The Bourgeoisie in 18th Century France* (Princeton: Princeton University Press, 1955).

ferred)? Was the highest of revolutionary ideals to be liberty, or was equality so crucial as to be sought at any price?[9]

In contrast to the Russian Revolution of 1917, where a tightly disciplined Communist Party structured the new order, the French Revolution had no cohesive leadership party capable of defining and organizing the Republic. Moreover, there were no firmly rooted representative institutions comparable to the British Parliament around which to build the Republic. It is not surprising that the Revolution's self-declared heirs in the twentieth century — Radicals, Socialists, and Communists among them — interpret the Revolution in very different terms.

At the opposite end of the French political spectrum, aristocrats, traditionalists, and clericalists emerged from the revolution too insecure, too embittered to provide the humane and flexible leadership necessary to national reconciliation. French conservatives have been called, not without cause, "the stupidest Right in the world." Charles X is said to have declared: "I would prefer to saw wood rather than reign in the manner of the English King." He succeeded in destroying a monarchy which might conceivably have become a valuable symbol of national unity, as in Britain. Others on the Right (which was itself divided) behaved with equal rigidity, whether in defense of property against working-class demands, in support of a powerful and conservative church, or in periodic conflict with the Republic. Once the Revolution had shaken French society, Frenchmen of different social classes, or of different religious or political beliefs, emerged too fearful and embittered ever again fully to trust each other. Clearly one of the legacies of the Revolution was pervasive *mistrust* — between nobility and bourgeoisie, between bourgeoisie and workers, between clericals and anticlericals, and between republicans and antirepublicans.

In this climate of mistrust, the major political issues of the day lay unresolved, piling one on top of the other until stalemate became an accepted state of affairs. As Philip Williams puts it,

> . . . In France, three issues were fought out simultaneously: the eighteenth century conflict between rationalism and Catholicism, the nineteenth century struggle of democracy against authoritarian government, and the twentieth century dispute between employer and employed.[10]

[9] The contradictory "strands" of the Revolution are explored in David Thomson's excellent *Democracy in France since 1870,* 4th ed.; (New York: Oxford University Press, 1964).

[10] Williams, *Crisis and Compromise,* p. 3. The same problem of "issue pile-up," viewed as a major source of instability in Europe, is explored in Seymour Martin Lipset, *Political Man* (New York: Doubleday Anchor, 1963), Ch. 3.

While in Britain the church-state issue had been largely retired from politics by the end of the eighteenth century, before the industrial revolution reached full force, and democracy had been generally confirmed by the end of the nineteenth century, in France these issues lived on and mixed with the new tensions of an industrializing society to excite and to divide the citizenry. On the Left, a revolutionary political tradition and an anticlerical religious outlook tended to deepen the alienation of the working class. On the Right, the higher bourgeoisie tended to acclaim the church, scorn the Republic, and cling desperately to their vested interests. Religion, politics, and class did not always divide Frenchmen along the same lines, however. Peasants tended to be anticlerical and Leftist in the South, but Catholic and conservative in Brittany and in Vendée. The middle class harbored traditional conservatives, Bonapartists, and center republicans. Even when they overlapped, the multiple political, religious, and economic cleavages in French society tended to complicate rather than moderate the search for consensus and legitimacy.

Not all of the causes of French political instability are to be found in her history and society. Three French regimes have fallen in European wars since the Revolution. France's vulnerable geographic position, in contrast to Great Britain's, tends to involve her in continental wars such as those which felled Napoleon Bonaparte in 1814, Louis Napoleon in 1870, and the Third Republic in 1940.

Lest the picture of instability drawn above be exaggerated, two qualifications are in order. First, beneath the froth of changing regimes was a relatively stable bureaucracy and an equally stable middle class. From 1830 until the 1930's, when communism, naziism, and depression combined to shatter whatever meager measure of consensus Frenchmen had achieved, the struggle for political power tended to be fought out by factions of the growing middle class, most of which eventually accepted the Republic as the form of government least dangerous to their interests.

A second type of French political consensus is to be found in those periods when France turned outward, united by a nationalist spirit which reached above social, political, and religious cleavages. Napoleon Bonaparte temporarily achieved such national unity, as did republican leaders in the 1870's after the Franco-Prussian War and again in 1914, and as Charles de Gaulle did in recent years.

Max Weber, the German sociologist, described three basic means by which governments legitimize their authority: tradition, legality, and personal charisma. None of the three provided a firm base for French governments after the Revolution of 1789. Various segments of French society developed loyalties to quite different strains in the

French political tradition. A government which claimed to be the heir of the Revolution, for example, was sure to alienate those who regarded the Bourbon monarchy as the traditional and rightful form of government for France. Similarly, strict adherence to legal procedures — as in election to office — legitimized government leaders only with that portion of French society which believed the enabling document, the constitution itself, to be proper and good. Lastly, a rare individual leader like Napoleon, with magnetic, charismatic powers, might establish the legitimacy of his own personal regime but fail to transfer his authority to institutions capable of surviving him.

Charles de Gaulle took power in a crisis which again demonstrated the failure of the Republic to win strong popular support. His effort to transfer his personal, charismatic authority to the Fifth Republic is but the most recent episode in France's long quest for political legitimacy.

2

Society and Politics

In nineteenth century France political regimes came and went like waves on the surface of a slowly changing but fundamentally stable society. In direct contrast, postwar politics under the Fourth Republic clung tenaciously to the familiar prewar pattern of stalemate at a time when the French economy and society were undergoing rapid change. In both periods, however, the social and economic structure of French society set certain limits to the exercise of political power, while political leaders and institutions contributed, in some degree, to the nature of social change. To understand the problems of political transition in contemporary France, one must understand something of the nature of the "New France" as it has emerged since 1945.[1]

The Economy

In some respects the postwar French "economic miracle" has been more remarkable than the widely admired German counterpart. Unlike the Germans, who had built a highly industrialized economy prior to the war, the French had not participated fully in the European industrial revolution. French economic growth in the nineteenth and early twentieth centuries had been slow and erratic, especially in comparison with that of Great Britain. In adopting the steam engine, in modern-

[1] For a description of social change in contemporary France, see Georges Dupeux, *La Société Française, 1789–1960* (Paris: A. Colin, 1964), Collection U; Stanley Hoffmann *et al., In Search of France* (Cambridge, Mass.: Harvard University Press, 1963); Société Française de Sociologie, ed., *Tendances et Volontés de la Société Française* (Paris: SEDEIS, 1966); John Ardagh, *The New French Revolution* (New York: Harper & Row, 1969); and Edward R. Tannenbaum, *The New France* (Chicago: University of Chicago Press, 1961).

izing their textile industry, in developing their steel industry, and in most other fields the French lagged behind the British.[2]

Although France gradually experienced most of the fruits as well as the social strains of industrialization, in comparison with Britain, Holland, Belgium, and Germany, she still seemed in 1939 to be essentially a country of farmers, of small towns, of innumerable small and relatively inefficient family firms. As late as 1946 only one third of the French population lived in cities of more than 10,000, as compared with 70 per cent in Great Britain and 47 percent in Germany. In that same year, some 35 percent of all employed Frenchmen were farmers, as opposed to approximately 15 percent in the United States and 5 percent in Great Britain.

Numerous writers have remarked the cautious, fearful outlook of French businessmen prior to the war, as well as the pessimism of French industrial workers regarding prospects for self-improvement within the existing structure of society. The sluggishness of French economic growth (to which entrepreneurial conservatism may have contributed) tended to reinforce the businessman's reluctance to share profits with employees while persuading a goodly portion of the working class that their aspirations could be fulfilled only by forcibly redistributing a fixed national income. In a society like that of prewar France, where the economic pie appeared fixed in size, the notion of equality tended to take on the revolutionary meaning of "levelling down," whereas across the Atlantic, in a society of affluence, American workers and employers alike usually assumed that economic growth would allow more for all.[3]

Emerging from the second world war, the French proceeded to disprove the legend that they are by nature condemned to economic inefficiency.[4] Spurred on by American aid, by enthusiastic government planners, and by a national consensus on the need for economic expansion, the French economy regained its prewar level by 1949, then surged on through the 1950's and into the 1960's at an unprecedented annual growth rate of 5 percent of the Gross National Product (GNP). By 1963 France's per capita GNP of $1,760 had surpassed that of both

[2] Two good studies of French economic growth are John Clapham, *The Economic Development of France and Germany, 1815–1914,* 4th ed. (Cambridge: Cambridge University Press, 1936); and Charles Kindleberger, *Economic Growth in France and Britain 1815–1950* (Cambridge, Mass.: Harvard University Press, 1964).

[3] This contrast is explored in David Potter, *People of Plenty* (Chicago: University of Chicago Press, 1954).

[4] On the postwar boom, see Charles Kindleberger, "The Postwar Resurgence of the French Economy," in Hoffmann *et al., In Search of France.*

Britain ($1,600) and West Germany ($1,640), as shown in Table 2.1, and more people owned automobiles in France (7,950,000) than in either Britain (7,300,000) or Germany (7,560,000), despite the larger populations of these latter two countries.[5] In the next five years (1963–1968), the French economy continued to grow faster than most other European economies. From 1954 to 1965 farmers poured into the cities at a rate of over 130,000 per year, driven from the land by mechanization or lured by well paying jobs in expanding industries. From 1946 to 1965, the proportion of farmers among employed

Table 2.1

Gross National Product (GNP) — Total and Per Capita

	GNP at 1963 Prices and Exchange Rates (in billions of dollars)		Percent Change in GNP		GNP Per Capita at Current Prices and Exchange Rates	
	1958	*1968*	*1958– 1963*	*1963– 1968*	*1963*	*1968*
Italy	36.58	63.92	6.6	4.9	$ 980	$1,390
United Kingdom	72.56	99.53	3.5	2.9	1,600	1,850
Germany	67.50	117.06	5.7	4.3	1,640	2,200
France	62.31	108.11	5.6	5.2	1,760	2,530
Sweden	13.29	20.59	4.8	4.2	2,210	3,230
United States	488.60	770.90	4.2	5.2	3,170	4,380

Source: Organization for Economic Cooperation and Development (OECD), *Main Economic Indicators,* June/July 1970, p. 138.

Frenchmen dropped from 35 percent to under 18 percent. By 1957, technological advances in French industry had strengthened France's competitive position to a point where her businessmen could accept, indeed often welcome, the eventual elimination of all tariffs between France and her new Common Market partners: Italy, Germany, and the Benelux countries.

In the cities in particular, automobiles, washing machines, refrigerators, ready-to-wear clothing, installment buying, even supermarkets,

[5] République Française, Institut National de la Statistique et des Etudes Economiques (INSEE), *Annuaire Statistique 1964* (Paris: PUF, 1965), p. 33.

have begun to transform the traditional French style of life. In general, residents of the more industrial areas of France — the Paris region, the North, Alsace-Lorraine, and the Lyons region — enjoy a higher average income than do residents of the western, the central, and the southwestern provinces. Farmers have profited only meagerly from the boom, especially in the South and in the West, where many of them cling to traditional ways of cultivating fragmented, minuscule plots.

Government and the Economy

Capitalism was never so pure in France as it once was in Great Britain and the United States. Since well before the Great Revolution, French businessmen have been protected, yet restricted, by high tariffs, state monopoly concessions, government loans, and a host of direct and indirect subsidies. True to the tradition of Colbert (Louis XIV's great minister) and Saint-Simon (the early nineteenth century prophet of the managed economy), government ministers generally have had less faith in the invisible hand of the market than in their own economic judgment and foresight. Sometimes their judgment has been abysmal, as in the decisions of the late nineteenth century to build canals and to subsidize sailing ships, just at the time when railroads and steamships were making them obsolete.[6] Even their successes have been clouded by the stultifying effects of the accompanying centralized governmental controls. The tradition has survived, however, reinforced by the seeming failure of unmanaged capitalism in the great depression.

In 1945, when their economy lay in a shambles, destroyed by depression, war, occupation, and liberation, it was understandable that the French should turn to government for guidance. The de Gaulle government's first major economic innovation, in 1944, was the nationalization of the coal mines, Air France, and the Renault automobile firm (whose owner was accused of collaboration with the Germans). In 1946, electricity, gas, the Bank of France, the four largest commercial banks, and thirty-four major insurance companies became government property. When one adds to this list the armaments industry and the railroads, both nationalized in 1936, the traditional government monopolies: the tobacco, match, gunpowder, and potash industries, the postal, telegraph, and telephone services, radio (and then television), plus the steamship lines and oil companies in which the government is part owner, the extensive and direct role of government in the economy becomes apparent. The nationalizations of 1944–1946 did

[6] Clapham, *Economic Development of France and Germany, 1815–1914,* pp. 243–245, 351–352.

not arouse great political controversy, nor is there now much sentiment in favor of returning them to private ownership.

There is no standardized form of organization for these public industries and services. Some, like the post office and the National Savings Bank, are run on civil service lines under the direct authority of a minister. Others, like gas, electricity, and mining, are organized like the British public corporations, with their own governing boards. Still others, like the transportation and petroleum companies, are "mixed" public and private enterprises, similar in structure to private firms. Some have great autonomy, but all remain to some extent under the tutelage of a government ministry. In France as elsewhere in the none-too-capitalist world, the difference between a subsidized private industry operating under tight government regulations and a public corporation with wide autonomy is not as great as the capitalism vs. socialism debate might imply.

The second economic innovation of the first de Gaulle government of 1944–1946 was systematic planning.[7] A dynamic one-time cognac salesman with long experience in the United States, Jean Monnet, helped to persuade de Gaulle and others that only by means of "indicative" planning and a "concerted economy" could France be guided into the twentieth century. Surrounded by a team of bright and enthusiastic young men, Monnet became the first director of the newly created Planning Commission. French planning, as it evolved pragmatically after the second world war, has very little in common with the Soviet variety. The commission does not set firm production goals by fiat; it consults widely with representatives of labor and management in each major sector of the economy before setting goals for investment and increased production. In the course of preparation of the Fifth Plan, which was in effect from 1966 to 1970, twenty-five "modernization commissions" drew some four thousand people into the planning process.

Once complete and approved by the government, a plan is legally little more than wishful thinking. Neither the government nor the private businessman is legally required to invest as the plan indicates; and yet the government makes use of tax incentives, government loans, and a variety of carrot-and-stick devices to reinforce the entrepreneur's sense of moral responsibility to follow the plan. Through its control over investments in the large public sector of the economy, the govern-

[7] On French economic planning, see Stephen Cohen, *Modern Capitalist Planning: The French Model* (Cambridge, Mass.: Harvard University Press, 1969); Pierre Bauchet, *Economic Planning: The French Experience* (London: Heinemann, 1964); and John and Anne-Marie Hackett, *Economic Planning in France* (London: Allen and Unwin, 1963).

ment has some of the means necessary to implement the plan on its own initiative. In an average year, some 50 percent of all funds invested are controlled by the government.

In its efforts to implement a plan, the government has had considerable success with respect to big business (which has begun to abandon some of its traditional mistrust and secretiveness), less with small businessmen (who often feel they have been neither adequately consulted nor protected), and less still with organized labor (which generally rejects the capitalist framework which the plan takes for granted). In the early postwar years the goal of the First Plan (1946–1952) — the reconstruction of basic industries like coal, electricity, transportation, and steel — seemed so obvious a priority that the politicians were quite willing to defer to the experts. As the scope of the planners' goals expanded to include target-setting for the whole economy, and then to the determination of priorities in such fields as welfare and housing, the technocrats on the Planning Commission came under increasing attack. Beginning with the Fourth Plan (1962–1965), some efforts have been made to democratize the planning process. Parliament has examined and approved the plans before they went into effect, and regional planning and development commissions — the "CODERS" — have been created to temper the overcentralization of the economic planning. Yet many critics, like former Prime Minister Pierre Mendès-France, still believe that the citizenry has too weak a voice in the planning process.[8]

The French experience with planning is generally considered successful, both at home and abroad, although economists disagree as to whether it helped to create the postwar economic boom, or merely coincided with it. At the least the plan seems to have encouraged businessmen both to think in terms of industrial growth and to recognize the relationship of their firms to the whole economy. But planning has not solved all of France's basic economic problems, including recurring inflationary pressure, resistance to efficient modes of organization (both in production and distribution), and weakness in applied science and technology.[9] It is no accident that the booming French computer industry is almost completely dominated by American firms.[10]

[8] See Pierre Mendès-France, *A Modern French Republic* (New York: Hill and Wang, 1963), especially Ch. 7.

[9] On this last subject, see the crusading book of Jean-Jacques Servan-Schreiber, *The American Challenge* (New York: Atheneum, 1968), and the more scholarly (and more reliable) book by Robert Gilpin, *France in the Age of the Scientific State* (Princeton: Princeton University Press, 1968).

[10] IBM is the largest. The largest French firm, Machines Bull, was taken over by General Electric in 1964, to the regret and dismay of the French Government.

The efforts of the planners to modernize France's economy have been strongly seconded by the Common Market, membership in which has forced French businessmen to operate more efficiently in order to survive against strong German, Dutch, Belgian, and Italian competition. If the Common Market has encouraged modernization, it has also complicated the work of the planners, who have no control over those investments in other Common Market countries which may vitally affect the French economy.

With prosperity has come continuing inflationary pressure. When the Gaullists came to power in 1958, they vowed to re-establish international confidence in the franc and to make French goods more competitive in the international market by controlling the inflation which had averaged almost 7 percent per year in the decade before 1958.[11] A new franc was issued worth one hundred old francs. By means of near-balanced budgets and by exercising controls on some prices and wages — especially the wages of over three million workers who are employed by the government and its nationalized industries — the governments of the Fifth Republic managed to hold inflation to an annual rate of 2 to 4 percent. By early 1968, however, if the stabilization program had managed to control inflation, it had also roused the tempers of workers whose salaries were rising more slowly than their expectations, and it had contributed to the growth in the number of unemployed from 195,000 in 1962 to 437,000 in March 1968. Although the unemployment rate was still lower than that in the United States, it was the highest France had seen since immediately after the second world war and was particularly high (three times the average) among young workers under twenty years of age. These problems undoubtedly underlay the grievances which were voiced during the strikes and demonstrations of May 1968. The wage increases which came out of that crisis had a part in increasing inflationary pressures, which in turn set off a rapid outflow of gold and created the strong pressures for devaluation of the franc to which de Gaulle dramatically refused to yield in the fall of 1968. Unlike the General, for whom politics commonly took precedence over economics, de Gaulle's successors looked hard at France's dwindling gold reserves, swallowed their Gaullist pride, and in August 1969 devalued the franc by 12.5 per cent. The touted stability of the new franc was broken. Long experience had accustomed the French to view devaluation as a precursor to more inflation. In order to control the effects of an inflation psychology, the government felt obliged to tighten credit, control some prices, cut government spend-

[11] The percent rate was calculated from figures in INSEE, *Annuaire Statistique 1965*, Annex, p. 9.

ing, and discourage a wage increase. One result was to set off a new cycle of labor discontent. Thus, the steady increases in GNP which continued through the 1960's clearly did not eliminate the interlocking problems of inflation and social unrest.

Social Welfare

Neither affluence nor the expansion of the public sector has made of France an equalitarian society. Indeed, a recent United Nations' study shows that the income gap between the wealthy and the poor is greater in France than in most other European countries. As the graph on p. 26 reveals, the bottom 30 percent of all French families, ranked by income, earned only 4.8 percent of total personal income, as opposed to the 36.8 percent earned by the top 10 percent of families. The share of the top 10 percent was 7.7 times as great as that of the bottom 30 percent — a ratio considerably greater than in most other Western European countries.

The income gap between the rich and the poor in France is not final proof of an inequalitarian society. Government may redistribute income through steep progressive income taxes and extensive social welfare programs, as in Sweden and Great Britain. Indeed, government expenditure in France amounts to more than a third of the gross national product — more than in any other country in the North Atlantic area.[12] And yet the French taxation and social welfare systems do not achieve much income redistribution. Tax fraud is notoriously widespread in France, leaving workers and managerial personnel, who are on fixed salaries and who cannot cheat, to pay more than their share. Moreover, indirect taxes, which are added to the prices of consumer goods for the poor as well as the rich, make up 46.6 percent of all tax revenue in France, as compared with 38.8 percent in Germany and 34.5 percent in the United States.[13]

As for social welfare, the social security system created, belatedly, in 1946 and since extended, provides benefits which are more extensive than those in the United States.[14] For social security payments amounting to 21 percent of salary up to a fixed ceiling (6 percent paid by the employee and 15 percent by the employer), the employee and his family are entitled to coverage in case of illness, accident, unemployment, death of the wage-earner, and retirement. The health plan allows

[12] Henry Ehrmann, *Politics in France* (Boston: Little, Brown, 1968), p. 37.

[13] *Ibid.*, p. 38.

[14] The most complete description is Roger Jambu-Merlin's *La Sécurité Sociale* (Paris: A. Colin, 1970).

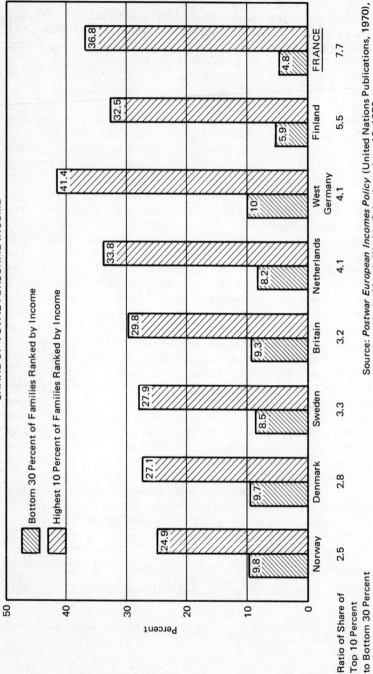

SHARE OF TOTAL PERSONAL INCOME

Bottom 30 Percent of Families Ranked by Income

Highest 10 Percent of Families Ranked by Income

	Norway	Denmark	Sweden	Britain	Netherlands	West Germany	Finland	FRANCE
Bottom 30%	24.9	27.1	27.9	29.8	33.8	41.4	32.5	36.8
Highest 10%	9.8	9.7	8.5	9.3	8.2	10	5.9	4.8
Ratio of Share of Top 10 Percent to Bottom 30 Percent	2.5	2.8	3.3	3.2	4.1	4.1	5.5	7.7

Source: *Postwar European Incomes Policy* (United Nations Publications, 1970), as reported in *Le Monde Weekly Selections*, June 10, 1970.

the patient to choose his own doctor, then reimburses him for all medical bills, including hospitalization and drugs, at the rate of 75 percent for short illnesses and up to 100 percent for prolonged illnesses. The French pattern is closer to private medicine than the British, for in Britain the doctor is paid directly by the government. The major problem which the French health plan has had to deal with has been the tendency of doctors to charge more than the fees authorized by the national and regional social security boards, leaving the patient to pay considerably more than 75 percent of the bill.

In addition to the customary social security benefits, the French government also offers monetary incentives for population growth. All pregnant women are entitled to a $15 per month allowance, plus reimbursement of all medical expenses.[15] If a woman has more than one child, she receives a monthly check of approximately $15 for the second child and $22 for each additional child. If she stays home with the children rather than taking a job, she receives another allotment of up to $25 per month, depending on the number of children in the family.

When added to government rent subsidies and public housing projects — the "Moderate Rent Housing" (H.L.M.) developments which have mushroomed in none too esthetic architectural styles in French cities and towns since the war — these benefits substantially add to the financial security of low income families. However, most of the government services mentioned are paid for by the employee himself and his employer (who tends to consider his share as part of the employee's salary), rather than out of general tax funds, as is more common in Great Britain. They resemble insurance plans more than income redistribution programs. So that crushing poverty remains the lot of millions of elderly people, whose social security pensions are at or little above the official minimum of some $30 per month.

Population

Prior to World War II, the stagnation of French society was reflected more in its stable population than in its slowly growing economy. In the century from 1846 to 1946, the population of France grew only from thirty-five to forty million. During the same period, the population of Europe as a whole nearly doubled. From 1800 to 1939, France experienced a continuous decline in birth rate. She could ill afford the loss of those 1,400,000 men — 4 percent of the entire French population — who were killed in the butchery of trench warfare in World

[15] All allowances are those in effect in 1970.

War I. Had it not been for a dramatic decline in peacetime death rates as a result of medical advances, France would have suffered serious losses in population.

Abruptly after 1945 the French birth rate rose to a level unknown since the nineteenth century. With the single-child family definitely out of style, the French population swelled from forty million in 1946 to over fifty million by 1968. And yet despite government subsidies of various sorts for *familles nombreuses,* the birth rate began dropping again after 1964. After leading most of Europe in birth rates for two decades after World War II, by 1968 France again found herself lagging behind.[16]

Social Structure

The Family

With urbanization, economic growth, and population expansion have come important changes in the character of French society. Perhaps the most cherished of institutions in traditional France, particularly in the middle class and among farmers, was the extended family.[17] No goal in life was deemed more important than protection of the continuity, security, and status of the family. If the family owned a business, the father's duty was to manage it cautiously, taking no risks which might jeopardize the security of his dependents. Decisions which affected the status and security of the family, like the education and occupation of the children, often were considered too important to be left to the whims of the immature; even marriage partners frequently were chosen by the families. Once married, the children often moved in with the husband's parents, prolonging the period of dependency and interdependency. The family was a secure though confining haven from which the Frenchman looked out on what he tended to regard as a hostile world.

Modernization gradually is breaking through the insulation of the extended family unit.[18] Industrialization has provided an abundance

[16] INSEE, *Annuaire Statistique Rétrospectif 1966,* Annex, p. 11; and J. P. Dumont, "Birth Rate Approaches the Low Pre-War Level," *Le Monde Weekly Selection,* April 22, 1970.

[17] On this subject see, for example, Rhoda Métraux and Margaret Mead, *Themes in French Culture* (Stanford: Stanford University Press, 1954).

[18] The most dramatic view of this process is to be had through community studies, of which three of the best are Laurence Wylie, *Village in the Vaucluse* (New York: Harper Colophon, 1964); Wylie, *Chanzeaux: A Village in Anjou* (Cambridge, Mass.: Harvard University Press, 1966); and Edgar Morin, *Une Commune en France* (Paris: Fayard, 1967).

of jobs in the cities for sons and daughters who seek greater independence than the family allows. Social security makes aged parents slightly less dependent upon the support of their children. Motorbikes and motorscooters allow adolescents and young adults to seek friends and recreation far away from father's protective view. Throughout France the nuclear family of father, mother, and children is replacing the extended family as the basic social unit. Within the nuclear family both children and wife (whose government family allowance payments may total more than her husband's paycheck) enjoy greater freedom than in the past. It may well be that the breakdown of the extended family, by giving individuals a greater need for and an interest in outside associations, will help to produce a more open and participant French society.

The Church

Even within the French Catholic Church — long regarded as one of the fortresses of social and political conservatism — there are striking signs of change.[19] Although first the old aristocracy and then the wealthy bourgeoisie rediscovered religion as a defense against the social and political ambitions of the lower classes, urbanization and the spread of republicanism brought an overall decline in church attendance, especially among men. In the present day over 80 percent of all Frenchmen consider themselves Catholics. (Approximately 2 percent are Protestants, 1 percent Jews, and the remainder mostly without religion.) Apart from baptism and marriage, however, many French Catholics rarely set foot in church. Opinion polls indicate that less than 25 percent of all Frenchmen attend mass regularly, that is, weekly or more often.[20] In a national poll take in April 1968, 35 percent of the respondents declared that they had taken communion for Easter or intended to do so.[21] The proportion of practicing Catholics varies by region from a strong majority of the population in Brittany, Alsace-Lorraine, the Basque country, the southern fringe of the Massif Cen-

[19] For a summary of groups and tendencies within the Church, see William Bosworth, *Catholicism and Crisis in Modern France* (Princeton: Princeton University Press, 1962). Relations between church and society are examined in René Rémond, ed., *Forces Religieuses et Attitudes Politiques dans la France Contemporaine* (Paris: A. Colin, 1965), No. 130 in the series Cahiers de la Fondation Nationale des Sciences Politiques; and Aline Coutrot and François Dreyfus, *Les Forces Religieuses dans la Société Française* (Paris: A. Colin, 1965).

[20] See *Sondages,* 1966: No. 2, pp. 15–19, and 1967: No. 2 (a special issue on religion and politics).

[21] *Sondages,* 1968: No. 2, p. 56.

tral and other scattered areas to less than 5 percent in the working-class suburbs of Paris. In addition to these sharp regional differences, in general women attend church more often than men, rural people more than urbanites, and, within the cities, the middle and upper classes much more than the working class.

With few exceptions, the church in the nineteenth century tended to view republicanism as an open threat to its social and spiritual mission. There are still numerous Frenchmen who believe that one belongs to the Right if he is sympathetic to the church and to Catholic schools (whatever his other opinions may be) and to the Left if he is staunchly anticlerical. Since the second world war, at least, Catholics and the church itself have rendered that mode of classification inadequate. As early as the 1890's, a republican and reform-minded group appeared within the Catholic community, led by Marc Sangnier. In the early 1900's, however, relations between the Republic and the church had been so poisoned by the Dreyfus Affair, by the outlawing of many clerical orders, by formal separation of church and state in 1905, and by papal disapproval of republican Catholics, that Sangnier could reach no more than a small group of reformists.

The moment of lasting reconciliation between the church and the Republic came in the anti-German Resistance during World War II, when Catholics, Socialists, and Communists found themselves allied in the same cause. The Catholic party which emerged out of the Resistance — the Popular Republican Movement — was by declaration both republican and socialist, as well as Catholic. The church itself finally made its peace with democratic government and gave its blessing to social reform. No longer was the church wedded to the social ideal of a passively obedient flock in a stagnant society. Under church sponsorship, two organizations founded between the wars, the Catholic Workers Youth organization (JOC), and especially the Catholic Agricultural Youth organization (JAC), became significant forces for social and economic reform. Among Catholic businessmen the Committee of Young Employers set out to inspire among employers a greater sense of responsibility toward their employees and toward their communities. As never before, Catholic laymen were given positions of authority within the parish and in a host of Catholic Action groups which deal not only with traditional religious instruction but also with the application of Catholic principles to professional and civic problems. Quite naturally, these reforms met resistance from conservative elements within the Catholic community. The Catholic youth associations, for example, have taken serious membership losses since reaching their postwar high mark, partly, no doubt, because of disagreement over their proper relationship to the church.

In the countryside and within the urban middle class, the church has contributed since the war to a growing social consciousness and to a wider participation in cooperative civic ventures. Yet even were its most reform-minded leaders to prevail, the church would be prevented from building a truly effective bridge between antagonistic groups in French society by virtue of the vigorous anticlerical outlooks both of the majority of the urban working class and of the political parties of the traditional Left. On the surface, it almost appears that religion has disappeared as a political issue, save when the problem of state aid to church schools arises. Underneath, the Frenchman's attitudes toward the church and toward its polar rival, the Communist Party, still seem to be fundamental in shaping his political attitudes. As we shall see in Chapter Four, there was no better predictor of a Frenchman's attitude toward de Gaulle than the extent of his attachment to the church.

The Working Class

In the introduction to his classic *Democracy in America,* written in the 1830's, Alexis de Tocqueville argued that the trend toward ever greater equality of social classes is one of the fundamental characteristics of modern nations. Up to the present, at least, his observation has held true. In France as in other Western democracies, mass education, popular democracy, rising wages, the welfare state, and an expanding middle class have blurred once clear distinctions between the attitudes and styles of life of the various classes, however one chooses to define them. In comparison with the United States, however, class distinctions in France still seem strikingly clear. In this respect, France has more in common with Britain than with the United States, although the contrasts between France and Britain are significant. Whereas British class relations generally have been characterized by social deference of inferiors to superiors, French class relations more often have been characterized by mistrust, antagonism, and fear.

Many of the members of that industrial working class which emerged in France in the nineteenth century came to feel themselves alienated from society. In their eyes the bourgeois property owners and businessmen who replaced the noble aristocracy as France's ruling class were as self-interested and as lacking in social conscience as their predecessors. The equalitarian society promised in the Revolution seemed still in the future, achievable only by yet another revolution. When nation-wide unions finally were permitted to form after the legalization of associations in the law of 1884, their leaders displayed little of that faith in peaceful reform which characterized British unionism.

In its famous charter of Amiens, adopted in 1906, the General Confederation of Labor (CGT) affirmed that "The class struggle places the workers in revolt against all forms of capitalist exploitation and oppression, material and moral. . . . [The Union Movement] prepares for the complete emancipation which can be achieved only by expropriating the capitalist class."[22]

The first creed adopted by the CGT was "syndicalism" — a loosely integrated doctrine which prescribed direct, often violent, action in a first stage, followed ultimately by a massive general strike, which presumably would destroy both capitalist enterprise and the state which protected it. Unlike the socialists, syndicalists tended to envision the future utopian society as one built around decentralized workshops, linked only through local union organizations. On the first three major occasions on which it was attempted, 1920, 1938, and 1947, the general strike failed miserably, leaving the labor movement in a shambles.

Following the first world war, the CGT (like the French Socialist Party) split into two competing unions, Communist and non-Communist, united again in 1945, then split once more in 1947. Although the non-Communist CGT flirted with reformism between the wars, the economic failure of the popular front governments of 1936–1938 (despite the material, though temporary, gains which they produced for labor) and the eventual Communist takeover of the united CGT in 1945 reaffirmed the alienation from French society of the larger part of organized labor.

Among the major factors which seem to have contributed to the failure of reformism in French labor, two have already been mentioned: the relative stagnation of the French economy prior to 1940 and the revolutionary historical tradition with which labor leaders identified. Two other factors were equally important. The first was the intransigence of French employers. In 1936 massive sit-down strikes and a new and determined popular front government forced employers' representatives to accept the "Matignon Agreements," which included compulsory collective bargaining, the forty-hour week, and pay increases. Humiliated and resentful, many French employers set out to sabotage the agreements, and, as soon as the popular front government was gone, to dismiss union activists from their establishments. A warlike climate of class struggle prevailed on both sides of the bargaining table, with the militancy of each party reinforcing that of the other.

---

[22] As cited in Val Lorwin, *The French Labor Movement* (Cambridge, Mass.: Harvard University Press, 1954), p. 30.

A second reason for labor militancy was the organizational, numerical, and financial weakness of French unions. In order to bargain effectively both with employers and with the government, labor needed unity and strength. It had neither. From the 1880's onward, the French labor movement was hampered by internal political conflict among syndicalists, reformists, socialists, Communists, and Catholics. Political infighting was one reason for the failure of organized labor to attract the majority of French workers, save in such extraordinary periods as the popular front in 1936 and the Liberation in 1945.

To the present, French unions have never been able to gain a lasting hold over more than one-fifth of the industrial labor force. On three occasions, after short periods of euphoria (1919–1920, 1936–1938, and 1945–1947) had drawn several million workers into the unions, a disastrous general strike led to a massive loss of membership. The outlook of the typical worker seemed to alternate between hostile indifference and unrealistic hope. Even those members who stayed with the union tended to be undisciplined and lax in payment of dues. Out of weakness came frustration, and out of frustration a penchant for revolutionary solutions.

After 1947, when the Communist Party went into permanent opposition, the party and its captive CGT worked hard and long to prevent French workers from being integrated into a non-Communist French society. Nevertheless, although the Communist Party remains the choice of more workers than any other party, sustained prosperity gradually has made inroads into traditional working-class attitudes. Before May 1968, sociologists talked of the increasingly realistic, bourgeois, security-minded outlook of French workers.[23] In the chemical, electrical, and steel industries — and increasingly in others as well — automation is producing a "new working class" of well-trained technicians who are more active union men than traditional French workers. Once a firm has trained a worker for a technical and specialized job, it has every interest in keeping him as long as possible, for example by offering him job security and regular pay raises.

To be sure, highly trained workers in automated industries still compose a minority of the industrial labor force. Throughout private industry, however, sustained prosperity and a shortage of skilled labor have encouraged employers to be more generous with their employees than in the prewar period. The purchasing power of the average French worker rose 94 percent from 1949 to 1964. It is significant that the crisis of May 1968 came at a time of rising unemployment after a long

[23] For a bibliography of recent studies of the French working class, see Gérard Adam, "Où en est le débat sur la nouvelle classe ouvrière?" *Revue Française de Science Politique,* XVIII: 5 (October 1968), pp. 1003–1023.

period of full employment. In opinion polls conducted in March 1968, the French Institute of Public Opinion (IFOP) found that 54 percent of all respondents and 61 percent of all workers expected unemployment to increase in the coming months. Forty-four percent expected to save less in 1968 than in 1967, as opposed to only 8 percent who expected to save more.[24] Only 30 percent of the respondents felt that the government was well informed on "the economic problems which concern people like you," as opposed to 57 percent who felt the government was not well informed on such problems.[25] As students of revolution are aware, an economic recession in a time of rising expectations can be dangerous for the government in power.

The strikes and demonstrations of May 1968 provided a clear reminder that in France as in the United States, well-paid and highly skilled workers are no less militant than low paid and unskilled workers. On the contrary, skilled workers and technicians in modern industries — aviation plants, refineries, chemical plants — were in the forefront in occupying plants and in demanding more worker participation in the management of the plant.[26] Yet in comparison with the traditionally revolutionary style of labor protest in France, their demands were less political and more exclusively focused on reforms within their places of work. Lest the point be exaggerated, it must be noted that this evolution in the style of labor protest owes at least as much to union leadership as to the rise of the technician.

The French labor movement remains politically divided and numerically weak. Between the exaggerated claims of union leaders and the underestimates of employers and of rival union leaders, it is extremely difficult to arrive at accurate appraisals of the size of union membership. In the mid-1960's the CGT probably had in the neighborhood of 1,000,000 members and the French Democratic Confederation of Labor (CFDT) and the socialist-oriented Force Ouvrière (FO) some 500,000 each.[27] Even adding in the major teachers union, the Federation of National Education (FEN), with some 400,000 members, and the white collar workers union, the Confédération Générale des Cadres (CGC), with some 200,000 members, the total French trade union

[24] "Problèmes économiques," *Sondages,* 1968: No. 2, p. 29.

[25] *Ibid.,* p. 27.

[26] Alain Touraine, *Le Mouvement de Mai ou le Communisme Utopique* (Paris: Seuil, 1968), pp. 166–169.

[27] At the end of 1967, commentators varied in their estimates of CGT membership from a low of 700,000 to a high of 2,000,000. Estimates for the CFDT ranged from 400,000 to 800,000 and for the FO from 350,000 to 1,000,000. The number of paid-up members very likely was nearer the lower figures than the higher. See Georges Lefranc, *Le Syndicalisme en France* (Paris: Presses Universitaires de France, Que sais-je series, 1968 ed.), p. 119.

membership in the mid-1960's was under 3,000,000, far below the levels of trade union membership estimated in 1965 for Britain (10,-180,000), Germany (7,450,000) and even Italy (8,350,000).[28] Within a single French plant, several unions normally will be found competing for the workers' loyalty, while the majority of workers shun membership altogether (there being no union shop in France). Although these relatively low memberships are a sign of weakness, they are not an accurate gauge of the unions' influence among workers. In the December 1963 elections of governing committees under the social security program, for example, CGT candidates won 44 percent of workers' votes, over twice as many as any other union, demonstrating that its following is wider than its membership.[29]

In the 1960's, inter-union rivalries, though far from dead, seemed less acute than before. In 1964 the Catholic union changed its name to the French Democratic Confederation of Labor (CFDT), a change designed to separate religion from unionism and to attract non-Catholics to the fold. During the miners' strike of the spring of 1963, all three major unions — the CGT, the FO, and the CFDT — joined efforts in support of the strikers. In January of 1966 the CFDT and the CGT signed an agreement calling for permanent coordination of their activities.[30] Economic as well as political cooperation among unions has multiplied in recent years, partly, no doubt, because of the Communist Party's efforts to revive the popular front. Opposition to the government's policy of wage restraints in government-controlled industries has also tended to bring the unions together.

The growing tendency of organized labor to give priority to wages and working conditions over social revolution was strikingly demonstrated in the crisis of May 1968, when the Fifth Republic was shaken to its very roots. The crisis was initiated by those thousands of students, and the thousands of police sent in to control them, who turned the Latin Quarter into a battleground in the first two weeks of May. The CGT, the CFDT, and the National Federation of Teachers (FEN) demonstrated their general support for the students by calling a twenty-four-hour general strike on May 13. The general strike began in a series of spontaneous wildcat strikes. The CGT lent its support after the strike was well on its way to becoming general and time and again seemed to drag its feet, only adopting a militant tone to regain control of its workers, especially the younger ones. In general it seemed more interested in preventing the students from contaminating workers than

[28] Roger Broad and Robert Jarrett, *Community Europe: A Short Guide to the Common Market* (London: Oswald Wolff, 1967), Table 12, p. 50.

[29] Lefranc, *Le Syndicalisme*, p. 114.

[30] Gérard Adam, "L'Unité d'Action CGT-CFDT," *Revue Française de Science Politique*, XVII: 3 (June 1967), pp. 576–590.

in overthrowing the Gaullist regime.[31] When the CGT and the CFDT reached a tentative wages and hours agreement in bargaining with the government and the National Managers' Council (CNP), the workers at the Renault automobile factory angrily rejected them. The CGT then called for continuation of the fight. When on May 30 de Gaulle called for new parliamentary elections, the CGT continued to talk of the need for a "popular government" but in fact did nothing to create one nor to prevent elections which produced a landslide Gaullist victory. Eventually, beginning in mid-June, the workers returned to their plants.

So far as organized labor is concerned, there are two strikingly new features to this entire "psychodrama," as Raymond Aron described the events of May.[32] First, unlike earlier general strikes, this one produced major wage increases, averaging 14 percent. The unity of rival unions and the massive number of workers who joined the strike (over eight million at the peak) clearly contributed to that success. Second, the CGT, which proved less radical than the non-Communist CFDT, was willing to abandon all of its political demands, including abrogation of the government's unpopular social security reforms. Why? The explanation given by the CGT secretary general, Georges Séguy, was that de Gaulle was only waiting to "drown everything in blood" with harsh military repression had the working class attempted to take power by force.[33] But surely there were options open to the CGT other than armed insurrection. Two unstated reasons help explain why they were not taken. First the Communist Party and its affiliate, the CGT, were reluctant to threaten their alliance with the Federation of the Democratic and Socialist Left (FGDS), which they had been nurturing for several years on the electoral and parliamentary levels. Second, it seems clear that the CGT feared that it would not be able to control those militant students and young workers who often bore the black flag of anarchy rather than the red flag of communism and who viewed the Communist Party as a bureaucratic, even a conservative body, almost as deserving of contempt as the Gaullists themselves. When students marched from the Sorbonne to the suburbs of Billancourt to join hands with the workers at Renault, they found the CGT had bolted the gates to keep them out. CGT leader Benoit Frachon later explained that organized labor could not permit nonunionists to

[31] For an inside story of the CGT during this crisis, by a union leader who broke with the CGT after May, see André Barjonet, *La C. G. T.* (Paris: Seuil, 1968) pp. 145–166.

[32] Raymond Aron, *The Elusive Revolution: Anatomy of a Student Revolt* (New York: Praeger, 1969).

[33] Quoted in André Barjonet, *La C. G. T.,* p. 160.

approach the workers with the purpose of insulting the unions and attempting to "replace them in their task of directing the struggles of the working class."[34]

Organized labor in France remains divided and politicized, although to a lesser degree than before 1960, and interest in immediate social revolution seems to continue its decline while interest in the defense of workers' interests here and now increases.

Farmers

It is not easy to generalize about the French farmer.[35] He is a practicing Catholic in Normandy, Brittany, and Alsace but a militant anti-clerical in much of the South. He cultivates large and prosperous farms in the North and the Parisian Basin, but generally small and poor farms elsewhere in France. He votes Gaullist in one district, Socialist in another, and Communist in a third, frequently despite the similar economic interests of the three districts.

There is nevertheless a certain evolution in the character of French agriculture which has brought marked changes to the life of the typical farmer. Prior to the second world war, most farmers resisted mechanization; after the war the number of tractors in use jumped from 46,000 in 1946 to 630,000 in 1960. Before the war, each farmer tended to go his own way, prizing his individualism above all else; since the war (and partly because of Vichy's efforts at organizing farmers), he more frequently has joined cooperatives, in some areas even to the point of buying farm equipment in common with nearby farmers. Prewar farmers defended their interests vigorously and often effectively, as in the case of sugar beet farmers and winegrowers, who distilled their produce into alcohol and sold it at highly subsidized prices to the government, which mixed it with gasoline for automobile consumption.[36] Postwar farmers are equally militant in self-defense, as they demonstrated on several occasions in the 1960's by blocking national highways with thousands of tractors in protest over declining farm prices and

[34] Quoted in *ibid.*, p. 165.

[35] A good introduction to the problems of the French farmer in this century is Gordon Wright's *Rural Revolution in France* (Stanford: Stanford University Press, 1964). Other useful sources include Jacques Fauvet and Henri Mendras, *Les Paysans et la Politique dans la France Contemporaine* (Paris: A. Colin, 1958, Cahiers de la F.N.S.P., No. 94); Jean Meynaud, *La Révolte Paysanne* (Paris: Payot, 1963); and Henri Mendras, *Sociologie de la Campagne Française* (Paris: Presses Universitaires de France, Que sais-je series, 2nd ed. 1965).

[36] For an account of the alcohol lobby, see Bernard Brown, "Alcohol and Politics in France," *American Political Science Review,* LI: 4 (December 1957), pp. 976–990.

the abolition of government subsidies; yet many are also more willing to accept such structural reforms as the regrouping of scattered parcels of land into larger, contiguous plots. A new generation of leaders (many trained in the Catholic Agricultural Youth) has come of age, threatening the conservative, prosperous farmers who have dominated the major farm association, the National Federation of Farmers' Associations (FNSEA).

France has indeed experienced a minor rural revolution in the postwar era. Many further reforms will be needed, however, including the joining of many small farms and the retraining of many more farmers for nonagricultural employment, if those who stay on the farms are to catch up with rising urban standards of living. In 1962, 80 percent of all French farms were less than 50 acres in size, and more than half were under 25 acres.[37] Undoubtedly these reforms will produce more explosions of political protest from farmers who wish neither to give up their farms nor to remain poor in an age of affluence.

The Middle Classes

In the course of the nineteenth century, the French noble aristocracy lost its political power, and much of its social preeminence as well, to the wealthy, property-owning bourgeoisie. Even when the masses were given the vote, in 1848 and again in the 1870's, a conservative peasantry tended to defer to the leadership of the wealthy. After the turn of the century, with the rise of the Radical Party, the petty bourgeoisie — the shopkeepers, artisans, and small businessmen who were so numerous in France — won greater influence in government. With rare and brief exceptions, the democratization of the social bases of French government stopped there. So long as the working class remained small and divided, so long as fear of revolution from below brought "right-minded people" together, France's socially conservative middle-class governors (whatever their party labels) remained secure from effective challenge from a British-style labor party.

In the twentieth century, and especially after 1945, however, economic changes began a thorough transformation of the French middle classes. The National Council of French Management (CNPF), which is essentially the organ of larger businesses, overcame its traditional biases against government and competition and accepted both government planning and the Common Market.[38] Modern factories gradually

[37] Wright, *Rural Revolution in France*, p. 178.

[38] The old passion for secrecy and fear of competition were still strong when Henry Ehrmann wrote *Organized Business in France* (Princeton: Princeton University Press, 1957). More recent developments are reported in Ardagh's *The New French Revolution*, cited above.

squeezed out the self-employed blacksmith, cabinetmaker, and shoe-maker. Shopkeepers were threatened by competition from larger stores. In the mid-1960's France had almost a million small shops, one for every 56 inhabitants, as compared with one for 86 inhabitants in Britain and one for 100 in the United States. Under the Fourth Republic, their major organizational representative, Small and Medium-Sized Enterprises (PME), fought vigorously and often effectively against all reforms which might jeopardize their vested interests. Since 1959 the PME and its leader, Léon Gingembre (whom the Swiss journalist Herbert Leuthy once chose as a symbol of the stagnant economy), have worked to adapt small business to survive in a modern economy. Despite their efforts, even in the prosperous years from 1955 to 1965, the number of self-employed merchants declined from 809,500 to 703,-000, while the number of salaried employees in commerce was rising from 948,900 to 1,376,400.[39]

When Pierre Poujade, the proprietor of a stationery shop in central France, called for a tax strike in the mid-fifties, thousands of angry shopkeepers joined him in forcibly preventing tax inspectors from examining the stock and bookkeeping of merchants suspected of fraud. When Poujade launched his own political party in 1956, there undoubtedly were hundreds of thousands of shopkeepers among the two and a half million voters who elected forty-two of his followers to the National Assembly. The Poujadist revolt subsided rapidly; yet with the gradual spread of supermarkets and department stores, and the inevitable extinction of more inefficient small shops, angry political protest from this quarter is a recurrent phenomenon. It seems likely that the discontent of small businessmen in the spring of 1969, expressed in antitax strikes and demonstrations (including seizure of tax records in the town of La Tour du Pin) played a part in de Gaulle's ultimate defeat and resignation.

The most striking postwar change in the character of the middle class has been the rapid increase in the number of salaried professional men and the relative decline in numbers and influence of the propertied bourgeoisie. With the emergence of larger and more modern firms, and with the growth of the government bureaucracy, the number of engineers, management personnel, and salaried professionals of various sorts has increased enormously. Like the Soviet Union and the United States, although belatedly, France is experiencing her own "managerial revolution." This group tends to be less ideological, more pragmatic, better educated in the natural sciences, and less resistant to change than the older, propertied bourgeoisie. Yet the "technocrat," whether

[39] INSEE, *Annuaire Statistique Rétrospectif 1966*, p. 108.

in government service or in private industry, has shown that citing expertise he can be as resistant to sharing power with subordinates as was the owner of the old family firm.

By the 1960's neither the "bourgeoisie" nor the "proletariat" looked much as Marx had described them more than a century before. And yet like Marx, many Frenchmen continued to believe that the relationship between the classes, even under France's much-modified version of capitalism, was one of conflict. In a national poll conducted in January 1967, 44 percent of the respondents responded "yes" to the statement that "in France at the present time, the class struggle is a reality." Thirty-seven percent replied "no," while the remaining 19 percent expressed no opinion.[40] The class antagonisms reflected in these responses were brought to the surface by the riots and strikes of the spring of 1968. The resentments of workers against the felt injustices of a capitalist society were forcefully expressed, as in those cases where workers held their managers prisoner within the factory, and where, as in the Sud Aviation plant in Nantes, sit-in strikers wrote on the walls of the buildings, "Yesterday slaves, today free men."[41] The threat of revolution from the Left in turn aroused the fears of the middle classes and attracted them in record numbers into the Gaullist camp in the June 1968 elections. Not since the 1930's had class relations been so tense.

Education

The weakness of class consciousness in the United States frequently is attributed not simply to the vagueness of class boundaries, but also to the relative ease with which the talented and ambitious son of a working-class father can make his way up the social pyramid. Contrary to the prevailing legend, recent research has shown that just as many white-collar workers are sons of manual workers — approximately 30 percent — in France as in the United States.[42] The expansion of commerce and the growth of large bureaucracies, both public and private, have created white-collar jobs which could be filled only with sons of manual workers, whose places in the factories often are taken by farm boys moving into the city. The similarity between the United States and France with regard to social mobility ends, however, when one examines the chances of a manual worker's son becoming

[40] *Sondages,* 1968: No. 1, p. 44.

[41] Barjonet, *op. cit.,* p. 151.

[42] See Seymour Martin Lipset and Reinhard Bendix, *Social Mobility in Industrial Society* (Berkeley: University of California Press, 1959), pp. 11–23.

a doctor, a lawyer, a high civil servant, or a teacher. Until very recently, the French worker's son was effectively blocked from the university education required for entry into the professions. The ascent from manual laborer to the professions normally took two or three generations.

Indeed, in France as in Great Britain, the educational system has helped to maintain class barriers, despite the ultrarepublican political values of most French public school teachers in the twentieth century.[43] Primary education in France has been free and compulsory since the 1880's. Secondary and university education, however, remained the almost exclusive preserve of a social and (for the university) intellectual elite. In 1951, 98 percent of all French thirteen-year-olds were still in school, as compared to 96 percent of all American thirteen-year-olds; among sixteen-year-olds, the proportion still in school dropped to 29 percent in France, but only to 81 percent in the United States.[44] In 1953 only some 19 percent of French working-class children ever entered a secondary school, as opposed to 60 percent of clerical-class children and 90 percent of those with fathers in the liberal professions.[45] Well over half those children of modest social origins who did continue school past the age of fourteen went to technical schools or to terminal "complementary courses" rather than to the more prestigious *lycées* and *collèges,* which offered the only means of preparing for the state secondary certificate, the *baccalauréat,* which in turn was a prerequisite for entrance into a university. Among French university students, only 1.6 percent were sons of workers in 1939.[46]

Since 1945, French education has begun to respond to economic and political pressures for democratization. In the two decades after the war, secondary school enrollment tripled, with the most dramatic increases coming in technical programs and in terminal general education. Secondary enrollment is expanding even further as funds become available to implement the government decree of 1959, which extended the legal school-leaving age from fourteen to sixteen. By 1962, the proportion of working-class children going on to some type of secondary

[43] See Pierre Bourdieu, "L'Ecole conservatrice," *Revue Française de Sociologie,* VII: 3 (1966); Bourdieu and Jean-Claude Passeron, *Les Héritiers* (Paris: Editions de Minuit, 1964); and the articles by Michel Crozier and Alain Touraine in Société française de sociologie, *Tendances et Volontés de la Société Française.*

[44] Bendix and Lipset, *Social Mobility,* p. 94.

[45] W. R. Fraser, *Education and Society in Modern France* (London Routledge and Kegan Paul, 1963), p. ix.

[46] Minister of Education, Alain Peyrefitte, to the National Assembly, *Journal Officiel, Débats, Assemblée Nationale,* June 1, 1967, p. 1521.

school had reached 42 percent (more than doubled from 19 percent in 1953), and was still rising.[47] Even in the universities, by 1964–65, 8.3 percent of all students were children of workers and another 6 percent were children of farmers or farm laborers.[48] By the 1960's the majority of university students were no longer from the higher bourgeoisie, but rather from the lower middle class.[49] Very likely democratization would have progressed more rapidly were it not for the reluctance of laboring parents to send their talented children on to advanced studies (particularly to the *lycée*) because of the risk of cutting them off from class and family.

Since the *lycées* remain the only means of entry into the universities, the decision as to who will attend them is critical. Until 1959, entrance was normally by examination at age eleven. In order to provide greater flexibility and greater opportunity for the late bloomer, the government decreed in 1959 that henceforth in all state schools there would be a two-year "observation cycle" for twelve- and thirteen-year-old pupils, prior to their admission to a *lycée,* to a technical school, or to a general education program. In 1967 the government announced the creation of a program of specialized counseling units in each district, designed to orient the child into the program for which he is best suited. The government seems aware that if children of working-class background are simply dumped into terminal general education programs, the secondary schools will continue to perpetuate sharp class distinctions. Gradually, although only against sharp resistance from teachers and administrators determined to maintain the traditional elitist *lycée,* French education is adapting to a more technically-oriented and more equalitarian society.

In addition to its elitist bias, the traditional French educational system possessed two striking and significant characteristics. For generations teacher-pupil relations have been stiff and authoritarian; text and teacher were not to be contradicted. From the time of Napoleon, the Ministry of Education in Paris has dictated to teachers from the Pyrenees to the Rhine exactly what should be taught and when. The authoritarian style of instruction limited opportunities for students to learn the skills of cooperation and participation associated with one facet of the democratic citizen's role. Centralization in education, as throughout French society, limited opportunities for decision-making at the local level.

[47] Fraser, *Education and Society,* p. ix.

[48] Peyrefitte, to the National Assembly, p. 1521.

[49] Raymond Boudon, "Quelques causes de la révolution estudiantine," *La Table Ronde,* December, 1968–January, 1969, pp. 172–173.

Like so many other features of the French educational system, centralization and authoritarianism were vigorously challenged and perhaps permanently modified by those angry students in the crisis of May 1968.[50] The student revolt began on the suburban Nanterre campus of the University of Paris, where the growing pains of French higher education were very much in evidence. As the postwar population boom reached the universities, their enrollment swelled from 202,000 in 1960–61 to 514,000 in 1967–68. The Nanterre campus, designed as an experimental university, opened its doors with 2,300 students in 1964. By 1967 its faculty and equipment clearly were incapable of offering the full program intended to the 12,000 students who were then enrolled. On a relatively new campus, where high expectations were being frustrated, there were widespread grievances which could be nurtured and exploited by student leaders, notably by Daniel Cohn-Bendit, "Danny le rouge."

For one group of students, the student rebellion of May 1968 was primarily an attack upon the university, upon the inadequacy of its traditional programs and methods in a modern society. For another group, in which the most prominent student leaders belong, there was no question of simply adapting an outmoded university system to the needs of what they regarded as a corrupt and oppressive ruling class. Rather, the university revolt was to be used as the opening wedge by which the whole of the Gaullist and capitalist establishment was to be weakened and overthrown.[51] An attitude survey conducted among students in September 1968 offers some evidence on the probable size of these two groups. The student respondents were asked to rank in order of importance three possible reasons for the student demonstrations of May: anxiety over finding employment in their fields of specialization, the inadequacy of the programs, methods, and financial means of the university, and rejection of the "consumers' society" (that is, rejection of the materialism and injustices of capitalist society). Only 7 percent gave a first-place ranking to "denial of the consumers' society," while 80 percent ranked it last, even though this was a primary slogan of the May revolutionaries. Anxiety over finding jobs in their field was ranked highest by 56 percent, while another 35 percent gave

[50] The student role in that crisis is examined sympathetically by Alain Touraine, *Le Mouvement de Mai ou le Communisme Utopique,* and by Edgar Morin, Claude Lefort, and Jean-Marc Coudray, *La Brèche* (Paris: Fayard, 1968). For a more negative view, see Aron, *The Elusive Revolution.*

[51] On the two kinds of motives, see Edgar Morin, "La Commune Etudiante," four articles in *Le Monde,* May 17–21, 1968.

highest ranking to the inadequacy of the university.[52] In response to another question, only 12 percent of the respondents identified themselves with those students who wanted radical transformations in French society; 54 percent identified with those who wanted to reform the university; and another 31 percent with those who wanted first simply to pass their examinations.[53] Apparently the revolutionaries were a minority within the student population as a whole, and probably among the tens of thousands of student demonstrators as well.

The revolutionaries were not only a minority group; they also were poorly organized and badly divided among orthodox Communist, Maoist, anarchist, and utopian Communist factions. Only a few weeks before the crisis, in April 1968, the general assembly of the largest and Leftist student association, the National Union of French Students (UNEF) had ended prematurely in a melee of verbal and physical battles between rival political factions.

If students could not agree upon the ultimate ends of their movement, at least most were united in a general hostility toward the government for its failure to reform the universities. In early May, after student demonstrations in the Latin Quarter produced violent confrontations between students and police, the unity of the student community was solidified around the banner of police brutality. Before the crisis was over, the contagion of rebellion had spread to the *lycées,* where demonstrations, occupations of administration offices, and displays of red and black flags became common occurrences.

When secondary school and university students returned from vacation in the fall of 1968, with the Gaullists still in firm control of the government and the Parliament, many wondered if the authority of teachers and administrators could ever be restored. The answer of the new Minister of Education, Edgar Faure (a skilled politician of long experience in the Fourth Republic), was to create in all schools and universities councils of administration in which elected student representatives have a major voice.[54] Collegial administration of the schools became a major part of de Gaulle's response to the May revolt: his "society of participation." The gigantic University of Paris was split up, and provincial universities were given greater autonomy than ever before. If the resistance of student ideologues and threatened

---

[52] The survey was conducted by IFOP and is reported in "Les Etudiants et la Nouvelle Université," *Réalités,* November, 1968, p. 71. This and other evidence on the May crisis is examined by Philippe Bénéton and Jean Touchard in "Les Interprétations de la crise de mai–juin 1968," *Revue Française de Science Politique,* XX: 3 (June, 1970), pp. 503–544.

[53] *Réalités,* op. cit., p. 71.

[54] For a case study of the Faure reforms, see below, Ch. 8.

teachers can be overcome, if indeed the authoritarian, hierarchical, centralized character of the French educational system gives way to governance by collaboration and cooperation, French education will emerge transformed.

In the past the educational system has reinforced not only class distinctions among Frenchmen, but religious distinctions as well. Approximately four-fifths of French children attend state schools, administered in a highly standardized fashion from Paris. The remaining one-fifth attend private schools, 90 percent of which are Catholic. Religion remains a subject of high political volatility in France largely because of the emotion surrounding the question of government aid to church schools. In 1951, the Barrangé law provided indirect subsidies to the private schools through parents' associations, and in 1959, the Debré law added direct subsidies to those private schools which accepted certain state controls. On both occasions, bitter charges and countercharges were exchanged by such groups as the largest teachers' association, the Federation of National Education (FEN) and the National Committee for Secular Action on the one hand and the Association of Parents of Pupils in Free Schools (APEL) on the other. Both camps flew the banner of "freedom": one meant freedom *from* religious instruction in all tax-supported schools, the other freedom *for* religious instruction, without a double educational cost to the parent.

The battle continues to rage; yet it would appear that some of the turn-of-the-century fury is gone from the debate. In the Third Republic, the priest and public school teacher were captains, respectively, of the Catholic and anticlerical teams in villages all over France. Since the war, a large number of Catholics (particularly women elementary teachers) has been been recruited into the teaching corps of the public schools, and young priests not infrequently have been among the most progressive, reform-minded people in town. Along with the religious question generally, the church school problem, although still alive, seems to divide Frenchmen less bitterly than in the past. According to a national attitude survey done in 1964, of those respondents who declared themselves of the "moderate Left," 64 percent of those with an opinion opposed repeal of state aid to private schools.[55]

The structure of French society has undergone, and is still undergoing, rapid and fundamental change. Sustained prosperity, the gradual blurring of class distinctions, the liberalization of the church, the decline in intensity of religious conflict, the reform of education — all of these changes create a potential for a more consensual, cooperative

---

[55] E. Deutsch, D. Lindon, and P. Weill, *Les Familles Politiques* (Paris: Editions de Minuit, 1966), p. 27.

society.[56] At the same time, however, rapid social and economic change creates new potential grounds for political conflict. One new ground for conflict centers on the "Americanization" of French society. Because America achieved a relatively high stage of affluence before the European countries, it has become a symbol of mass production, impersonality, materialism, and generally what the French call the "consumers' society." However angrily this model is rejected by French students and intellectuals, it seems to be acceptable to most Frenchmen, including workers, so long as they can partake of its riches.

Save perhaps in the areas of economic planning and educational reform, government has had relatively little part in shaping the new French society. Inflation, depression, and war were more important than political leadership in persuading Frenchmen to give up their hopes of clinging to a past style of life. Conversely, at least until the end of the Fourth Republic, social change had little impact upon French government and politics. In France, as in all countries, however, the political system is interrelated with other facets of the society in which it is imbedded. Political parties which cease to adapt their programs and tactics to a changing electorate eventually begin to appear dated, if not irrelevant. As we shall see, the successes of Gaullism and the decline of many of the older parties owe something to the character of the new France as well as to the personality of General de Gaulle.

Beginning with Aristotle, students of politics often have remarked that stable, nontyrannical democracy (Aristotle's "polity") seems to survive best in societies in which the middle class is large and in which the economic gap between the wealthy and the poor is moderate. Prosperity and industrialization tend eventually to extend the middle class and to give an ever larger proportion of the population a stake in stability and moderation. Should this theory hold true for France, the long-term prospects for stable democracy there would seem better than ever before. To be sure, the social and political explosion of May 1958 was clear evidence that affluence is no guarantee of social harmony. Political attitudes, political leadership, and political institutions all may restrict the political effects of changes in social structure. The following chapters will examine these factors.

[56] Harvey Waterman explores this theme in *Political Change in Contemporary France* (Columbus, Ohio: Charles E. Merrill, 1969).

3

Political Culture

Why have the Swiss and the Scandinavians been able to maintain stable and effective democracies with governmental institutions and party systems outwardly similar to those of the French? Why has constitutional engineering so rarely produced the intended changes in French political behavior? For clues to the answers to such questions, one must look beyond institutions to French historical experience and its legacy in the typical beliefs, symbols, and values which shape the outlook of the French upon politics, both at the mass and at the elite levels. In the current terminology of comparative politics, one must examine French "political culture."

Clearly differences in political culture have something to do with the contrast between democracy as practiced in France and Italy on the one hand and in Britain, Switzerland, and Scandinavia, for example, on the other. Yet the student of French political culture must beware on three counts. First, as in all complex societies, French society includes a wide variety of personality types and political attitudes. In some cases, differences in political attitudes between regions, between social classes, or between ideological groupings may be greater than average differences between nations. Stereotypes of national character may obscure more than they illuminate. Second, political attitudes may be as often the *products* of experience with certain kinds of institutions and leaders as their cause.[1] Third, there is relatively little precise evidence from attitude surveys which might allow confident judgments regarding the proportion of the population holding certain attitudes. Often our discussion of necessity will be impressionistic; at times, attitudes will have to be inferred from behavior — a risky procedure. Nonetheless, the topic is too important to be ignored simply

[1] On this point see Dankwart Rustow, "Transitions to Democracy: Toward a Dynamic Model," *Comparative Politics,* II: 3 (April 1970), pp. 337–363.

because the evidence is not all in. The following discussion will proceed in dialectical fashion, focusing first upon a trait which is generally attributed to the French, and then upon the qualifications to the traditional image suggested by recent evidence and apparent trends in French political culture.

The French Character

Individualism

It is a commonplace, noted by almost all observers, domestic and foreign, that the French tend to be individualists.[2] Theirs is not an individualism distinguished by open and flagrant nonconformism to established cultural patterns, however. In dress, in manners, even in opinions on social and political matters, the self-professed French individualist may conform very closely to the norms of his social milieu. He is an individualist not so much because of what he does (although he is a staunch defender of his family, his economic interests, and his personal independence) as because of what he *refuses* to do. Typically, in the past, he has shunned any type of group affiliation which might place restrictions and social obligations upon him. Although sociable enough in casual encounters, he has viewed detachment from all social commitments as the ideal means of safeguarding his independence. It was this kind of individualism which the Radical philosopher, Alain, had in mind when he wrote that "The most striking characteristic of democracy is that it is anti-social."[3] Individualism in this sense of social detachment seems to have been common to most segments of French society. Workers have been reluctant to tie themselves to unions in the same way that small businessmen have rebelled against associational bonds.

Very likely the relative meagerness and peculiar character of group life in France is related to the difficulty of achieving compromise and cooperation in French politics. A certain proportion of Frenchmen have long been accustomed to joining associations for the defense of their interests, such as trade associations, farmers groups, and trade unions. One 1951 survey indicated that 41 percent of all Frenchmen belonged to at least one voluntary association; in 1959 and 1960 a cross-national survey produced comparable figures of 57 percent in the United States, 47 percent in Great Britain, 44 percent in Germany, and

[2] See, for example, André Siegfried's lively and perceptive analysis of French society and politics, *France, A Study in Nationality* (New Haven: Yale University Press, 1930).

[3] Alain, *Eléments d'une doctrine radicale,* p. 139.

29 percent in Italy.[4] Scattered evidence from more recent surveys suggests that something like half of all Frenchmen now belong to an association of some sort, not counting church affiliation.[5] Yet one finds in France relatively few community service organizations of the League of Women Voters variety. French associations, more frequently than American and British associations, have been of a type described by one sociologist as "delinquent communities," hostile to government authorities and devoted to the uncompromising defense of a particular interest with complete disregard for the claims and welfare of other portions of the community.[6] As Laurence Wylie remarked, "This phenomenon is not uniquely French, of course, but it is acutely French."[7]

In the early 1960's, a number of students of French society saw signs of increasing willingness among the French to participate in educational, professional, cultural, religious, and other types of voluntary associations.[8] Among the signs was the mushrooming after 1958 of dozens of new political but nonpartisan clubs. Farmers and businessmen seemed to be more interested in professional cooperation, even on occasion between groups of differing ideological outlook. Before the war it would have been difficult to imagine the scene at the 1959 convention of the National Club of Young Farmers (CNJA), where a banner at the rostrum proclaimed: "Individualism: there is the enemy."[9] According to official records, in 1968 nearly 20,000 associations, clubs, and fraternal organizations were formed — 5,000 more than were created in 1967.[10]

One must not exaggerate the importance of this trend, however. French associations typically have commanded only minimal and sporadic participation on the part of their members. Most of the political

[4] The French figure is from Arnold Rose, *Theory and Method in the Social Sciences* (Minneapolis: University of Minnesota Press, 1954), pp. 50–115. Figures for other countries are from Gabriel Almond and Sidney Verba, *The Civic Culture* (Princeton: Princeton University Press, 1963), p. 302.

[5] A survey on agriculture by the French Institute of Public Opinion (IFOP) in 1964 found that 58 percent of farmers interviewed belonged to a professional association (*Sondages,* 1964: No. 1, p. 27). Another preliminary survey by the present author and associates (Ambler, Michelat, and Percheron) found that 53 percent of the members of a rough national sample of 241 belonged to an association.

[6] Jesse Pitts, "Continuity and Change in Bourgeois France," in Hoffmann *et al., In Search of France,* pp. 235–304. See also Orvoell R. Gallagher, "Voluntary Associations in France," *Social Forces,* XXXVI: 2 (December 1957), pp. 153–160.

[7] In Hoffmann *et al., In Search of France,* p. 223.

[8] See especially Laurence Wylie, "Social Change at the Grass Roots."

[9] Wright, *Rural Revolution in France,* p. 155.

[10] "Letter from Paris," *Le Monde Weekly Selection,* April 15, 1970.

clubs now have only a handful of regularly active members. If one probed into the farm cooperative movement, one might well find, as did Edgar Morin in a Breton village, that it works best when most of those cooperating are either young, committed Catholics, or members of the same extended family.[11]

A number of factors apparently have contributed to the poverty of constructive group life in France. Until very recently the church seemingly preferred a passively obedient band of believers, in sharp contrast to the numerous self-governing religious congregations which strongly influenced both social and political life in England and the United States. As de Tocqueville pointed out, the Old Regime purposefully discouraged the formation of voluntary associations and left a legacy of highly centralized government which has severely limited opportunities for participation at the local level. The central importance and social self-sufficiency of the independent family in French society also has discouraged participation in nonfamily groups. Lastly, until the past few years, French schools have seen no purpose in student government, clubs, and other recognized peer group activities.

Even when the Frenchman deigns to join an organization, he usually doesn't leave his taste for individualism behind. In his delightful and revealing book, *The Notebooks of Major Thompson,* Pierre Daninos explains that ". . . for every Frenchman who wakes up as a nudist in Port-de-Bouc, you may be perfectly certain that another Frenchman will arise an anti-nudist in Malo-les-Bains. You might think the antagonism would end there. Hardly. The nudist founds an organization, which elects an Honorary President (himself) and a Vice President. Then the Vice President, having quarreled with the aforesaid President, forms a neo-nudist Committee rather more leftish than the first one. For his part, the anti-nudist, having taken the chair at an Honorary Committee. . . ."[12] The internal schisms which plague French organizations were common occurrences among political parties in the Third and Fourth Republics. From 1945 to 1958, every party represented in the National Assembly, save the Communists, suffered at least one split, including the Gaullists.

The distaste of the French for the obligations of membership in voluntary associations would appear to have political importance, given the abundance of such training grounds for cooperation and compromise in most stable democracies. Yet one must not exaggerate that importance, as some have done, and conclude that France is a "mass society" in which isolated and alienated individuals are easy targets for

[11] Morin, *Une Commune en France,* pp. 116–120.
[12] Pierre Daninos, *The Notebooks of Major Thompson* (New York: Knopf, 1955), p. 38.

totalitarian movements.[13] The bonds of family as well as the pride which Frenchmen traditionally have taken in maintaining their personal independence have substituted for voluntary associations as shields against mass movements.[14] Even in the case of the urban working class, which is indeed attracted to a totalitarian movement, the Communist Party, the appeal seems based more upon a sense of class solidarity than upon a desire to escape from individual alienation.[15]

Mistrust

As a form of government based upon majority vote and upon choice between alternative majorities, democracy in a complex society inevitably requires compromise and cooperation, and hence a certain degree of trust in one's fellow citizens.[16] If there is to be a majority, factions must place their faith in a set of leaders. If election winners are to be accepted by those who voted against them, there must be general confidence that normal democratic procedures will be observed. A recent comparative study reveals that trust in one's fellow citizens is in fact considerably higher in the United States and Great Britain than in Germany and Italy.[17]

Although the evidence does not all point in the same direction, as we shall see, the French usually have been viewed as a mistrustful people who barricade themselves in their fortress-homes behind triple-locked doors and who hide their business affairs behind a thick cloak of secretiveness. Students of French culture repeatedly have remarked upon the Frenchman's suspicion of *"les autres"* — all of those outside his immediate circle.[18] To the Frenchman, it is argued, the social environment is essentially hostile; the safe and appropriate attitude of

[13] William Kornhauser, *The Politics of Mass Society* (Glencoe, Ill.: The Free Press, 1959), pp. 84–89.

[14] On this point I would agree with Duncan MacRae, *Parliament, Parties, and Society in France, 1946–1958*, pp. 28–31.

[15] Gabriel Almond, *The Appeals of Communism* (Princeton: Princeton University Press, 1954), Ch. 9.

[16] On the relationship between social trust and stable democracy, see Morris Rosenberg, "Misanthropy and Political Ideology," *American Sociological Review*, XXI (1956), p. 691; and Almond and Verba, *The Civic Culture*, Ch. 10. Huntington, in *Political Order in Changing Societies,* argues that a minimal level of mutual trust is a requirement of any kind of stable and effective government (pp. 28–32).

[17] The percentages of respondents who believed that "Most people can be trusted" was 55 percent in the United States, 49 percent in Great Britain, 30 percent in Mexico, 19 percent in Germany and 7 percent in Italy. Almond and Verba, *The Civic Culture,* p. 267.

[18] See, for example, Métraux and Mead, *Themes in French Culture;* Wylie, *Village in the Vaucluse;* and Pitts, in Hoffmann *et al., In Search of France.*

the cautious man is to assume that all who are not of the family or close friends are not to be trusted. When business is bad, farm prices low, or wages stagnant, certainly *"les autres"* are to blame, primary among them being politicians and government officials.

Mutual mistrust might be attributed in part to France's divisive and inconclusive revolutionary tradition. It is reinforced and perpetuated by the family and the school. From his earliest years the child is taught to believe in the security of *le foyer* (the household), and the potential threat of outsiders, particularly strangers. In middle-class homes, parents tend to select playmates for their children — often cousins — and to frown upon contacts with outsiders unknown to the family. In school the child who misbehaves or is badly prepared soon feels the sting of ridicule. In its authoritarian style of instruction, in its exclusive stress upon individual rather than group achievement, in its frequent use of ridicule as a motivational device, and in its manipulation of social pressure to reinforce sanctions imposed by the teacher, the school tends to feed and to maintain mutual suspicion in French society.[19]

It may be that this picture of suspiciousness approaching paranoia is overdrawn, or at least dated. In a preliminary attitude survey conducted in the summer of 1969, 241 adult Frenchmen from seven regions of France were asked whether in general it is better to have confidence in people or to mistrust them. Forty-six percent felt that it is better to have either "complete confidence" or "some confidence" in other people, 50 percent thought it better to mistrust them either "a little" or "completely," and the remainder offered no opinion.[20] Comparing these responses with those to a similar but not identical question

[19] The military-type discipline of the traditional French school is described vividly by Jean Boorsch, "Primary Education," in *Yale French Studies,* No. 22 (Winter–Spring, 1958–1959), pp. 22–30. On the use of ridicule, see Wylie, *Village in the Vaucluse,* Ch. 4.

[20] This survey, organized by the author in collaboration with Guy Michelat and Annick Percheron, was a pilot study. A survey of a larger sample will follow. The major bias in the rough quota sample used in the pilot study is its overrepresentation of Left voters. In the first ballot of the presidential elections on June 1, 1969, 47.3 percent of those of our respondents who said they had voted chose a candidate of the Left. Those candidates actually won only 31.4 percent of the votes cast. Since slightly more of the Left voters in this sample had confidence in people (53.5 percent) than did Center and Right voters (48.5 percent), the results of this survey may slightly exaggerate the level of mutual trust of the French population as a whole. As might be expected, nonvoters, and those who refused to divulge their vote, less often declared trust in people (36.2 percent) than either Left or Right voters. A portion of the findings of this survey are reported in John Ambler, "How Frenchmen View Authority: Ambivalence and the Participant Society," a paper delivered at the Western Political Science Association meetings, April, 1970.

posed to German, Italian, British, Mexican, and American samples in 1960, the French respondents offered more "trustful" responses (46 percent) than the Italians (7 percent), Germans (19 percent), and Mexicans (30 percent), but fewer than the British (49 percent) or the Americans (55 percent).[21] Although the French sample is too small and roughly drawn to permit generalization about the attitudes of the whole French population, the results do suggest that the commonplace image of the mistrustful Frenchman needs more empirical testing.

Incivisme

In the realm of politics, individualism, detachment, and suspicion become what the French call *incivisme,* or lack of civic spirit. One measure of *incivisme* is mistrust of the national government and of the politicians and administrators who run it. Laurence Wylie catches this flavor of *incivisme* in his fascinating study of a small village in Southern France. "Theoretically," he writes, "Government may be an alter ego of *la patrie,* but in point of fact it is made up of men — weak, stupid, selfish, ambitious men. It is the duty of the citizen *not* to co-operate with these men, as the civics books would have people do, but rather to hinder them, to prevent them in every possible way from increasing their power over individuals and over families."[22] A national survey conducted by the French Institute of Public Opinion (IFOP) in 1962 found that 77 percent of the respondents felt that political candidates in their districts were "not at all" motivated by a desire to serve their fellow citizens, while 87 percent had "no confidence at all" that their deputy or senator would defend their interests."[23] In other surveys conducted from September 1962 to March 1969, IFOP found that never fewer than 48 percent and sometimes as many as 60 percent of their interviewees felt that the administration of justice was functioning badly in France.[24]

Some of the results of the 241-interview pilot study conducted in 1969 and referred to earlier are suggestive on the subject of political mistrust, although the inadequate size and representativeness of the sample, as well as its Leftist bias, require extreme caution in general-

---

[21] Almond and Verba, *The Civic Culture,* p. 267. In these surveys, the respondent was asked to agree or disagree with the statement: "Most people can be trusted."

[22] Wylie, *Village in the Vaucluse,* p. 207.

[23] Guy Michelat, "Attitudes et Comportements Politiques à l'Automne 1962," in *Le Référendum d'Octobre et les Elections de Novembre 1962,* Cahiers de la Fondation Nationale des Sciences Politiques, No. 142 (Paris: A. Colin, 1965), p. 256.

[24] *Sondages,* 1969: Nos. 1 and 2, p. 35.

izing from these results. Like the IFOP figures cited above, they suggest that mistrust of government is indeed widespread in France. Of the 241 respondents 51 percent felt that the actions of the French administration are "often" or "always" unjust. When asked how they would be treated if they had occasion to deal with an office of the government administration, only 27 percent of the total sample felt their views would receive serious consideration.[25] The Almond and Verba Five-Nation study of 1960, which included a very similar question, found that "serious consideration" was expected by 53 percent of all Germans interviewed, 48 percent of American, 59 percent of British, 35 percent of Italian, and 14 percent of Mexican respondents.[26] In response to another question in the 241-interview study concerning how people feel generally about the government, 58 percent of those 228 respondents who offered an opinion selected the option that "in general people tend to mistrust the government, whatever kind it may be." Only 58 percent of all 241 respondents agreed completely (16 percent) or more or less (42 percent) with the statement that "the people decide how the country shall be run through the vote." A similar statement in the Almond and Verba study drew agreement from 71 percent of American, 83 percent of British, 62 percent of Italian, 78 percent of German, and 65 percent of Mexican respondents.[27] Even discounting for the Leftist bias of the French sample, these findings suggest that mistrust of government and a feeling of inability to influence government are roughly as widespread in France as in Italy and considerably more widespread in France than in the United States, Germany, or Great Britain.

Given this and corroborating evidence from larger surveys, it seems clear that the level of mistrust of government is relatively high in France. Yet one must not assume without further evidence that political mistrust is simply a manifestation of generalized mutual mistrust in French culture. Indeed, once Left voters and Center-Right voters were separated, the 241-interview study revealed little correlation between general trust in people and trust in government. Moreover, it seems likely that the level of trust in government in France varies by region and by level of government. Mark Kesselman has argued persuasively that there is less conflict, mistrust, and turnover in French local government — at least in smaller cities and towns — than in national government.[28]

[25] For a description of the survey, see p. 51, note 20 above.

[26] Almond and Verba, *The Civic Culture*, p. 109.

[27] Inter-University Consortium for Political Research, *The Five Nation Study* (Ann Arbor: University of Michigan Press, 1968), p. 92.

[28] Mark Kesselman, *The Ambiguous Consensus, A Study of Local Government in France* (New York: Knopf, 1967), especially Chs. 1 and 10.

A second expression of *incivisme* is in the "delinquent community" style of much pressure group activity, notably a total lack of concern for the rights of other groups or of the general public. Righteous defense of interests is so commonplace that Frenchmen found nothing particularly unusual in the refusal of striking miners to obey a government order to return to work in 1963, the tractor blockade of national highways by indignant farmers in 1961, or even the kidnapping of a mayor and three policemen by disgruntled shopkeepers in 1969.

A third striking manifestation is found in the extensive tax fraud which has plagued French governments. For example, in 1947 the government estimated the average doctor's income to be 400,000 old francs; doctors actually declared an average income of 153,000 francs.[29] When one rents an apartment in France, he often is asked to pay in cash in order to leave no trail for internal revenue. (*"C'est une question du fisc, vous savez."*) Small businessmen notoriously keep two sets of books, one accurate set to be carefully hidden away, and another set for the revenue service, often reducing actual receipts by half or more. When the government inspectors were instructed to look more carefully in the 1950's, small merchants ganged together under Poujadist leadership forcibly to prevent inspections. Public opinion seems not to consider tax evasion to be a very serious offense. In an opinion poll conducted in 1964, only 55 percent of respondents felt it was "normal" to declare all of one's income. Nineteen percent felt it normal to "leave out as much as possible," 11 percent to "make some omissions," and the remainder refused to express an opinion.[30] In the 241-interview pilot study, only 39 percent of the respondents were willing to criticize tax evaders. The most common view (held by over a third) was that "everyone manages as he can." In keeping with the lack of public indigation at tax evasion, the internal revenue service often bargains with the evader rather than throwing him in jail.

Once again, as in the case of mistrustfulness, the presumed *incivisme* of the French needs qualification. Tax fraud may be due in part to the unusually large proportion of self-employed persons in the French labor force. These, of course, are the people who can most easily doctor their figures. As an ever larger proportion of the working force moves into positions where wages and salaries are fixed and reported to the government, tax fraud should decrease. Nonetheless, its frequency in past years is evidence of French reluctance to fulfill willingly one of the normal obligations of citizenship.

As for the presumed apathy and cynicism of French citizens, it must

[29] Fabrice Marpier, "Epargne forcée, impôt voluntaire et solidarité nationale," *Esprit*, January 1949, p. 20.

[30] *Sondages,* 1964: No. 4, pp. 19–20.

be noted that since 1945 an average of 78 percent of all registered voters and almost 70 percent of the total voting-age population have turned out to vote in national elections; almost three-quarters of registered voters show up at the polls for municipal elections.[31] The percentage of voter turnout in French national elections is very similar to the average turnout in Great Britain and far higher than that in the United States, where it is rare for more than 60 percent of the voting-age population to show up at the polls even in a presidential election. The American comparison is misleading, for residence requirements, racial discrimination, and cumbersome registration requirements all have discouraged voting. In France, as in most European countries, eligible voters are automatically registered by the local government, which revises the list of voters annually. Yet it seems only fair to admit that on this important measure of democratic citizenship, Americans at least have no greater claim to virtue than Frenchmen.

Yet another qualification to the *incivisme* image of the Frenchman is his underlying patriotism, which comes to the surface periodically. In the interwar period, it appeared that although tight with his tax contribution the Frenchman was eager to serve his country in time of crisis, as he had done so valiantly in World War I. As André Siegfried, one of the more acute observers of the French political style, put it in 1930:

> Ask a Frenchman for his money to save his country, and perhaps he will not give it to you, in fact at the very moment when he shows himself ready to sacrifice his life. But appeal to him if you are defending, not a political platform of interests, but ideals like liberty, equality, or the Republic, and you will find yourself surrounded by hundreds and thousands of enthusiastic supporters.[32]

[31] For example, on the first ballot of the legislative elections of March 1967, 22,887,151 voters turned out: 81 percent of the 28,291,838 registered voters or 71 percent of the voting age population of 31,992,000. (The voting-age population was calculated from data in République Française, Institut National de la Statistique et des Etudes Economiques, *Annuaire Statistique, 1968,* p. 30.) For a detailed discussion of national election turnouts, see Alain Lancelot, *L'Abstentionnisme Electoral en France,* Cahiers de la Fondation Nationale des Sciences Politiques, No. 196 (Paris: A. Colin, 1968), especially Ch. 1; and Marie-Thérèse and Alain Lancelot, "Atlas des Elections Françaises de 1968 et 1969," *Revue Française de Science Politique,* XX: 2 (April 1970), pp. 312–328. On turnouts in local elections, see Kesselman, *The Ambiguous Consensus,* pp. 19–26.

[32] *France, A Study in Nationality,* p. 20. On the same theme, see Carlton J. Hayes, *France, a Nation of Patriots* (New York: Columbia University Press, 1930).

The crises of the 1930's, the debacle of 1940, and the postwar strength of the Communist Party have all revealed that the antagonisms between Frenchmen are sometimes more powerful than the common loyalties which unite them. And yet Gaullist successes in the Fifth Republic have demonstrated that when circumstances are right a large proportion of the French population still responds warmly to a nationalist appeal.

Attitudes toward Authority

One of the most critical, yet least studied ingredients in any political system is the distribution of attitudes toward political authority. Particularly in a democracy, where the powers of coercion must be kept within legal bounds, widespread rebelliousness against authority may jeopardize either the effectiveness of the political system, if individual liberties are respected, or the very survival of democracy if they are not. Judging from the behavior of the French, their attitudes toward political authority appear to be characterized by serious ambivalence. At times smoldering rebellion and obedient submission seem to co-exist, as in the Third and Fourth Republics when public opinion tended to mock parliament and scorn government leaders while it deferred to a powerful and highly centralized bureaucracy. Sometimes the contradictory attitudes are seen in sequence, as when opinion seems to fear strong government in peaceful times, then turns enthusiastically to a national saviour (be he named Napoleon, Clemenceau, Pétain, or de Gaulle) in times of crisis. The events of the springs of 1968 and 1969 offer poignant examples. The anti-authoritarian individualism which exploded in the street demonstrations of May 1968 (apparently with broad public sympathy at the outset among Parisians) gave way in June 1968 to a landslide electoral victory for the Gaullists, those staunch defenders of governmental stability. Then the patricide of April 1969, when the electorate rejected de Gaulle's referendum proposal knowing his resignation would follow, was almost undone less than two months later by the victory of Gaullist candidate Georges Pompidou in the presidential elections. In both Gaullist victories, the fear of disorder played a major role.

Evidence from attitude surveys also suggests an ambivalence toward governmental authority. We have seen how little confidence the French have in politicians and in government. Yet in a major national survey conducted in 1967, 51 percent of the respondents expressed the view that government stability is "very important," 28 percent that it is "fairly important," and less than 5 percent that it is "rather unimportant" or "not at all important," with the remaining respondents offering no opinion.[33] A similar question concerning the government's task in maintaining order was asked in the 241-interview survey in 1969. Of those respondents who offered an opinion, 40 percent felt that responsibility to be "a very important thing," and another 46 percent a "fairly important thing," as against 11 percent who found it "of little importance" and 3 percent "of no importance." These are hardly the responses one would expect from latent anarchists.

Michel Crozier, a leading French sociologist, has proposed a solution to these paradoxes. In *The Bureaucratic Phenomenon* he suggests that the Frenchman's passion for personal independence and his fear of being caught in dependency relationships lead him whenever possible to avoid direct, face-to-face contacts, especially with superiors. Whether the problem be one of labor-management relations or of a tenant-landlord dispute, the Frenchman tends to feel that in direct, face-to-face bargaining he may be treated as an inferior, he will risk humiliation if he loses, and in the event of an agreement he will have sacrificed some of his freedom of action.

Counterbalancing this passion for personal independence, in Crozier's view, is an equally strong desire for order in society, and hence a recognition of the need for authority. The French resolve their dilemma by shunting most of the problems of human relations off onto an impersonal and centralized bureaucracy. "Authority is converted, as much as possible, into impersonal rules. The whole structure is so devised that whatever authority cannot be eliminated is allocated so that it is at a safe distance from the people who are affected."[34] When conflicts between groups arise, government is expected to intervene and arbitrate, sparing the antagonists the unpleasantness of direct personal encounter. And yet bureaucracy itself is restricted by the rigid and impersonal rules by which it functions. It is incapable of changing the rules in order to face up to new economic, social, and international problems. As a result, problems build into crises, until the nation eventually must turn to a powerful political leader who can unite the citizenry and resolve the crisis, before giving way to yet another bureaucratic era.

[33] A preliminary report on portions of this study is contained in Roy Pierce and Samuel Barnes, "Public Opinion and Political Preference in France and Italy," a paper presented to the American Political Science Association meetings, September 1970. The figures cited are estimated from Figure 1.

[34] Michel Crozier, *The Bureaucratic Phenomenon* (Chicago: University of Chicago Press, 1964), p. 222. French ambivalence toward authority is also explored by Stanley Hoffmann in "Heroic Leadership: The Case of Modern France," in Lewis J. Edinger, ed., *Political Leadership in Industrialized Societies* (New York: Wiley, 1967).

This thesis is an engaging one, although it remains speculative. There are scattered bits of evidence which seem not to fit. For example in 1970 four trade unions and the major employers association (the CNPF) met and came to an agreement on the creation of a job-training and retraining program. One of their reasons for settling the problem "face-to-face," it was reported, was to avoid government intervention. A more significant exception to the Crozier model of French society is the so-far successful effort of the Gaullists to institutionalize strong government leadership. Lastly, the 241-interview pilot study of 1969 failed to reveal any positive relationship between individualism (the passion for personal independence) and dislike for face-to-face relationships with superiors.

In view of this contrary, but far from conclusive, evidence, it would seem wise to pursue alternative explanations to the French authority paradox. Could it be that French ambivalence toward authority is rooted more deeply in historical experience with politics than in some general cultural or psychological trait? Such an explanation (which is just as speculative as Crozier's) might run along the following lines. In France, in contrast to the United States, belief in strong government is generally regarded as typical of the political Right rather than of the Left. Individual liberty and minimal government controls were the natural ideals of those middle-class republicans who turned conservative once the privileges of the nobility had been destroyed and once Napoleon had embroiled the nation in perpetual war; yet they often felt obliged to defend strong government, and especially strong executive leadership, in order to protect the status quo against the lingering monarchist threat and, more important, against the egalitarian claims of a growing proletariat. The ideal of maximum liberty conflicted with the practical need for strong authority in defense of order.

Among democrats of the Left, the Jacobins of the revolutionary period favored strong government, but largely for negative reasons: they feared that weak government would permit local reactionary movements to undo the accomplishments of the Revolution. Following the Revolution, experience with a long chain of antirepublican men on horseback, from Napoleon Bonaparte to Marshal Pétain, overshadowed the Jacobin legacy to the Left of social reform through strong government. The Socialists, like the Radicals, came to fear and despise strong executive leadership, even though concentrated governmental authority again would be essential, as it was during the Revolution, were the Socialists ever able and willing to effect broad social reforms.

On both the Left and Right, the French have learned to mistrust strong political leadership; yet both camps, for differing reasons, at times have had need of it. The instability and relative ineffectiveness of government under the Third and Fourth Republics (which the public judges severely in opinion polls) tended to reinforce mistrust of the quarrelsome politicians; at the same time political instability reminded Frenchmen of the importance of order. To add to the ambivalence, ever since the Revolution, numerous Frenchmen of the Left as well as the Right have been willing periodically to forget their antagonism to political authority in response to a nationalist appeal.

More research is needed to reveal whether the answer to the French authority paradox lies in the link between a general cultural pattern and politics, or whether it is hidden in the distinctive political past of the French.

Ideology and Politicization

Americans and Englishmen, who are accustomed to a pragmatic and largely nonideological style of politics, frequently are struck by what seems to be a constant and dramatic confrontation between political doctrines in France. Indeed, Frenchmen not infrequently find Anglo-Saxon politics to be muddled and illogical; ideological consistency and the ability to follow first political principles to their logical conclusions are qualities of mind more esteemed and refined in France than across the channel. When the first principles of rival political groups clash as sharply as they do in France, however, the consequence of ideological politics is conflict and stalemate.

Since in the Third and Fourth Republics no party could ever exercise full power, doctrine tended to become divorced from action. Robert de Jouvenel once remarked of the Third Republic that "Our legislators are far less interested in the content of the bills before them than in the resolution closing the debate."[35] In similar fashion, many of those farm owners in certain parts of France who proudly exhibit their Leftist leanings and anticlericalism by voting for the Communist Party would be horrified if that party ever won enough votes actually to attempt a Communist reconstruction of French society.

The French taste for abstract political ideals and the French difficulty in effecting practical reform seem to be products of a number of historical and sociological factors, most of which have already been mentioned. The accumulation of issues — church-state relations, legitimate constitutional form, and employer-worker relations, no one of which has been solved — tends to infuse ideological issues into all sorts of otherwise mundane questions. Lack of experience in local self-government or in voluntary associations deprives most Frenchmen of experience in achieving compromise solutions. The pattern is reinforced

[35] *La République des Camarades* (Paris: Grasset, 1914), p. 89.

by an educational system which prizes abstract rationality and consistency and which gives little attention to the practical aspects of collective problem-solving.

In the past and still to an extent today, mutually hostile political camps have been able to create self-perpetuating political subcultures, largely isolated from their rivals. Until the political conservatism of the church began to soften, conservative Catholics were able to live in communities of like-minded persons, send their children to Catholic schools (to be taught the evils of republicanism), read only Catholic newspapers, and shun all organizations in which they might confront ideas different from their own. Still today the Communist worker often lives in such a ghetto, for example in the "red-belt" suburbs around Paris, with the Party — the proletarian church — attending to his every need for companionship, for recognition, for information, and for the designation of appropriate targets on which to vent his hostilities. However, many Frenchmen were never fully isolated in such a subculture, for ideological lines and class lines have never coincided, and mass communication as well as social and geographical mobility are threatening those ideological ghettos which remain. Nonetheless, France continues to lack a set of political symbols capable of creating an affective bond between the government and all of her people. Laurence Wylie described vividly how the people of Chanzeaux, a small village in Western France, continue to attend mass and to vote for parties of the Right in respect for an antirevolutionary tradition which dates from the Vendéen uprising against the revolutionary government in the 1790's. With equal respect for tradition (in this case a revolutionary tradition), the people of Rousillon, a village in the South of France, pride themselves on their anticlericalism and on their Leftist politics.[36]

In 1962–1963, some four hundred children in the French city of Grenoble, ranging in age from ten to fourteen, were asked, among other things, "Was the French Revolution of 1789 a good thing or a bad thing?" Of the children in public schools, 66 percent replied a "good thing" and 21 percent a "bad thing"; yet of those in private Catholic schools, just as many felt it was "bad" (41 percent) as "good" (41 percent).[37] In general the differences between Catholic and public school attitudes reported in this study are not as dramatic as the "two

[36] Wylie, *Village in the Vaucluse,* pp. 206–239; and Wylie, *Chanzeaux,* pp. 245–278.

[37] Charles Roig and Françoise Billon-Grand, *La Socialisation Politique des Enfants,* Cahiers de la Fondation Nationale des Sciences Politiques, No. 163 (Paris: A. Colin, 1968), p. 115. For a summary and critique of this book in English, see Fred I. Greenstein and Sidney G. Tarrow, "The Study of French Political Socialization: Toward the Revocation of Paradox," *World Politics,* XXII: 1 (October 1969), pp. 95–137.

Table 3.1

Opinions by "Political Family"

	Extreme Left	Moderate Left	Center	Moderate Right	Extreme Right	"Marais" (Uninvolved, floating Center)
	N=269	N=333	N=243	N=312	N=205	N=719
Government aid to private schools should be abolished						
Agree	63%	31%	15%	8%	12%	10%
Disagree	33	54	74	82	82	64
No Opinion	4	15	11	10	6	26
It is regrettable that France lost all her colonies						
Agree	32	47	50	54	76	52
Disagree	57	41	40	28	14	20
No Opinion	11	12	10	18	10	28
We should try to build socialism						
Agree	84	69	58	38	32	31
Disagree	6	11	15	21	31	9
No Opinion	10	20	27	41	37	60
Private big businesses should be nationalized						
Agree	58	34	23	25	29	22
Disagree	22	42	57	50	47	29
No Opinion	20	24	20	25	24	49
The authority of the government must be maintained						
Agree	19	30	48	54	62	36
Disagree	73	58	42	30	26	24
No Opinion	8	12	10	16	12	40

Source: Emeric Deutsch, Denis Lindon, and Pierre Weill, *Les Familles Politiques Aujourd'hui en France* (Paris: Les Editions de Minuit, 1966), pp. 109–112.

Frances" interpretation would imply; and yet it is hard to imagine anything near this proportion of American children, whatever school they might attend, replying that the American Revolution was a "bad thing," or English children responding that the Glorious Revolution of 1688 had been a mistake. With few exceptions, the political symbols and political traditions which do exist in France are divisive and die hard, even in a period of rapid social change.

Clearly political antagonisms are greater in France than in Britain and the United States. Whether the average French citizen is more ideological, in the sense of judging all political issues in terms of a fixed doctrine, is another question. Indeed, James Bryce, in his classic *Modern Democracies,* published in 1921, noted that "A large section of the population, especially in rural districts and in the smaller towns, cares little about politics unless when some question arises directly affecting their occupation, and . . . many of those who vote at a general election, because they are brought up to the polls, give so slight attention to public matters that definite opinions cannot be attributed to them."[38] Modern survey research has tended to support this view and to suggest that the average Frenchman is not significantly more doctrinaire or ideological in his approach to political issues than the average American.[39] As shown in Table 3.1, a national survey of French political attitudes, conducted in June 1964, discovered a remarkable lack of agreement among those who declare themselves to be of the Right as well as among those who declare themselves to be of the Left. State aid to church schools — one of the issues often thought to be a supreme test of "Rightness" — is favored by 54 percent of those who think of themselves as belonging to the Moderate Left, and even by 33 percent of those on the *Extreme* Left! If the Left is more united in favor of "building socialism," (69 percent of the Moderate Left and 84 percent of the Extreme Left), surprisingly enough this objective also wins more favor than disfavor among those of the Right. When socialism is defined more precisely as nationalization of big businesses, the Moderate Left opposes it by 42 percent to 34 percent and support on the Extreme Left drops to 58 percent. Moreover, 63 percent of the respondents declared themselves "very little" or "not at all" interested in politics.[40]

With the exception of the nationalization of industries question,

[38] James Bryce, *Modern Democracies* (New York: Macmillan, 1921), Vol. I, pp. 287–288.

[39] Philip E. Converse and Georges Dupeux, "Politicization of the Electorate in France and the United States," *Public Opinion Quarterly,* XXVI: 1 (Spring, 1962), pp. 1–24.

[40] Deutsch, *et al., Les Familles Politiques Aujourd'hui en France,* p. 16.

there is a gap of at least 43 percent between the level of agreement to these survey statements among those identifying with the Extreme Left and those identifying with the Extreme Right, which indicates that the Left-Right spectrum does still have some meaning, although some probably think the distinction is based primarily on one's attitude toward the church, while others think it is based on economic philosophies and still others think it is based on the now dated decolonization issue. The responses to the last question in Table 3.1 reveal that another traditional issue separating Left and Right is still alive: the Right insists more strongly than the left upon strong governmental authority, primarily for the purpose of defending law and order against the radical advocates of change. Other survey evidence suggests that those who identify with the Right are also still more concerned with maintaining hierarchy and discipline throughout society and hence are less sympathetic than the Left to the suggestion that subordinates, children in the family, students in school, or workers in the factory, be allowed to participate in the decision-making process.[41]

Fuzzy as the concepts of Left and Right are, they may be the most stable anchor available to a Frenchman as he tries to find and maintain his position in the turbulent sea of French politics. In the United States, the customary anchor has been partly loyalty, which grossly simplifies politics and voting for many of the 75 percent of Americans who identify with either the Democratic or Republican parties. In France, since 1947 all parties have lost from two-thirds to three-fourths of their members, and a survey conducted in the fall of 1958 showed that in that year (one, to be sure, in which parties were out of favor), less than 45 percent of those who agreed to answer identified themselves with one of the numerous and changing political parties on the scene.[42] So long as the political loyalties of French citizens are not institutionalized (that is attached to a political party), their voting choices may fluctuate widely from election to election, with unsettling effects on the political system.[43]

Given the fuzziness and overlap of attitudes on the Right and Left, the term "ideological" seems too strong to apply to the French electorate. It may be that the ideological aspects of the French political style are due more to the attitudes and habits of a small minority of political activists than to those of the general public. Nevertheless, at

[41] Ambler, "How Frenchmen View Authority," p. 18.

[42] Converse and Dupeaux, "Politicization of the Electorate," pp. 9–10.

[43] Philip Converse has argued that party loyalty is one important measure of the level of institutionalization, and hence of the stability, of a democracy. "Of Time and Partisan Stability," *Comparative Political Studies,* II: 2 (July 1969), pp. 139–171.

the mass level the symbolism and tradition attached to the church and to the Communist Party continue to evoke strong and divisive sentiments even among Frenchmen who know very little about the ideologies which the symbols presumably represent.

The "Political Class"

A democracy which lacks consensus at the level of mass attitudes is not necessarily condemned to instability. The examples of Holland and Austria show how leaders of contending factions of a divided society can cooperate sufficiently to make democracy work, if they feel the stakes are high enough.[44] Yet it may be that when antagonisms at the mass level surpass an undefined threshold, it becomes impossible for leaders to cooperate with the enemy without losing the support of their own communities. As we shall see, French elites did cooperate in the Fourth and Fifth Republics, but not in such a way as to maximize governmental effectiveness.

Since French politics often seem ideological to the outsider, and since the masses are not highly ideological, one might conclude that French politicians and party cadres are inflexible ideologues, who view all political problems in terms of class struggle, or Christian mission, or some other universal key. Only a portion of the Communists and a few politicians of the extreme Right fully fit this description. Inflexibility is common enough on a few symbolic issues, as in the cases of traditional Leftist hostility to church schools and to the strong executive, and fundamental divisions persist with regard to economic policy. On a host of lesser questions, however, members of the National Assembly long ago learned to exchange favors with political foes, to fight doggedly in defense of the local interests of their constituencies, and to divorce practice from principle occasionally in the interest of reelection. Before the Communist Party was created, one of the Assembly's most entertaining critics, Robert de Jouvenal, was able truthfully to remark that "There is less difference between two deputies, one of whom is a revolutionary and the other of whom is not, than between two revolutionaries, one of whom is a deputy and the other of whom is not."[45]

The clublike atmosphere of the Assembly and the common interest

---

[44] See Arend Lijphart, *The Politics of Accommodation: Pluralism and Democracy in the Netherlands* (Berkeley: University of California Press, 1968); and, by the same author, "Typologies of Democratic Systems," *Comparative Political Studies*, I: 1 (April 1968), pp. 3–44.

[45] *La République des Camarades*, p. 17.

of deputies in holding on to their seats produced what appears to the cynical observer as a conspiracy against the public. Throughout the Third and Fourth Republics, the tacit rules of the political game called for procrastination and evasion of responsibility whenever major problems arose, on the theory that "those who crawl do not fall."[46] Deputies quickly learned to guard jealously against premiers and ministers who might expand executive powers at the Assembly's expense.

This game of politics was not so completely cynical as it might appear. In the Third and again in the Fourth Republic, enemies of the Republic on both the Left and the Right forced all who wished to save the regime to live together in what inevitably was an unholy and ineffective alliance, joining men as different in political outlook as are, for example, conservative Republicans and Socialists in the United States. Presumably in order to defend a higher ideal, the Republic, a few men like Socialist leader Guy Mollet were willing virtually to ignore their political principles in order to hold a cabinet together. But whenever it was suggested that the "Third Force" of Center and Center-Left parties fuse into a single party capable of supporting stable government, party officials revived the church school issue and the question of socialism to prove the impossibility of union.

As we have noted, party loyalty appears to be relatively weak in France at the mass level. Throughout the Fourth Republic, however, party workers and officials were so strongly attached to traditional party platforms and to the old party structures that attempts at federation repeatedly failed.[47] Even when overcome by Gaullist majorities in the Fifth Republic, the Popular Republicans, the Radicals, and the Socialists have strongly resisted any federation which would mean the disappearance of their familiar "old houses."

The attitudes and habits acquired by active politicians prior to 1958 are by no means dead. Evasion of responsibility, jealousy of executive leadership, attachment to the old party structures, and fascination with the old and divisive issues of French politics were some of the characteristics of a parliamentary game over which the general public had very little control. Unless these attitudes and habits are changed permanently, there remains the possibility of reversion to the earlier

---

[46] Nathan Leites, *On the Game of Politics in France* (Stanford: Stanford University Press, 1959), p. 145, quoting from *La Nef*, February 1958, p. 6.

[47] The impact of the partisan and ideological rigidity of party militants is a recurrent theme in MacRae, *Parliament, Parties, and Society in France, 1946–1958.* For a contrary view, which insists more strongly on the politician's desire for reelection as a primary motivation, see Howard Rosenthal, "The Electoral Politics of Gaullists in the Fourth French Republic: Ideology or Constituency Interest?" *American Political Science Review,* LXIII: 2 (June 1969), pp. 476–487.

French political style in the post-Gaullist era, however great the transformations in the larger French society.

A New French Political Culture?

Although changes in political attitudes are not as readily observable
as changes in social structure, there are occasional signs of change in
this arena as well. Beginning soon after the Liberation, the French
Planning Commission set out to break down mistrust between businessmen and government administrators. The moment was propitious, for
Frenchmen in all walks of life seemed eager to help rebuild the economy and to share in a new kind of prosperity. Out of hundreds of
meetings at the regional and national levels, held anew each time a
four-year plan is constructed, there gradually has emerged an unprecedented spirit of cooperation. As labor and farm representatives
were brought into the advisory committees, antagonistic groups have
been given an opportunity to exchange points of view in a private and
informal setting, keeping the needs of the overall economy ever in
view. Mistrust and antagonism certainly have not disappeared through
these sessions; yet a greater sense of economic reality and a greater
mutual understanding between antagonists do seem to have emerged.[48]
Despite the limited number of people involved, this is a significant innovation in a society where face-to-face relations have so long been
avoided. Very likely these planning conferences have had some part in
the gradual mutation of negative "delinquent-community" type farm
and business groups into what at times appear to be more constructive
professional associations.

And yet, if there are more examples of cooperative behavior by organized interests than in the past, the old style of bitter confrontation
is still alive. The new style of labor-management relations acclaimed
in the mid-1960's gave way to another massive confrontation in the
highly political general strike of May 1968. The trade unions have
become increasingly disillusioned by the planning process, which they
view as dominated by conservative businessmen and government technocrats. The Norman farmers who "kidnapped" Education Minister
Olivier Guichard and then harangued him with their grievances for
over an hour and the truck drivers who chose to dramatize their demand for higher wages by blocking the exits from Paris at the begin-

---

[48] See Michel Crozier, "Pour une analyse sociologique de la planification
française," *Revue Française de Sociologie*, VI: 2 (April–June 1965), pp.
147–163; Crozier, "Indications of Change in the Pattern of French Administration," *Human Relations*, XIX: 3 (1966), pp. 323–335; and *La Planification comme Processus de Décision*, Cahiers de la Fondation Nationale des
Sciences Politiques, No. 140 (Paris: A. Colin, 1965).

ning of the August 1970 vacation period both were behaving in the traditional manner.

As suggested earlier, the passing of the extended family and the democratization of relations within the nuclear family ought to contribute to a more participatory and cooperative society. However, until May 1968 the philosophy of the schools — particularly the *lycées* — changed less rapidly than that of the family, despite the rapid expansion of their enrollments. There was limited experimentation with student government and some adoption of inductive learning techniques; but in the main the school offered little opportunity for discussion and even less for open dissent from a teacher's opinion. In the universities as well, the instructor frequently remained a distant, unapproachable, and authoritative source of wisdom. There was indeed incongruence between authoritarianism in the classroom and democracy in the political arena.[49] This is not to say that the teacher's authority was never challenged; but challenges took the form of raucus classroom disturbances (the classic *chahut*) rather than open discussion and debate. Indeed the demonstrations of May 1968 were in part a gigantic protest against school authorities, a monumental *chahut*.

It is still too early to tell whether the educational reforms which followed the events of May 1968 will change these characteristics of French education. The representative councils of administration which were created in each school were intended to create an institutionalized means for exchange of views among teachers, administrators, parents, and students. If successful, this reform could add a new dimension to the socialization of French children into the citizen's role in a participatory democracy. At the moment, one can only predict that lasting changes will come slowly and against the strong resistance of tradition.

Perhaps the most important change in French political attitudes has been the declining popular appeal of the old political parties and their doctrines, with the partial exception of the Communist Party. Although party leaders bemoan the new political apathy of the French, a glance at the high election turnouts of recent years suggests that the French have only lost interest in parties, not in politics.[50]

[49] One knowledgeable French political scientist, Alfred Grosser, attributes much of the French aversion to the constructive participation to the French school's typically authoritarian climate and stress upon individual competition. "France: Nothing but Opposition," in Robert Dahl, ed., *Political Oppositions in Western Democracies* (New Haven: Yale University Press, 1966), p. 291.

[50] This was the conclusion of a conference of French political scientists, held in 1961. *Cahiers de la Fondation Nationale des Sciences Politiques,* No. 120, *La Dépolitisation, Mythe ou Réalité?* (Paris: A. Colin, 1962). See also Alain Lancelot, *L'Abstentionnisme Electoral en France.*

With the Gaullists in the lead, the parties are beginning to talk more about housing, schools, highways, and wages and less about the church, the Revolution, and class struggle. De Gaulle contributed to these changes in French political style. As a nationalist, he stressed the importance of national unity, appealed continually to national pride, played down the old divisive issues, and among the trinity of revolutionary virtues placed greatest emphasis on fraternity. His own political battle with the older political parties of course produced a new line of cleavage: that between Gaullists and anti-Gaullists. Although a Catholic, and hence representative of tradition, de Gaulle was also a vigorous modernizer, intent upon keeping France abreast of technological advancement. His followers have helped to infuse a more concrete, pragmatic spirit into the French political style. It may be that one of Gaullism's most notable accomplishments is the creation of a stable party loyalty for many of those hitherto free-floating souls on the Center and Right. There are indications from surveys of the late 1960's that party identification in France is now more prevalent than in 1958, though still less prevalent than in most other democracies.[51]

How far have the changes gone? The Communist Party maintains its hold over a fifth of the electorate. Officials of the old parties continue to resist fundamental changes in a game of politics which they dominated for so long. If new attitudes are to lead to permanent changes in French politics, the French system of political parties must undergo still further transformation.

All that one can conclude at present is that there is greater potential for cooperation and participation in French society than in the past. If political leaders do not obstruct, this new style should contribute to a more stable political system. In France, as in most other parts of Western Europe, sustained economic prosperity and the gradual democratization of society seem to go hand in hand with a decline in the intensity of ideological conflict. To be sure, in France as elsewhere, affluence breeds new ideological discontent, especially among educated youth. However, the meager electoral successs of the militant new groups on the French Left (Alain Krivine and the Trotskyists; Michel Rocard and the United Socialist Party) suggest that the new ideology has little appeal for the masses.

American students of comparative politics frequently contrast the "fragmented" and conflictual nature of French political society with the presumably consensual nature of such societies as Great Britain, the United States, and Sweden. The notion of consensus, although critical to an understanding of stable democracy, leads to confusion unless

[51] Pierce and Barnes, "Public Opinion and Political Preference," p. 3.

clarified in two ways. First, if it is to have operational meaning, consensus must be defined as widespread agreement, for example, an agreement of three-fourths of the population, rather than unanimity. The Irish Nationalists of Northern Ireland and the militant American Black Nationalists, for instance, clearly do not feel themselves part of the consensual society in Great Britain and the United States. Second, as David Easton has suggested, there are at least three significant *levels* of political consensus: the community (the continued unity of the nation itself), the regime (the fundamental constitutional form), and the government of the day.[52] In a competitive democracy, and Great Britain, France and the United States all fall in this category, there is no lasting consensus in support of the party which happens to control the government at any point in time. At the same time there seems to be a consensus in support of the nation as a lasting political community in each of these three countries. Competing parties may wish to change the nation's policies or even its institutions; very few want to break up the nation, as do opposition movements in a number of African countries. It is at the middle level — that of the regime or constitution — where the consensus seems less certain in France. One of the more critical ingredients of stable democracy is still lacking in that country: there is no consensus on an appropriate constitutional form. The partisans of the all-powerful Assembly remain fundamentally hostile to a strong executive such as the one provided for in the present constitution. Until a constitutional consensus emerges, the Fifth Republic (as opposed to an abstract, mythical republic) will not be able to count upon the kind of instinctive support which buoys up the British and American political systems in times of crisis.

[52] David Easton and Robert D. Hess, "Youth and the Political System," in Seymour Martin Lipset and Leo Lowenthal, eds., *Culture and Social Character* (New York: Free Press, 1961), pp. 229–231.

4

Parties and Elections

From the founding of the Third Republic in the 1870's until the legislative elections of 1962, when the Gaullists won an absolute majority of seats in the National Assembly, the French prime minister always had been obliged to rely upon at least the passive support of a coalition of parties. Throughout the Third and Fourth Republics the National Assembly (and the Chamber of Deputies before it) invariably had incorporated at least eight separate political party groups, some of ephemeral character. Since the first world war, no single party had ever won more than 28 percent of the popular vote or more than 30 percent of the seats (both by the Communists in November 1946).[1]

Governmental stability in the Fifth Republic initially was the result of Charles de Gaulle's unusual popularity and his ability to parlay that popularity into parliamentary majorities. But without fundamental and permanent changes in this system of political parties, it seems unlikely that the Fifth Republic's efforts at producing governmental stability and effectiveness through constitutional engineering will succeed any better than those of the Fourth. In order to afford some perspective on the forces of change which may perpetuate governmental stability based upon stable parliamentary majorities, and on the forces of resistance to change, which could force an unwanted return to the old pattern of instability and deadlock, we will examine the electoral system, the individual parties, and trends in the present party system.

The Electoral System

Whatever may be said about roses, a vote is not a vote is not a vote. The way it is counted makes all the difference. Take, for example, the

[1] Peter Campbell, *French Electoral Systems and Elections 1789–1957* (New York: Praeger, 1958), pp. 90–126.

district of Côte-du-Nord in the French legislative elections of 1956. The results were as follows:

Party	Votes
Communist:	67,694
Popular Republican Movement:	49,953
Socialist (SFIO):	45,276
Center coalition, including UDSR, RGR, & Ind.:	41,357
Poujadist:	26,873
Radical Socialist:	18,442
Young Republic:	16,064
Social Republican:	9,043

Since seven deputies were elected in this district by proportional representation (the *apparentement* agreements which will be described later were not made here), the Communists won two seats, the Popular Republicans two, and the Socialists, Centrists, and Poujadists one each. Had this been a single-member district in a winner-take-all-style American or British election, the Communist candidate would have been the sole victor, although probably the votes would have been distributed differently in that case. Had a second, run-off election been held to elect a single deputy, the winner might have been a Communist, a Popular Republican, a Socialist, or a Centrist, depending upon how party alliances developed. By structuring the competition among candidates, the electoral system influences both the parties and the voters. A straight proportional representation system offers much less incentive to the parties to form coalitions than does a single-member-district system. Proportional representation also offers the voters a wide range of party choices, while a single-member-district system more often requires him to choose between two candidates, neither of whom may quite suit his tastes. One must not conclude, however, that the electoral system is the major determinant of the pattern of party competition.

As in other western democracies, dominant parties in France have tended to devise election laws which they believe will help them maintain or increase their strengths. The double ballot (or run-off) system in use throughout most of the Third Republic allowed parties of the Center and Right to survive as separate parties and still join forces on the second ballot to keep the Left underrepresented. When three strong national parties emerged out of the Resistance and the Liberation —

the Communists, the Socialists (SFIO), and the Popular Republicans (MRP) — they agreed on an electoral system which would handicap loosely organized parties built around local notables, like the Radicals and the Moderates. An average of five deputies was elected by proportional representation in each legislative district. The voter cast his ballot for a party list rather than for individual candidates, allowing the party to control the nomination and rank ordering of candidates. Smaller parties could survive and elect a deputy in a district by winning as little as 20 percent or less of the popular vote.

After 1947 the government parties found themselves under attack on two fronts. On the Left was the powerful Communist Party, now in permanent opposition. On the Right were the Gaullists, who sought to show that the constitution in force was unworkable. The government's response was a familiar one in the annals of French republican history: it altered the election law to handicap its rivals. Beginning with the 1951 elections, any two parties were allowed to conclude an alliance (*apparentement*) in a given district. If between them they won a bare majority of popular votes, they received *all* of the seats in that district. In the 1951 election, the Gaullists entered relatively few *apparentement* alliances and won 118 seats (19 percent) with 21 percent of the popular vote. The Communist Party rarely could find alliance partners and dropped from 187 seats in 1946 to 103 seats in 1951, although its popular vote declined only from 28 percent to 26 percent. In the 1956 election, under the same election laws, the Center parties were more divided, fewer *apparentement* agreements were made, and the Communists won 150 seats based on 26 percent of the popular vote.

When de Gaulle came to power in 1958, his advisors, who had little sympathy for national party machines, chose to return to the system used during most of the Third Republic: the *scrutin d'arrondissement*. Deputies are now elected in single-member districts, as are members of the British House of Commons and the United States House of Representatives, but when no candidate wins an absolute majority on the first ballot there is a second, run-off election a week later. In the Third Republic this system helped to keep alive a large number of loosely structured parties. Since it was rare for any of the numerous candidates to receive an absolute majority on the first ballot, the parties would engage in an elaborate horse-trading process before the run-off ballot (usually the following week). The Radicals, for example, would consent to withdraw their candidate in district A in favor of the Socialist candidate; in return the Socialists would withdraw their candidate in district B, where a Radical was more likely to defeat a conservative candidate in the run-off.

Although in the Fifth Republic this electoral system again has pro-

Table 4.1

French Election Results — National Assembly
(Showing Percentage of Popular Vote (pv) and Seats Won)

	1956 pv	1956 seats[1]	1958 pv*	1958 seats	1962 pv*	1962 seats	1967 pv*	1967 seats	1968 pv	1968 seats
Communist	26	150	18.9	10	21.8	41	22.5	73	20.0	34
Socialist (SFIO)	15	95	15.5	47	12.6	66				
Federation (FGRS)							18.8	121	16.5	57
Radical	13	91	8.3	41	7.6	39				
Center (MRP, CD, PDM)	11	83	11.7	65	8.9	59	12.8	41	10.3	33
UNR (Gaullist)	3.1 (RS)	22	17.5	204	31.9	230				
UD Vè, UDR							37.8	200	43.6	292
Indep. Repubs. (Gaullist)					5.9	34		42	4.1[3]	61[3]
Independent	14	97	20.1	115	[2]					
Poujadist	11	52								
Other	7	6	8	96	10.3	11	8.1	9	5.5	8
Total		596		578		480		486		485

* First Ballot

[1] Group strength varies, sometimes radically, within the lifetime of each Assembly. Party names have changed frequently among Center, Moderate, and Gaullist deputies. Unaffiliated deputies are not included. Splinter parties are omitted or grouped with their usual allies.

[2] Most Independents who stayed out of the Gaullist camp joined the Centre Démocratique group in 1962 and its successor, Progrès et Démocratie Moderne in 1967.

[3] The popular vote indicated for Independent Republicans in 1968 includes only those who did not run under the Democratic Union for the Republic (UDR) label. The number of seats (61) refers to the total elected with or without that label.

duced extensive bargaining among the parties and again has helped some small parties to survive, it has not prevented a tendency toward polarization of the electoral battle between the Gaullists and their opposition on the Left. Under the *scrutin d'arrondissement* the nature and consistency of party alliances are of critical importance. In the 1958 elections the Communist Party found few alliance partners and, as shown in Table 4.1, suffered serious losses as compared with 1956, winning only ten seats in the National Assembly (less than 5 percent) with almost 19 percent of the first-ballot popular vote.[2]

By 1962 the Socialists, battling for survival, were willing to conclude local agreements with the Communist Party in order to pool their votes against the Gaullists. With Communist support in many run-off races, the Socialists rose from 47 seats to 66 seats in the National Assembly, even though they won fewer votes on the first ballot (12.6 percent) than in 1958 (15.5 percent). The Communists also made significant gains with 41 seats based on 21.8 percent of the popular vote in the first ballot. In terms of seats won, the bargain clearly was more favorable to the Socialists than to the Communists. Rather than vote for a Communist on the second ballot, a good number of Socialist voters apparently preferred to abstain, to vote for a Popular Republican, or even for a Gaullist, despite the advice of their party leaders. With the opposition still divided, the Gaullists won a solid majority in the National Assembly, even though they had received only 38 percent of the popular vote on the first ballot.

This surprising Gaullist victory, plus a direct confrontation between de Gaulle and the candidate of the Left, Francois Mitterrand, in the presidential election of December 1965, helped to forge a tighter electoral alliance among Radicals, Socialists, and Communists. The popular front alliance worked more effectively in 1967 than in 1962. Although the Gaullists did as well on the first ballot as in 1962 (almost 38 percent of the vote), they emerged from the second ballot with twenty-two fewer seats and a very slim parliamentary majority. The Popular Republicans also lost seats, while the Communists picked up thirty-two seats with only a fractional gain on the first ballot. Appar-

---

[2] The Fondation Nationale des Sciences Politiques has published (or is publishing) major studies of most national elections since 1956. See the Fondation's *Cahiers* series, No. 82, *Les Elections du 2 janvier 1956;* No. 109, *Le Référendum de septembre et les élections de novembre 1958;* No. 142, *Le Référendum d'octobre et les élections de novembre 1962;* and No. 169, *L'Election présidentielle des 5 et 19 décembre 1965.* Hereinafter cited as *Elections 1958, 1962, or 1965.* See also Philip Williams, *French Politicians and Elections, 1951–1969* (Cambridge: Cambridge University Press, 1970); and *Revue Française de Science Politique,* XX: 2 (April 1970), special issue on the 1969 presidential election.

ently the major change from 1962 was the greater willingness of Socialist voters to vote for Communist candidates when the Socialist candidate was withdrawn after the first ballot.[3]

The elections of June 1968 again demonstrated that the *scrutin d'arrondissement* is sensitive to changes in the solidity of party alliances. The crisis which shortly preceded the elections set off a conservative, anti-Communist reaction, which the Gaullists actively encouraged. In that altered climate of opinion, fewer Federation voters rallied behind run-off Communist candidates than in 1967, and fewer Center voters fell Left rather than Right after the first ballot. As a result, the popular front's total of 36 percent of the first-ballot vote (down from 41 percent in 1967) won it only 94 seats (compared with 194 in 1967).

The single-member-district election system, with a run-off ballot, presently provides the French parties with some motivation to form coalitions for the run-off election. Yet the nature of the alliances may differ from region to region. The Socialists, for example, may ally with the Communists in one district, yet join an anti-Communist coalition in another district. The election of the president by direct, popular vote, which the constitution of the Fifth Republic has required since 1962, allows no such flexibility. In the United States, popular election of the president is one of the reasons why two large, coalition-type parties dominate the political scene; the single prize of the presidency tends to force those who would seek it into one of two competing coalitions. In France, such a polarizing effect seemed in fact to be one of the results of the December 1965 presidential election, when François Mitterrand, the candidate of the united Communist and non-Communist Left, won an unexpected 45 percent of the vote in the run-off against de Gaulle. The presidential election of June 1969 demonstrated that if the electoral law encourages the formation of broad political coalitions, it is only one factor among many. The nature and high stakes of the election did indeed encourage the Gaullists, despite their family quarrels, to rally together in order to elect Georges Pompidou. Yet the election only exacerbated the disunity of the French Left. The Left this time split its votes among four candidates (Trotskyite, orthodox Communist, Left Socialist, and SFIO), allowing the Center candidate, Alain Poher, to reach the run-off. The Communists then chose a "plague on both your houses" policy and asked their supporters to abstain, hence contributing to Pompidou's 58 percent to 42 percent victory.

[3] Philip M. Williams and David B. Goldey, "The French General Election of 1967," *Parliamentary Affairs*, XX: 3 (Summer, 1967); and the IFOP poll reported in *Le Monde*, March 15, 1967.

Clearly the electoral system does make a difference. The decline of the Communists and the rise of the Gaullists in the legislative elections of 1958, 1962, and 1968 would have been less abrupt and far less pronounced under a straight proportional representation system. The Gaullist government realized the significance of electoral laws when in December 1966 it pushed through Parliament an amendment requiring that a candidate for the National Assembly win a vote equal to 10 percent of the registered voters in his district in order to enter the run-off, rather than 5 percent of the actual vote, as previously required.[4] As predicted, the ten percent barrier eliminated over six-hundred opposition candidates, but only two official Gaullist candidates after the first ballot on March 5, 1967. Premier Georges Pompidou announced further that the American and British-type single ballot system (which is even harder on small parties) might one day become "useful, indeed necessary" in France.[5] As for the direct presidential election system, it clearly strengthened Gaullist unity in the critical period after de Gaulle's resignation.

And yet other factors — social cleavages, political tradition, and leadership among them — are ultimately more important than election laws in shaping a party system.[6] The emergence of a parliamentary majority and the uncertain tendency toward polarization in the Fifth Republic are not primarily the result of the electoral system (witness the Third Republic), but rather of the challenge of de Gaulle and the Gaullists.

Since 1958, Guallism has produced a major simplification of the choices offered the French voter. Most representatives of the traditional Right — the Independents, or Moderates — have been either defeated or absorbed by the two major Gaullist parties, the Union of Democrats for the Republic and the Independent Republicans. Since the Algerian war, the extreme Right has almost disappeared. The Popular Republican Movement (MRP), continuing a decline in fortunes begun under the Fourth Republic, dropped from 83 seats in 1956 to less than 20 in 1968. Most of the few surviving Radicals

---

[4] *Journal Officiel, Débats, Assemblée Nationale,* December 8, 1966, pp. 5310–5322.

[5] *Ibid.,* p. 5322.

[6] On this topic see Campbell, *French Electoral Systems,* especially pp. 43–45. For an analysis lending greater independent importance to electoral systems, see Maurice Duverger, *Political Parties* (New York: Science Editions, 1963), Part II. A rigorous statistical study of the whole question is Douglas Rae's *The Political Consequences of Electoral Laws* (New Haven: Yale University Press, 1967).

teamed with the Socialists in the Federation of the Democratic and Socialist Left, which, as we have seen, cooperated closely with the Communist Party in the 1967 and 1968 elections. Before heralding the imminent emergence of a French two-party system, however, one must look carefully at the durability and rigidity of the French Communist Party, as well as at the rifts within both the Gaullist and the Left coalitions.

The Communist Party

The Appeals of Communism in France

To American observers it often seems paradoxical that the second largest Communist party in the Western world (second only to the Italian Communist Party) should be found in a land of proud individualists and staunch nationalists. The first key to this seeming paradox is the success of French Communists in fitting their movement to the French revolutionary tradition. Addressing an election meeting at the Palais des Sports in Paris on June 10, 1968, Communist Party Secretary General Waldeck Rochet condemned the antinational "nihilism" of some would-be revolutionaries and insisted that "the workers [read the Communist Party] are consciously taking up and extending the national heritage of France. They have not only a feeling of love and pride for their country, but also a sense of responsibility. As the Communist Manifesto announced, they aspire to become themselves the Nation. . . . The *Marseillaise* is not a Gaullist anthem; it is the song of the French people, its song of struggle against oppression and for freedom."[7] Presuming to be the Jacobins of today, French Communists speak the language of equality, the language of the underdog, whether he be an industrial worker, a struggling small farmer, or even a hard-pressed shopkeeper. In those parts of France where the political tradition long has been Leftist, notably in many departments of Central and Southern France, the Communist Party now appears to be the most radical enemy of clericalism, the most intransigent foe of economic and social privilege. François Goguel has shown that the far Left (represented by different parties) has been powerful for almost a century in parts of southern and central France.[8] Even in conservative Brittany, one excellent community study suggests, the Communist Party

[7] As quoted in Cahiers de la Fondation Nationale des Sciences Politiques, No. 175, *Le Communisme en France* (Paris: A. Colin, 1969), pp. 76–77.

[8] Cahiers de la Fondation Nationale des Sciences Politiques, No. 27, *Géographie des Elections Française, 1870–1951* (Paris: A. Colin, 1951), p. 105.

of today is the direct heir of the much older Radical Republican Party.[9]

The French Communist Party (like Communist parties throughout the world), has been most popular when, like the Jacobins which it claims as forefathers, it has identified with nationalistic causes. As one acute observer put it, "The Communist Party is like an accordion that contracts when it plays a Russian air and expands when it plays a French one."[10] When the Socialist Party formally accepted Lenin's twenty-one conditions and became the French Communist Party in 1920, it had 110,000 members and had in 1919 drawn almost 23 percent of the popular vote. The Comintern soon began fashioning its conquest into a true Bolshevik party which would be ruthless and monolithic in its internal affairs and an obedient instrument of the U.S.S.R. in foreign affairs. Although a solid and disciplined organization emerged from a decade of "bolshevization," the party dropped to 30,000 members in 1932 and to 8 percent of the popular vote in the elections of that year.[11]

It took a major depression, an alliance with other parties of the Left, and a firm Communist stand in defense of the nation against the fascists to revive the party's fortunes. By 1936 the party had over 300,000 members and 15 percent of the popular vote. Then, in 1939, it abruptly abandoned its attacks on the Nazis, after Stalin's nonaggression pact with Hitler, and was quickly outlawed by the government and abandoned by all but its most disciplined supporters. Only a brilliant resistance effort, beginning in 1941, when Hitler attacked Russia, managed to blur memories of the Communist Party's treason of 1939. The Communist Party emerged from the war a party of resistance heroes, a "party of martyrs," a party which, more than any other, had mobilized all of its strength to eject the Germans. At a time when the old parties of the Third Republic seemed discredited, the Communists became the "first party of France," winning an all-time high of 28 percent of all votes cast in the National Assembly elections of 1946 and having a membership of almost one million by 1947. From 1944 to 1947, for the first time in its history, the party agreed to allow several of its leaders to participate as ministers in coalitions governments.

[9] Morin, *Une Commune en France*, pp. 189–193.

[10] Jean-Marie Domenach, "The French Communist Party," in Mario Einaudi, J.-M. Domenach, and Aldo Garosci, *Communism in Western Europe* (Ithaca: Cornell University Press, 1951), p. 149.

[11] Party membership figures are from Annie Kriegel, "Le Parti Communiste Français (1920–1939): Evolution de ses effectifs," *Revue Française de Science Politique,* February 1966, pp. 5–35.

With the onset of the Cold War after 1947, the Communist Party's slavish obedience to the Stalinist line, even during the 1956 Hungarian revolt, tended to dim its patriotic image. Partly as a result (though also in keeping with a general decline in French party memberships), the membership dropped steadily to a low point of 300,000 in 1961, although its popular vote has dropped below 20 percent in only one election since 1945, that of 1958. The party has continued to play upon nationalist sentiments with its warnings against German rearmament and its continual attacks upon America's presumed imperialistic designs. The Jacobin tradition is kept alive by faithful party observance of Bastille Day, July 14, 1789, of the massacre of the Paris Communards in 1871, and even of the feast day of Joan of Arc, a quite unMarxist French national hero. Since the fall of Khrushchev in 1964, the Communist Party has shown new, albeit timid, signs of independence from Moscow, culminating in the condemnation of the Soviets' armed invasion of Czechoslovakia in the summer of 1968.[12] Past experience suggests that anything which strengthens the party's nationalist appeal is likely to win it votes.

The Communist Party has taken root in French soil not only because of its intransigence and its nationalist appeal, but also because of the bitterness of class antagonisms in French society. Since the second world war, the industrial working class, including wives and retired workers, has given from 35 to 50 percent of its votes to the Communist Party, far more than to any other single party.[13] Although the evidence is spotty, it seems likely that when the party is losing votes (as from 1956 to 1962), Communist voters from the working

[12] On the party's relations with the Communist world through 1966, see François Fejto, *The French Communist Party and the Crisis of International Communism* (Cambridge, Mass.: M.I.T. Press, 1967).

[13] The determination of working-class voting choices is no simple task. First, the boundaries of that class are not at all clear. Second, respondents in opinion surveys often are reluctant to identify themselves as Communist voters. To take a striking example, the French Institute of Public Opinion (IFOP) found that only 4.4 percent of the respondents in their sample (which may have been badly drawn) claimed to have voted Communist in 1958, whereas official figures showed that 14.3 percent of all eligible voters did in fact vote for the Communist Party in that year. (*Elections 1958*, p. 144). Surveys taken from 1962 through 1967 picked up more declared Communist voters, suggesting a declining fear of admitting Communist allegiance. For a report on such a survey prior to the 1967 elections (showing a 35 percent Communist vote within the working class), see Monique Fichelet, Raymond Fichelet, Guy Michelat, and Michel Simon, "Premiers Résultats d'un Programme de Recherche: Les Français, la Politique, et le Parti Communiste," reprint from *Cahiers du Communisme*, December 1967 and January 1968, p. 16.

class remain more loyal than those from farm and middle-class milieus.[14]

Although the Communist Party draws about half of its votes from workers, the working class is far from monolithic in its partisan preferences. The party typically draws 60 percent of its votes from men.[15] Some of the reasons are apparent and apply to Italy as well as to France: women workers and workers' wives vote less regularly than men, are more often closer to the church than are their husbands, and have fewer ties to unions and other class-related activities.[16] The Communist Party's popularity in the working class also varies greatly by region. In strongly Catholic areas like Alsace and Brittany, the Communist vote among workers often drops well below one-third, while in many of the "dechristianized" areas of France, as in the working-class suburbs of Paris where the Communist Party has been unbeatable for a generation, two-thirds or more of the working class regularly give it their votes. Many of the working-class communities which ring Paris

[14] Jean Ranger has used attitude survey findings to demonstrate that in the 1960's 50 percent of all Communist votes came from workers, as opposed to only 40 percent in the 1950's. ("Le Vote Communiste en France depuis 1945," in *Le Communisme en France*, pp. 243–245.) Viewing the question from the other side — the percentage of the working class which votes Communist — Mattei Dogan comes to the opposite conclusion that the Communist Party is losing its hold over the working class. Dogan holds that the Communist vote within the working class was over half in 1946, 49 percent in 1956, and 38 percent in 1962. Even though the working-class Communist vote could have been declining in this period, but less rapidly than in the electorate as a whole (hence increasing the proportion of Communist votes coming from workers), the opposite trends could not have been as sharp as Dogan and Ranger describe them. Unfortunately it is impossible to determine who is right with any certainty, for both labor under methodological handicaps. The serious underreporting of Communist vote intentions in surveys taken in the 1950's casts suspicion on Ranger's evidence, while the necessary element of guesswork involved in Dogan's method of figuring working-class votes from aggregate district voting results deprives Dogan's conclusions of their certainty. I would guess that the Communist vote in the working class was never as much as half and hence has declined less than Dogan contends. See Dogan, "Le Vote Ouvrier en France: Analyse Ecologique des Elections de 1962," *Revue Française de Sociologie*, VI: 4 (October–December, 1965), pp. 435–471; and "Political Cleavage and Social Stratification in France and Italy," in Seymour Martin Lipset and Stein Rokkan, eds., *Party Systems and Voter Alignments* (New York: Free Press, 1967), pp. 131–141.

[15] *Elections 1962*, p. 228; and Dogan, in Lipset and Rokkan, *Party Systems and Voter Alignments*, pp. 160–161.

[16] Dogan in Lipset and Rokkan, *Party Systems and Voter Alignments*, pp. 163–165; and M. Dogan and J. Narbonne, *Les Françaises Face à la Politique* (Paris: A. Colin, 1955).

— Saint-Denis, Ivry, Aubervilliers, and many others — have been governed by Communists since at least the 1930's.[17] In 1966, of the 39 communities of over 30,000 population in the Paris suburbs, 21 had Communist mayors. In the traditional bastions of Communist strength, like the Paris region, the extreme northern departments, and the northern and western sections of the Massif Central, the Party can maintain its appeal even when it is losing heavily elsewhere, as in 1958 and 1968.[18]

The American observer is tempted to believe that the continuation of the era of prosperity which France has enjoyed for almost two decades eventually will ease class antagonisms and lure workers away from the Communist Party. On closer examination, however, one finds that prosperity is not all bad for the Communists. To be sure, since 1946 the party has lost almost two-thirds of its members (in a time of generally declining party memberships) and five-sixths of the readers of its daily newspapers.[19] Yet, as we shall see, its voters have remained strikingly loyal. Affluence may sometimes calm the revolutionary zeal of a working man, but it also tends to draw him out of small shops and into large factories in metropolitan areas, where the Communist trade union, the Communist press, and the more homogeneous "proletarian" community constantly reinforce his loyalty to the "workers' party." Indeed, for many a French or Italian worker newly arrived in the big city, "Membership in the Party is then felt to be an entrance ticket into industrial society."[20] Industrialization inevitably produces frustrations and difficult adjustments as well as greater overall productivity. Unlike most other parties, the Communist Party stays close to the masses, championing their cause in even the most minor grievances. One former Communist leader has observed that "The story of Lenin, who organized the workers of Petrograd on the basis of their demand for hot tea, is often quoted."[21]

Within the working class, the findings of survey research conducted in the mid-1960's indicate, as one researcher put it, that "It is the better qualified workers, the skilled workers and lower level technicians, often trained within the factory, in short the aristocracy of the working

[17] "Questions au parti communiste," *Esprit,* October 1966.

[18] Jean Ranger in *Le Communisme en France,* pp. 215, 234, and 246.

[19] Annie Kriegel, *Les Communistes Français,* (Paris: Seuil, 1968), pp. 21 and 31.

[20] *Ibid.,* p. 65. For an excellent article on the "urbanizing" role of the Italian Communist Party, see Robert C. Fried, "Urbanization and Italian Politics," *Journal of Politics,* XXIX: 3 (August 1967), pp. 505–534.

[21] Quoted by Charles Micaud, *Communism and the French Left,* (New York: Praeger, 1963), p. 82.

class, who vote communist."[22] Another study based upon a survey of voter intentions before the 1967 election suggests that the Communist Party got less than its share of votes from citizens at the lowest income level (only 11 percent of Communist voters claimed monthly incomes of under 500 F, although 14 percent of the entire sample was in this group), but decidedly more than its share from middle income voters (52 percent of its supporters to 42 percent in the whole sample).[23] Again, within the formal membership of the party, highly skilled workers — especially metal workers and railroad workers — are more numerous than unskilled workers.[24]

The fact of increasing affluence seems less important than the worker's perception of that affluence. If he continues to feel unjustly rewarded in comparison with the salaries of middle-class managers and professionals, or if he believes that his employers have raised his wages only in response to Communist trade union pressure, he may continue to vote Communist as his wages go up.

It may be true nonetheless that in the long run sustained prosperity is bad news for the revolutionary workers' party. In this case the Communist Party may yet prosper and grow, but at the price of ceasing to be revolutionary. As we shall see, the French Communist Party since 1962 has been moving tentatively away from revolution, as its supporters are aware. In an attitude survey taken in early 1968, only 21 percent of those respondents who had voted Communist in 1967 agreed with the statement that "If it thought the situation were favorable, the Communist Party would be ready to start a revolution in order to take power."[25]

Communism in France often has been described as an ersatz religion for a de-Christianized working class, or as an escape from the crushing loneliness of at atomistic society.[26] Undoubtedly the party does have

[22] Alain Duhamel, "La Structure sociologique de l'électorat," *Sondages,* 1966: no. 2, p. 5. For an earlier series of studies showing equal alienation from bourgeois society and equal attachment to the Communist Party among well paid and poorly paid workers, see Richard F. Hamilton, *Affluence and the French Worker in the Fourth Republic* (Princeton: Princeton University Press, 1967).

[23] Fichelet *et al., Premiers Résultats d'un Programme de Recherche,* pp. 14, 17.

[24] Kriegel, *Les Communistes Français,* pp. 62–64.

[25] Alain Lancelot and Pierre Weill, "L'Attitude des français à l'égard du Parti Communiste en février 1968 d'après une enquête de la SOFRES," in *Le Communisme en France,* p. 289.

[26] Jules Monnerot, *Sociology and Psychology of Communism* (Boston: Beacon Press, 1960); Micaud, *Communism and the French Left,* Chs. 2 and 3; and Kornhauser, *The Politics of Mass Society,* pp. 84–88, 180, and *passim.*

its religious and fraternal aspects; yet one significant study suggests that these appeals are more important for middle-class recruits than for workers.[27] For a young worker in Saint-Denis, joining the Communist Party is an act neither of rebellion nor of escape. It is simply a demonstration of solidarity with the working class with which he identifies.

Psychological interpretations of communism's appeal may have greater saliency when applied to middle-class members, for whom the Communist Party is a more unusual choice. Intellectuals in particular have been drawn in considerable numbers either into party membership (as in the cases of Pablo Picasso, the artist, Louis Aragon, the poet, and Frédéric Joliot-Curie, the scientist) or into irregular collaboration with the party (as in the case of Jean-Paul Sartre). It seems likely that guilt, disgust, and loneliness all have had a hand in luring French intellectuals into the Communist sphere: guilt at being born into what they viewed as an unjust, class-bound society; disgust with the decadence and ineptitude of Republican France over the past generation; and longing for escape from loneliness and despair through a movement which offers purpose, community, and action.[28] On rational as well as psychological grounds, in the postwar years the Communist Party, despite its Stalinist defects, appeared to be the only movement willing and perhaps soon able to affect thoroughgoing reforms in French society. The Communist Party has prized its intellectuals, but since the 1920's has preferred to give leadership to Communists of working-class origin — men like longtime party secretary general, Maurice Thorez, a former miner, and his successor Waldeck Rochet, a former market gardener — whose sensibilities were less disturbed by Soviet censorship of the arts or by repression of the Hungarian Revolt.

As we have seen, manual workers provide on the average over half of the Communist Party's votes. The remainder come from farmers, white-collar workers, civil servants, and others attracted by the party's image as the party of the underdog. Many of these votes (like many working-class votes) undoubtedly are expressions of protest against all of those believed to be responsible for low wages, low farm income, high taxes, the indifference of governmental leaders, and a host of other perceived wrongs. Frenchmen from many walks of life look upon a vote for the Communists as an ideal means of venting their anger at the

---

[27] Almond, *The Appeals of Communism*, pp. 230–257 and 368–369.

[28] Raymond Aron, *The Opium of the Intellectuals*, trans. Terence Kilmartin (Garden City: Doubleday, 1957); and Micaud, *Communism and the French Left*, Ch. 4. For an alternative view, which focuses on rational more than psychological appeals, see David Caute, *Communism and the French Intellectuals 1914–1960* (London: Andre Deutsch, 1964).

governing parties and warning them to pay more heed. In a sense the Communist Party stands outside the political game, shaking its fist at those who choose to play. While other parties, including the Socialists, have shared in governing France, with all the compromises which that normally entails in a multi-party system, with two brief exceptions (1936–1937 and 1944–1947), the Communists have formed a relentless and seemingly incorruptible opposition.

In some cases the protest takes a temporary and individual form, as in the case of the usually conservative lycée teacher who voted Communist, as he had vowed to do, when the government failed to settle the Algerian war rapidly enough to suit him. More significant are the cases of sustained group protest, for example, in some Leftist farm communities. Laurence Wylie found that in one village in the department of Vaucluse, Communist voters did not feel they were voting for the creation of a totalitarian collectivist society; on the contrary, they were voting in the most forceful manner available *against* all of those ill-defined outside forces — government, wealthy, selfish interests, foreign powers — which they believed to be threatening their independence and well-being.[29] By taking up the cause of such groups as marginal farmers, the Communist Party encourages this type of Poujadism of the Left; yet it also offers an institutional and usually peaceful means of expression to the more helpless elements of French society.[30]

Are French Communists Really Communists?

The Party's adaptation to the French revolutionary tradition, its exploitation of class tensions, and its appeal to virtually all discontented groups in French society are some of the major reasons for its survival. But are the people drawn to the party for diverse reasons really Communists? Could they easily be lured away into another political movement? The party's twenty to thirty thousand militant organizers — trained in party schools and deeply committed to the movement — clearly are Communists. The man who votes Communist once in his life in a moment of anger or frustration clearly is not. The rest fall somewhere between these poles. Let us examine the evidence to determine something of their distribution.

A series of opinion surveys has clearly shown that Communist voters have more faith in their party and are more loyal to it than are the supporters of any other party. With the single exception of November

[29] Wylie, *Village in the Vaucluse,* pp. 218–220.
[30] Such is the thesis of Georges Lavau, "Le Parti Communiste dans le système politique français," in *Le Communisme en France,* pp. 7–81. See especially pp. 25–37.

1956, shortly after the Hungarian revolt, when only 68 percent of former Communist voters declared their intent to vote Communist again, all surveys since 1946 have found that at least 80 percent, and sometimes as many as 95 percent, of those who voted Communist in the last election intended to do so again in the next.[31] Intended repeaters in other parties were considerably fewer, ranging, for example, in 1962 from 40 percent of Independent party voters to 68 percent of Gaullist voters. A poll in 1952 showed that 62 percent of Communist voters, but only 48 percent of Socialist voters and 45 percent of Gaullist voters, had "total confidence" in their parties.[32] A 1962 poll revealed that 88 percent of Communist supporters — 20 percent more than in any other group — believed that their party best defended people like themselves.[33] Despite their limited education (which is usually correlated with low political interest), Communist supporters declare themselves to be more interested in politics than most Frenchmen and to engage much more frequently in such political activities as attending meetings, selling party newspapers, and giving money to the party.[34] (In absolute terms, Communists, like Frenchmen generally, participate far less often in political activities other than voting than they did in the late 1940's, although still more often than supporters of other parties.) One study, based upon a survey conducted in 1966, divided respondents into "participants" and "isolates," depending upon the level of their interest and involvement in politics. Of those who identified themselves as "extreme Left" (most of whom voted Communist), 63 percent were classed as "participants," as compared with only 37 percent in the entire sample.[35]

The attitudes of Communist voters differ, often sharply, from those of other Frenchmen on such issues as European integration (which Communists have been slow to accept), rearmament (which many saw as aimed at the peace-loving USSR), Soviet repression in Hungary (which shocked relatively few of them), the need for Algerian independence (which they accepted long before most other Frenchmen),

[31] Ranger, in *Le Communisme en France,* pp. 216–219.

[32] *Ibid.,* p. 220. For similar findings in a 1966 survey, see Deutsch, Lindon, and Weill, *Les Familles Politiques,* pp. 47–50.

[33] *Sondages,* 1952: No. 3, pp. 54–56, and 1963: No. 2, pp. 69–70.

[34] Ranger, in *Le Communisme en France,* pp. 226–227 and 230–231. In this case the usual tendency of limited education to produce low political interest apparently is overbalanced by the equally common tendency of those at the extremes of the political spectrum to be more interested in politics than those in the middle. See Angus Campbell, "A la recherche d'un modèle en psychologie électorale comparative," *Revue Française de Sociologie,* VII (Numéro spécial 1966), pp. 579–597.

[35] Deutsch, Lindon, and Weill, *Les Familles Politiques,* pp. 15–19.

and domestic wage policies (whose conservatism they blame exclusively on the capitalists).[36] In each case Communist voters were largely in agreement with the position of the Communist Party. Undoubtedly some of them simply followed the party's lead without understanding the ideology upon which these positions presumably were based.

Yet if Communist voters tend to be unusually loyal to their party, many of them still are not eager to see the Communist Party in control of France. In a poll taken in February 1968, 79 percent of those respondents who had voted Communist in the legislative elections of March 1967 were favorable to the appointment of Communists as government ministers, yet only 59 percent favored a Communist prime minister and only 52 percent a Communist president.[37] The ambivalence of Communist voters which these figures demonstrate did not disappear even with the June 1969 presidential elections, when Communist candidate Jacques Duclos campaigned his way to a striking 22 percent of the total vote in the first ballot (as opposed to the 20 percent which Communist legislative candidates had won a year earlier). Undoubtedly a number of Duclos voters would have modified their vote had they felt that he might actually win.

In sum, what answer can be given to the question, "Are French Communist voters really Communists?" Given the variety of grievances which bring them to the party and their low average level of education (in 1962, 79 percent of Communist voters had gone no further than primary school, as compared to 70 percent of Socialist voters and 60 percent of UNR voters), the mass of Communist voters could hardly be expected to be sophisticated Marxist theorists.[38] And yet, the Communist electorate is also considerably more than a patchquilt assemblage of malcontents. The striking loyalty and high political interest of Communist voters demonstrate that the party has been able to establish a lasting hold over a sizeable proportion of its voters, whatever their initial reasons for supporting it. The lack of enthusiasm of many Communist voters at the prospect of a Communist president seems to support the view that their party loyalty is only negative, that

[36] The views of Communist voters, as expressed in polls, are contrasted to those of non-communist voters in Pierre Fougeyrollas, *La Conscience Politique dans la France Contemporaine* (Paris: Editions Denoël, 1963), pp. 38–110.

[37] Alain Lancelot and Pierre Weill in *Le Communisme en France,* pp. 295–297.

[38] On the educational background of Communist voters, see *Elections 1962,* p. 233. On the generally low level of ideological sophistication among the poorly educated electorates of parties of the Left, see Philip E. Converse, "The Nature of Belief Systems in Mass Publics," in David Apter, ed., *Ideology and Discontent* (New York: Free Press, 1964), pp. 206–261.

is to say, reliable only so long as the party is a minority in opposition. And yet the results of another survey conducted in December 1966 suggest that this view is inaccurate. The respondents were asked, "If a Communist regime were established in France, do you think people like you would gain from it, lose from it, or neither?" Of the Communist voters in the sample, 68 percent replied "gain," only 4 percent "lose," 22 percent "neither," and 6 percent offered no response.[39] Although certain of the party's protest voters undoubtedly could be lured away by an attractive alternative, the loyal core of the Communist electorate seems large enough to insure the survival of the party as a major force in French politics for the foreseeable future.

Organization of the Communist Party

In France, as elsewhere where communism has met with some success, one of the party's major weapons has been its skill in the use of organization. In a country famed for extreme individualism, the Communist Party has created a body of dedicated, disciplined militants. As former Communist Party General Secretary Maurice Thorez once remarked, "Ours is not a party like the others." To be sure, it presents candidates for election and campaigns in their behalf. Yet it demands far more of its members than do other parties, and, in the past at least, has prepared them for clandestine and revolutionary activity as well as for open propaganda.

The basic unit in most French parties is the section, which brings together a hundred or more members for lectures and discussion. The Communist Party's basic unit, the cell, of which there were 18,600 in 1966, is smaller (3 to 60 members), more intimate, and far more demanding. Members are expected to study Marxist ideology, often to attend party schools, and always to devote much of their leisure time to distributing party literature, recruiting members, and agitating in support of party policies.[40] In 1966, the party had in operation a total of 1,923 elementary party schools with 16,097 students, 311 regional schools with 3,480 students, and 34 national schools with 1,286 students.[41] Despite this impressive effort, of the 23,000 to 48,000 new

[39] Fichelet *et al.,* "Premiers Résultats d'un Programme de Recherche," p. 265.

[40] One of the most authoritative and informative sources on the life of the Party is Kriegel, *Les Communistes Français.* See also Guy Rossi-Landi, "Le Parti Communist Français: Structures, Composition, Moyens d'Action," in *Le Communisme en France,* pp. 183–209. In English, see Micaud, *Communism and the French Left.*

[41] Rossi-Landi, in *Le Communisme en France,* p. 203.

members who joined each year from 1959 to 1966 (balanced by 30,000 leaving annually), the party was able to send only 35 percent through one of its schools.[42] It is certain that a much higher percentage of longtime members have had party school training in Marxist-Leninist doctrine, as well as in current party doctrine on such subjects as "the pauperization of the proletariat," "forms of transition to socialism," "the struggle for peace," and "the Communist Party."[43]

The party's drop in membership from over 700,000 in 1947 to approximately 300,000 in the late 1960's, the continuing rapid turnover in membership, the absence of the usual elected officials in over 6,000 cells in 1966, and occasional reports of low attendance at cell meetings all caution against concluding that the typical Communist Party member is a new type of Frenchman.[44] Yet it is clearly true that there is within the membership a nucleus of perhaps 30,000 true militants for whom all of life revolves around the party.[45]

According to rare reports by those who have attended, cell meetings often produce lively discussion and debate.[46] They serve as an important source of information for the party hierarchy and a vital contact with the masses. Once a decision is taken at a higher level, however, in compliance with the principle of democratic centralism, members are expected to accept it without complaint. Since individual cells have no contact with each other save through higher echelons, a rebellion within a cell is usually easy to contain, so long as leaders at the top remain united. On those rare occasions when a rebellious cell tries to rally support, as when the "Sorbonne-Lettres" cell sent a proposed program to all other cells in its section in January 1959, the central party organs are quick to discipline.[47]

Actual power within the party is tightly centralized in the hands of

[42] *Ibid.,* p. 203.

[43] Maurice Thorez, "L'Enseignement du marxisme-leninisme dans les écoles du parti," *Cahiers du Communisme,* November 1956, pp. 1198–1214.

[44] On cell "bureaux," see Rossi-Landi, in *Le Communisme en France,* p. 188. With regard to party membership, the only official figures issued by the party show simply the number of membership cards sent out. These show a postwar high of 907,785 in 1947, a low of 389,000 in 1955, and a gradual rise in the 1960's to 425,800 in 1966. Between 20 and 35 percent of these cards are not sold. By means of various calculations, Annie Kriegel estimates the actual 1967–1968 membership at 275–300,000. See her *Les Communistes Français,* pp. 31, 261 (n.8), 297–298.

[45] The image of monolithism and complete dedication is portrayed in Micaud, *Communism and the French Left,* pp. 78–79. For a critique of this image, see Hamilton, *Affluence and the French Worker,* pp. 24–29.

[46] Domenach, in Einaudi, Domenach, and Garasci, *Communism in Western Europe,* pp. 84–85.

[47] Rossi-Landi, in *Le Communisme en France,* p. 186.

the secretary general, his secretariat, the fourteen-member political bureau, and, to a lesser degree, the central committee to which it is theoretically responsible. The national leadership is organizationally linked to the membership through thousands of paid party officials, and through the elected party bodies: the National Congress, the Federation Convention (at the Department level), and the section convention. These bodies serve primarily as means of educating and arousing the membership. At each level, members are theoretically elected by the next lower body. While in practice the lists have always been drawn up in advance by higher party authorities, the introduction in 1964 of the secret ballot for voting within the National Congress makes genuine competition for party office technically possible.

For most of the party's history, from 1932 to 1964, leadership was firmly in the hands of a miner's son, Maurice Thorez. Thorez was consistently loyal to Moscow and allowed no factionalism within the party. Those whom he perceived to be challenging him, including such party luminaries as André Marty in 1952, Auguste Lecoeur in 1954, and Laurent Casanova and Marcel Servin in 1960, were quickly driven out of the party. Upon his death in 1964, Thorez was replaced by a lifelong party worker, Waldeck Rochet, who shared Thorez' Communist orthodoxy, but not his popular legend. In that same year, 1964, when Moscow's stern hand over the Communist world was relaxing, and when the French party's non-Communist allies were questioning the democratic character of democratic centralism, a leading member of the party's political bureau announced to the Seventeenth Party Congress that "For a long time it was necessary to place particular stress upon centralism in the life of the party. How could it have been otherwise under the difficult conditions in which the party was formed, in the period when the party was illegal, and at a time when the party had to hold off certain opportunist and revisionist attempts to challenge the Leninist conception of the party? . . . But today . . . we deem it necessary to place stress more on democracy in the internal life of the party."[48] Indeed, there very likely has been freer discussion within the party since 1964, especially at the higher levels, although nothing approaching competitive democracy in the usual Western sense.

The Communist Party's organizational reach is extended far beyond its 300,000 members through the activities of a host of party-controlled auxilliary associations for students, workers, veterans, women, scientists, intellectuals, ex-Resistance fighters, and numerous other categories. Of these, the most important clearly is the General Confederation of Labor (CGT), the largest French trade union. Long under the leader-

[48] Georges Marchais, "Intervention au XVIIe Congrès," *Cahiers du Communisme,* June–July 1964, pp. 286–330; quotation from p. 299.

ship of Benoît Frachon, a member of the political bureau of the Communist Party, the CGT usually has preferred revolutionary militancy to effective reform. Only after the death of Thorez in 1964 did it begin to seek the cooperation of non-Communist unions in improving the workers' plight here and now. Under the leadership of Georges Séguy, the CGT behaved in a most cautious fashion in the crisis of May 1968, as described in Chapter 2.

Until the mid-1960's the French Communist Party was known as the most Stalinist Communist party in Europe. Thorez waited five years after Khrushchev's famous secret speech of 1956 before finally denouncing Stalin's crimes. To the outsider, the party gave the appearance of a monolith in which public dissent was unthinkable. In recent years, however, a number of cracks have appeared, only to be patched over. In the late years of the Algerian war, the Movement of Peace, which had almost invariably hewed to the party line, defied the party by supporting some of de Gaulle's initiatives for ending that war. As the Sino-Soviet dispute came into the open, several splinter organizations were formed to champion the Maoist version of Marxism--Leninism. Their journals, including *La Voie Communiste* and *L'Humanité Nouvelle*, challenged the legitimacy of PCF leaders as the true prophets of the Marxist religion. In the last years before his death, Thorez was also criticized by orthodox Communists for fostering what some felt to be a "cult of personality."

Perhaps the most surprising challenge to party discipline came from the Communist student auxiliary. To the shock of party representatives, the Sixth Congress of the Union of Communist Students (UEC), meeting in February 1962 at Chatillon-Sous-Bagneaux, adopted a program calling for greater autonomy for the UEC and more rapid progress toward "destalinization" within the French Communist Party.[49] Over the next four years the party fought a running battle with both the "revisionist" right wing of the UEC, which called for more internal party democracy, and the pro-Chinese left wing, which deplored the party's loss of revolutionary zeal. A series of purges finally restored party control by 1966; yet a portion of the purged left wing formed the Jeunesse Communiste Révolutionnaire, which drew the party's wrathful denunciation for its important agitational role in the student riots of May 1968.

The Soviet occupation of Czechoslovakia in August 1968 provoked open quarreling within the party's own ruling body, the political bureau.[50] But despite these displays of division and independence, disobedience is still rare in the life of France's most disciplined party.

[49] Fejto, *The French Communist Party*, pp. 145, 165–66, 201–202.
[50] See *Le Monde,* Oct. 6–7, 1968.

Strategy and Alliances

The attitude of the French Communist Party toward democratic socialist parties has vacillated between one of total war against the betrayers of the working class and one of cautious alliance against common enemies. In 1962, after a fifteen-year period of Cold War enmity, the Communist Party and the non-Communist Left began a new flirtation which has been troubled by mistrust and frequent quarrels over the proper nature of their alliance. On the electoral level, the Communists cooperated with the Socialists in the legislative elections of 1962, then with the new Federation of the Democratic and Socialist Left in the presidential election of 1965 (when the Communists supported François Mitterrand, the Federation candidate, from the first ballot), and in the legislative elections of 1967 and 1968. The alliance worked to mutual advantage until 1968, when the May crisis and the following Gaullist landslide in the June 1968 elections destroyed both the Federation and the popular front alliance.

As we have seen, the non-Communist Left seemed to get the better of the bargain, especially in 1962, as a result of the inability of the Federation to deliver all its votes to a Communist in the runoff ballot in those districts where the Federation candidate had withdrawn in his favor.[51] The highpoint of the alliance came in 1967, when the Left won 41 percent of the popular vote in the first ballot and in the runoff ballot came close to denying the Gaullists their parliamentary majority. It seemed at last that the Communist Party was well on its way to being accepted as a legitimate player in the democratic arena. Far more than in 1962, Socialists, and even some Center voters, were willing to cast their ballots for a Communist in order to defeat the Gaullists. A national attitude survey taken in late 1966 showed that only 26 percent of the respondents felt that they had something to lose from the creation of a Communist regime in France, and 51 percent felt that the Communist Party had played a "useful" role in France since 1944.[52]

Aware of the importance of their votes to the Federation, the Communist Party insisted ever more strongly that if the Left were to continue to present itself to the voters as an alliance, it needed a minimal common program, one offering a truly socialist alternative. A lengthy

[51] See above, pp. 74–75.

[52] Nineteen percent felt they would gain from a Communist regime, 42 percent that they would neither gain nor lose, and 14 percent did not reply. On the question of usefulness, 21 percent declared that the Communist Party had played a harmful role, and 28 percent did not reply. Monique Fichelet, Raymond Fichelet, Guy Michelat, Michel Simon, "L'Image du Parti Communiste Français," in *Le Communisme en France*, pp. 260 and 263.

dialogue ensued, much of it in the pages of the Communist daily, *L'Humanité,* and the Socialist daily, *Le Populaire.* Before we tie our-selves to a formal alliance, the socialists asked in essence, can we be sure that you are finally independent from Moscow and that you believe in democracy as we understand it? It is not true that your party is run in an autocratic, anti-democratic manner? The Commu-nists replied that all Communist parties are "independent and equal in rights," and that the transition from capitalism to socialism now could be brought about by peaceful, democratic means, without outlawing non-Communist parties.[53] As for internal party affairs, did not the introduction of the secret ballot in the election of central party leaders further guarantee the democratic character of democratic centralism? The non-Communist Left wondered what the Party really had in mind when it talked of "true" or "advanced" democracy; was it to be "democracy" of the style of the democratic republics of Eastern Eu-rope? One could not be sure that the Party had truly abandoned the position taken by Thorez as recently as 1956 when he told the Fourteenth Party Congress that "Socialist democracy is rightfully called *dictatorship* of the proletariat because it is an instrument of the workers' struggle against the exploiters, against all of those efforts undertaken from outside or from within the country toward restoring the capitalist regime and the dictatorship of the bourgeoisie."[54]

Doubts notwithstanding, the Federation eventually agreed to negoti-ate and then, in February 1968, to publish a joint declaration with the Communist Party.[55] The two parties declared themselves "irreconcil-ably hostile to the regime of personal power," a regime which could be ended only by pruning the president's powers concerning referendums, national emergencies, and relations with Parliament. They declared their agreement on the need for an extension of "civil rights and public liberties," on the necessity for more democratic participation in French economic planning, on the high priority of raising the purchasing power of the masses, and on the need for tax reforms directed at shifting the burden to the wealthiest businesses and individuals. On specific means, the parties often differed, as in the Socialists' greater interest in main-taining a relatively strong presidency (one they hoped soon to fill) and the Communists' greater insistence upon rapid nationalization of private industry. The declaration revealed embarrassingly few areas of agree-ment on foreign policy matters, for, like the Soviet Union, the French Communist Party found more to admire in Gaullist foreign policy than in the views of its allies of the Left. Like de Gaulle, and unlike most

[53] For reports in English on these party stands, see *The New York Times,* January 16, 1964, May 18, 1964, and October 15, 1964.

[54] From the full text of Thorez' speech, *L'Humanité,* July 19, 1956.

[55] Quoted in full in *Le Monde,* February 25–26, 1969.

of their partners, they were opposed to European political unity, hostile to an American alliance, and highly critical of the Israelis.

The popular front alliance which gradually had been forged was weakened and finally shattered in the spring and summer of 1968. Even though the Communist Party had vigorously and repeatedly denounced Cohn-Bendit and the other "adventurers" and "anarchists" who joined him in the rioting of May 1968, even though the party had made no attempt to seize power by force (on the contrary it had helped get workers back on the job in early June), it nonetheless was widely blamed for contributing to the crisis. The elections of June 1968, in which the Federation and the Communist Party together lost one hundred seats, provoked the demise of François Mitterrand and his Federation, and with them the demise of the popular front alliance.

When the defeat of de Gaulle's referendum of April 27, 1969 led to his resignation and the call for new presidential elections, the Left, which had united behind Mitterrand in 1965, now divided its votes among five competing candidates. The Communists, having failed to persuade the non-Communist Left to discuss a common candidacy with them, this time ran one of its veteran leaders, Jacques Duclos. To the dismay of the Socialists, Duclos campaigned his way from an early opinion poll score of 10 percent to an eventual first-ballot vote of over 22 percent. Forceful yet reassuring, aggressive though good-humored, Duclos looked nothing at all like the fierce Bolshevik who might turn France into a dictatorship. He talked much of the weakness of his opponents and their programs, occasionally of social reform under "advanced democracy," and hardly at all of Marxism-Leninism. In the first ballot Duclos ran far ahead of the Socialist tandem of Gaston Defferre (the presidential candidate) and Pierre Mendès-France (Defferre's proposed prime minister), and came within 2 percent of outdistancing Centrist candidate Alain Poher. Having humiliated the Socialists, the Communists proceeded to demonstrate that without them the Left was helpless by calling on Communist voters to abstain in the second ballot, thereby insuring the runoff victory of Gaullist Georges Pompidou. The Communist Party had no interest in displacing the Gaullists only to find itself forced back into the ghetto in which it had spent most of the Fourth Republic. Their point was made: so long as the Gaullists hung together, they could not be beaten without Communist help. Yet a renewal of the popular front would have to await the reformation of a noncommunist Left, at that time still sharply divided, not least of all over the propriety of a Communist alliance.

If, as we have attempted to demonstrate, the French Communist Party remains a powerful and stable force on the French political scene, if, further, the Left opposition is helpless without Communist support, it becomes important to know whether the party has genuinely changed, especially whether it is now prepared to act independently of Moscow and within the framework of a liberal democracy. On both questions, unfortunately, the evidence is far from conclusive. The first hint of a change in the French party's traditionally servile attitude toward the USSR occurred at the time of Khrushchev's removal from power. The French Communist Party first demanded an explanation, then sent a team to investigate, and finally concluded in essence that this was an internal Russian affair and that it would abide by its own declaration of October 14, 1964, asserting the independence of each Communist party.

Much more dramatic was the French party's condemnation of the USSR for the latter's occupation of Czechoslovakia in August 1968. As in the case of several other Communist parties of Western Europe, the Czech occupation provoked their first public criticisms of the mother country. Yet the French Communist Party was moderate in its criticism and harsh against those in its own ranks who defended the Czechs too vigorously. One of the most outspoken party critics of the Czech occupation, the noted Communist theorist Roger Garaudy, was allowed to write in the party daily, *L'Humanité* that "it seems absolutely necessary to me to tell the French people: the socialism which our party wishes to install in France is not that which today is being imposed militarily upon Czechoslovakia."[56] An unprecedented public debate between Garaudy and the party leadership terminated, however, with Garaudy's removal from the central committee and his subsequent expulsion from the party in May 1970. Two months later another leading party member, Charles Tillon, a former resistance hero and Communist government minister, was expelled from the party also because of his liberal views on Czechoslovakia. Since the spring of 1969, when the party accepted the forced resignation of Czech premier Alexander Dubcek without protest, party leaders have seemed eager to file the whole affair.

In December 1970, party leaders twice within a week voiced criticism of the actions of Communist governments. On December 19, Etienne Fajon, a member of the party secretariat, publicly criticized the Government of Poland, whose policies had produced strikes and demonstrations in a number of Polish cities. On December 22, Georges Marchais, who as Assistant Secretary General was the real party leader during Waldeck Rochet's illness, deplored the "grave errors committed by the Polish leaders," as well as the "absence of social democracy" in Poland. Only three days later, the party daily, *L'Humanité,* criticized

[56] *L'Humanité,* January 2, 1970.

the judicial procedure and severe sentences of the Leningrad trials, in which several Russian Jews had just been found guilty of conspiring to escape from the USSR by hijacking an airplane. *L'Humanité* urged the Russian government to commute the death sentences awarded in that trial.

These actions were noted and approved by the Socialist Party leaders with whom the Communists were carrying on negotiations for political collaboration. On most foreign policy questions, however, the French Communist Party has deviated very little from the Soviet line, whether the issue has been European unification, the Atlantic alliance, the Middle Eastern crisis, or Maoist China.

On the question of liberal democracy, it must be said that in the past two decades the party has taken elections seriously and has made no serious attempt to foment revolution. And yet one may ask how a movement based on the Leninist doctrine that the bourgeois state, like any state, is the reflection of dominant economic interests, can ever genuinely believe in "bourgeois democracy."[57] Once in power could it in fact risk being replaced in elections by capitalistic "counterrevolutionary" parties operating freely and legally? Certainly not without either adjusting the basic doctrine or choosing to disregard it. The party has promised that there would be a place for non-Communist parties in the building of socialism; it has given no assurance that these parties could include staunchly anti-Communist parties. Might the party have in mind only the kind of docile, nominally non-Communist labor parties which were permitted in Communist Poland and Hungary? In sum, there are indeed signs of change within the French Communist Party, signs which suggest it might one day become a genuinely independent, democratic party. To assume that it already has would be hazardous, to say the least.

The Non-Communist Left

Since the Communist-supported strikes and the Gaullist municipal election victories of 1947 (one might push the date back much further), French politicians of the democratic Center and Left have toyed with the notion of a "Third Force," designed to preserve the progressive Republic against her enemies. Time and again Center-Left coalitions have been smashed upon the jagged rocks of vested party interests (loyalty to the "old houses" in which party leaders are comfortable and independent), of ideological quarrels (of which socialism and the

[57] For an interesting statement on communism and democracy by a Party leader, see Pierre Juquin, "Pour une Gauche Qui Gouverne," *La Nouvelle Critique*, June 1967, pp. 4–8.

church school issue are the most venerable), and of mutual suspicion. In the 1960's a series of Gaullist electoral victories intensified the pressure toward coalition. When the results of the legislative elections of 1962 were in, the Radicals had tumbled from their postwar high of 13 percent in 1956 (that figure representing a mere fraction of their all-time high of 28 percent of the popular vote and 41 percent of the seats in 1906) to 7 percent of the popular vote on the first ballot; the MRP had fallen from its 26 percent peak of 1946 to a mere 9 percent; and even the Socialist electorate had withered from 18 percent of the popular vote in 1946 to under 13 percent. Yet, as we shall see, even these dire circumstances were and continue to be insufficient to overcome the obstacles to federation among these parties. Since the Socialists hold many of the keys to the future of the democratic Left, let us begin with them.

The Socialists

From its founding in 1905, the French Section of the Workers International (SFIO) has had its reformist wing, led initially by Jean Jaurès, a warm and eloquent humanist, and its revolutionary wing, whose turn-of-the-century leader was an intransigent prophet of class violence, Jules Guesde. Even after the revolutionary wing (the majority wing) became the Communist Party in 1920, the remaining Socialists were not of one mind over the propriety of cooperating with "bourgeois" parties. Periodically the Socialists lent their support to non-socialist governments, although they refused to enter the cabinet until 1936, when the popular front victory allowed party leader Léon Blum to become prime minister of France. After the second world war, Socialists Félix Gouin, Léon Blum, Paul Ramadier, and Guy Mollet each served as prime minister. With the exception of a five-year Socialist retreat between the elections of 1951 and 1956, the SFIO was an indispensable building-block in the construction of cabinet coalitions. Social ministers sat in twenty of the Fourth Republic's thirty-two governments.[58] And yet while Socialist ministers conducted business as usual, while the Mollet government recalled thousands of draftees to help preserve French Algeria, Socialist party programs continued to condemn French capitalism and to call for a social revolution by democratic means.

Dissonance between political rhetoric and political action is nothing new to French politics. It arises naturally out of coalition politics where no party needs to take full responsibility for governmental policies. In the case of the SFIO, however, the effect was particularly striking. The

[58] Williams, *Crisis and Compromise*, p. 494.

SFIO National Council which met in November 1968 offers a poignant example. That council noisily rejected proposals from the podium that the time had come for the party to abandon the "Marxist scheme of 1905," when the party was founded, and to choose new policies and new leaders. The council preferred instead to follow Secretary-General Guy Mollet's lead in reasserting that

> . . . there will exist no real democracy until the capitalist regime is abolished. . . . It [The Socialist Party] proposes substituting for capitalist property a social property which can take a variety of forms, and for the management of which the workers must prepare themselves. It believes that the transition to a society of socialist character can and must be accomplished by democratic means through progressive stages of reform; . . . but it insists upon warning the workers: the socialist transformation cannot be the natural product of the sum of reforms correcting the effects of capitalism. It is not a question of adjusting a system but of substituting a better one for it. It is in this sense that the socialist party is revolutionary.[59]

At a time when Socialist parties in West Germany, in Great Britain, and in most other countries of Western Europe were making their peace with capitalism, on the condition that it accept certain governmental controls, the SFIO proudly renewed its declaration of war. At a time of general European prosperity (although marred in France by strikes and by financial crisis), Mollet concluded that "the present chances of socialism in the world are greater than ever."[60]

Why have French Socialists refused to follow the lead of those European Socialists who seem to have declared an end to ideology? It may be that the pressure of a powerful Communist Party on its Left (in a country where being Left is still more fashionable than being Right) has encouraged the SFIO to emphasize its own revolutionary nature. And whatever the cynics may say, the SFIO leaders are socialist believers of long standing, for whom abandonment of the socialist dream would be a painful experience. It is quite likely that in the judgment of party leaders an abandonment of the traditional creed would shake the loyalty of party members and voters.

This might well be an accurate assessment of the state of mind of the SFIO's remaining members, of whom there were said to be 60,000 in 1963, and undoubtedly far fewer by the late 1960's;[61] yet attitude surveys, like the one cited earlier, suggest that Socialist *voters* rarely

[59] Quoted in *Le Monde,* November 5, 1968.

[60] *Ibid.*

[61] The 60,000 estimate for 1963 is by François Goguel and Alfred Grosser, *La Politique en France* (Paris: A. Colin, 1964), p. 106.

view the world in systematic ideological fashion.[62] While in 1964 the Left agreed generally on the goal of "building socialism," it will be recalled that among the self-professed "Moderate Left" (not all of whom are Socialist voters, of course), 42 percent *opposed* nationalization of large private businesses and only 34 percent favored it.[63]

It is clear that the SFIO's staunch loyalty to socialism at the level of party doctrine has not prevented its gradual transformation into a party essentially of the middle class. From 1898 to 1940, an average of 47 percent of all Socialist members of the Chamber of Deputies were of working class origin (as opposed to 84 percent of Communist deputies). In the Fourth Republic the figure for Socialist deputies of working-class origin dropped to 5 percent.[64] The Socialist counterparts to the Communist Party's longtime leaders, Maurice Thorez, a former miner, and Waldeck Rochet, a former farm laborer, were first Léon Blum then Guy Mollet, both middle-class intellectuals and both alumni of the prestigious École Normale Supérieure. While the Communist Party prefers to train workers for leadership positions in party schools, the SFIO relies heavily upon public school teachers to administer the Party organization at all levels.[65] By the 1950's the working class made up only a fourth of the party membership and supplied only 11.4 percent of the party's departmental executive committee members and candidates for Parliament.[66]

In the 1960's the Socialists (plus their allies in the Federation of the Democratic and Socialist Left from 1965 to 1968) have received some 18 to 22 percent of all working-class votes, fewer than either the Communists (with 35 to 38 percent) or the Gaullists (with some 30 percent).[67] And yet working-class votes still represent over 30 percent of the shrunken Socialist electorate. The party's working-class support tends to be strongest in smaller cities and in departments like the *Nord* where the Socialist-oriented union, the *Force Ouvrière,* is particularly well organized.[68] The Socialists' most important base of electoral sup-

[62] See above, pp. 61–62.

[63] Deutsch, Lindon, and Weill, *Les Familles Politiques,* pp. 109–110.

[64] Mattei Dogan, "Political Ascent in a Class Society: French Deputies 1870–1958," in Dwaine Marvick, ed., *Political Decision-Makers* (Glencoe, Ill.: Free Press, 1961), pp. 72–76.

[65] Micaud, *Communism and the French Left,* p. 203.

[66] Pierre Rimbert, "Le Parti socialiste S.F.I.O." in M. Duverger, ed., *Partis politiques et classes sociales en France,* Cahiers de la Fondation Nationale des Sciences Politiques, No. 74 (Paris: A. Colin, 1955), p. 201.

[67] The "working class" referred to here includes workers' wives and retired workers. Figures are from Dogan, in *Revue française de sociologie,* VI: 4 p. 471; and Fichelet *et al.,* "Premiers Résultats, p. 16; *Sondages,* 1967: No. 3, p. 55.

[68] Michel Simon, "Attitudes politiques ouvrières dans le département du Nord," *Cahiers Internationaux de Sociologie,* XXXVI (1964), pp. 57–74.

port, however, is not so much in the working class as among white-collar workers and lower-level management personnel, in both cases particularly those who work for the government. According to one estimate, in 1951 civil servants and their families contributed 30 percent of the Party's votes.[69]

Like the voters whom it attracts, the SFIO's form of organization is strikingly different from that of the Communist Party. In place of the cell, with its ambiance of intimacy, commitment, and action, one finds as the base unit the section, a large group given to political discussion and to social conviviality. Again in contrast to the Communist Party, debate and dissent abound throughout the SFIO, in the sections, in the departmental federations, at the annual national congresses, and within the national council.

Although Secretary General Guy Mollet on occasion was charged with using dictatorial tactics, his power within the party depended not upon fear and coercion, but rather upon a skillful politician's blend of persuasion and patronage. From his election as Secretary General in 1946, until his resignation in 1968, when critical issues arose, he was always able to round up a majority within the party, beginning with his home department of Pas-de-Calais. Yet he could not prevent open battles within the party over such issues as the European Defense Community, the Algerian war, the recall of de Gaulle to power in June 1958, and the referendum on the new Constitution in September 1958. The battles over the SFIO's proper relationship with de Gaulle prompted the only serious schism of recent years. The new Autonomous Socialist Party, later renamed the Unified Socialist Party (PSU), has barraged the SFIO with criticism from the Left, yet it has never won more than 4 percent of the popular vote (in 1968) nor elected more than four deputies (in 1962).

Even as its percentage of the popular vote in national elections dropped from 18 percent in 1946 to 13 percent in 1962 and as its membership declined from almost 300,000 to 60,000 in the same period, the SFIO managed to retain many of its strongholds in local government. In 1961 it boasted more than 50,000 members on the town and city councils of France — more than the Communists and Gaullists combined.[70] After the 1965 municipal elections, socialist mayors were chosen to preside over 11 percent of all the cities and towns of France, and over 19.8 percent of towns with more than 2,000 inhabitants. The next most successful party, the Gaullist UNR, could claim only 6.8 percent of all mayors and 9.2 percent of those in towns of over 2,000

[69] Catherine, in Duverger, ed., *Partis politiques et classes sociales en France*, pp. 140–141.

[70] Roger Aubin, *Communes et Démocratie* (Paris: Editions Ouvrières, 1965), Vol. II, p. 212.

population.[71] After the 1965 and 1971 municipal elections, the Socialists controlled 40 of the 192 cities of more than 30,000 population.[72] Familiar Socialist candidates and the persistence of traditional voting habits at the local level have helped the SFIO to keep its organization intact in hopes of brighter national prospects in the future.[73]

After de Gaulle took on all of the traditional parties and defeated them in the referendum of October 1962 (over direct election of the president), and in the legislative elections of November, 1962, anti-Gaullists of the Left began talking of the need for alliance. Discussion, then action, centered on two partially contradictory forms: alliance between the Socialists and the Communists, whose voters seemed critical to the success of any anti-Gaullist movement on the Left; and a revival of some version of the "Third Force" concept. The political dialogue and the electoral alliances which followed between Communists and Socialists have already been discussed. The second strategy was pursued in parallel fashion. The first significant initiative came from the newsmagazine, *L'Express,* which launched a campaign in the fall of 1964 in favor of the presidential candidacy of one "Monsieur X," who turned out to be Gaston Defferre, the Socialist Mayor of Marseilles.

Defferre set out to create a new British-type labor party, uniting the remnants of the Radical Party, the MRP, and the SFIO. He won the support of his own SFIO, although Guy Mollet demonstrated no undue enthusiasm for the candidacy of a man who was a personal rival within the party and who had been launched by men outside it. What Defferre proposed was not simply a short term electoral alliance of the Third Force, but rather the eventual disappearance of the SFIO, the Radicals, and the MRP into the Democratic and Socialist Federation. He quickly aroused the hostility of the Communist Party by making it clear that he viewed the Federation as a rival rather than a partner of the Communists. The Defferre candidacy collapsed early one morning in June 1965, when Socialist and MRP leaders emerged from an all-night meeting to announce that they were unable to agree on the conditions of federation. The church-state issue and conflict over socialism were two ostensible causes of the break; the reluctance of party leaders to give up the independence of their separate parties very likely was the more important cause. Since interparty federation had been one of

[71] Jeannine Verdès-Leroux, "Caractéristiques des maires des communes de plus de 2,000 habitants," *Revue Française de Science Politique,* XX: 5 (October 1970), p. 976.

[72] *Le Monde,* March 23, 1971.

[73] For a general discussion of the SFIO in recent times, see Harvey G. Simmons, *French Socialists in Search of a Role, 1956–1967* (Ithaca: Cornell University Press, 1970).

Defferre's conditions for running, he immediately withdrew as a candidate for president.

Into the vacuum stepped François Mitterrand, long a leading figure in a small Center-Left group, the Union Démocratique et Socialiste de la Résistance (UDSR). It first appeared that Mitterrand, like Defferre, was entering the battle as a lone knight, without the support of established parties. Then on September 10, 1965, the day following Mitterrand's declaration of candidacy, representatives of the Socialists, the Radicals, the UDSR, and the Convention des Institutions Républicaines (itself a federation of some fifty political clubs) announced the creation of the Fédération de la Gauche Démocrate et Socialiste. The new Federation partners jointly declared that "Experience has shown that the dispersion of political formations constitutes a danger for the normal functioning of institutions, finally for democracy itself. There exists no remedy to this situation, from which our country still suffers, apart from the regrouping of existing formations. . . ."[74] Their immediate task was to destroy the Gaullist "regime of personal power" by electing Mitterrand president.

Defferre had opted for the MRP and against the Communists. Mitterrand dropped the MRP and successfully lured the Communists into an alliance. The MRP put up its own candidate, Jean Lecanuet, who won a surprising 16 percent of the vote on the first ballot of the December 1965 presidential elections. Yet Mitterrand, benefitting from the support of loyal Communist voters, drew another 32 percent of the vote, throwing de Gaulle into a humiliating runoff ballot. The runoff went to de Gaulle, as expected; but Mitterrand's 45 percent of the vote, against the greatest French hero of the century, demonstrated the potential power of a united Left.[75]

The Federation now began preparing for the next parliamentary elections. In the spring of 1965 the creation of a "shadow cabinet," British style, was announced with Mitterrand, the shadow prime minister, assuming the role of spokesman for the opposition. By the time of the elections in spring 1967, the Federation had accomplished the unprecedented feat of selecting in advance a single representative of the democratic Left to do battle with the Gaullists and Communists in each constituency. There was to be no more competition between Socialists and Radicals, even on the first ballot. After the first ballot, as described below, the Federation and the Communist Party each withdrew its

[74] *L'Année Politique, 1965* (Paris: Presses Universitaires de France, 1966), p. 66.
[75] On the election, see *Election 1965;* and Roger-Gérard Schwartzenberg, *La Campagne présidentielle de 1965* (Paris: Presses Universitaires de France, 1967).

candidate when in a given district the other's candidate was "better placed." In the interests of attracting votes to defeat the Gaullists, the Communists even withdrew their candidates in some fifteen districts where they had won more votes on the first ballot than had the Federation candidates. In 65 percent of the 366 constituencies where it was represented on the second ballot of the 1967 elections, the Left's sole candidates drew *more* votes than those obtained in the first ballot a week earlier by *all* candidates of the Left. Apparently the Popular Front alliance attracted some votes from the center in the runoff in 1967, as it had done in 1936.[76] The results — a gain of sixteen seats for the Federation on a smaller proportion of the vote than in 1962 — seemed to justify continuation of the popular front.

The Communist alliance, which was so useful in 1967, proved to be an albatross around the Federation's neck in June 1968, when public opinion had turned sharply against the Communists. The popular front alliance was renewed, but it produced a loss of 64 seats for the Federation, as well as a 39 seat loss for the Communists. On June 30, 1968, the Left's runoff representatives improved on the first-ballot performance of parties of the Left in only 40 percent of the 297 constituencies in which they ran. Fourteen Communist candidates and ten Socialist candidates — all sole candidates of the Left for the runoff — were defeated in districts where the combined first-ballot vote of the Left had been over 50 percent.[77] According to a national survey conducted by the French Institute of Public Opinion (IFOP), in districts where a Communist squared off against a Gaullist in the runoff ballot, he drew the votes of only 63 percent of first-ballot Federation supporters (as opposed to 70 percent in 1967), and only 10 percent of first-ballot Center party supporters (as opposed to 25 percent in 1967).[78] Outside Paris, anti-Communist sentiment was particularly strong. In the provinces only 55 percent of first-ballot Federation voters stayed with the Left when represented by a Communist on the second ballot.

The Federation's dilemma was obvious. Without the Communists and their loyal 20 percent of the electorate, the Left would be divided and overwhelmed by the Gaullists. With them, the Federation frightened off most of its potential runoff allies to its right, and in 1968 even some of its own supporters.

The elections of June 1968 effectively destroyed the Federation. Up

---

[76] On the comparison with 1936, see Raymond Barrillon, *La Gauche Française en Mouvement* (Paris: Plon, 1967), pp. 72–81.

[77] Raymond Barrillon, "La Défaite électorale de la Gauche vue à travers les chiffres," *Le Monde,* July 6, 1968.

[78] *Le Monde,* Nov. 7, 1968.

to that point it had made little progress toward the proclaimed objective of full fusion of its components into a true party. After the May-June crisis and the resulting Gaullist landslide, the Federation partners seemed disillusioned with their creation. The Federation had not only lost its momentum, but its parliamentary group had been reduced to 13 Radicals, 42 Socialists, and a mere 2 representatives of the Convention Républicaine, including Mitterrand. The Federation seemed to be hardly more than an alliance between the remnants of the Socialist and Radical parties.

In the fall of 1968 the Federation collapsed. Mitterrand resigned, proposing that the Federation be replaced by a single, unified party with a fresh set of leaders. The Socialists concurred with the proposal of a new party; but their insistence that that party adhere to traditional socialist doctrine implied that what Mollet had in mind was simply an expansion of the SFIO.[79]

When de Gaulle finally moved off center stage after his defeat in the April 1969 referendum, the non-Communist Left was too divided to take advantage of its opportunity. The Socialists were about to hold the inaugural conference of a new Socialist Party, to be built around the SFIO and François Mitterrand's Convention of Republican Institutions. Against the opposition of both Mitterrand and Guy Mollet, Gaston Defferre, Mayor of Marseilles, revived his presidential bid of 1965 and managed to secure the endorsement of the Socialist Party Conference. Even though he persuaded the once-popular Pierre Mendès-France to join his team as prime minister designate, Defferre managed to win only 5 percent of the votes cast on the first ballot of the presidential election of June 1969. Michel Rocard, whose Unified Socialist Party (PSU) refused alliance with either the Socialists or the Communists, was not far behind Defferre, with 3.7 percent of the vote, while the Trotskyist candidate, student leader Alain Krivine, trailed all other candidates with 1.1 percent of the vote. Losing votes to both Poher, the Centrist candidate, and Duclos, the Communist, the non-Communist Left was reduced to less than 10 percent of the votes cast.

The "new" Socialist Party which emerged during and after the presidential campaign was fundamentally the old SFIO, with the addition of a few new recruits, including its new First Secretary, Alain Savary, who had left the old Socialist Party during the Algerian war. The Radicals, the Convention, and the PSU all remained outside, although Convention representatives were invited to sit in on Socialist Party conferences.

After the trauma of the spring of 1968, which scarred the Left more

---

[79] *Le Monde,* November 5, 1968.

than it did the Gaullists, unity on the Left seemed beyond reach, either with or without the Communists. Not even the polarizing pressures of a presidential election could bring it about. And yet what remained of their survival instinct told the Socialists that they must not fight another election alone. Once again, after their electoral disaster in June 1969, the Socialists began planning and negotiating for a new electoral alliance with the Communists. Despite warnings from cautious members like André Chandernagor (who told the Socialist National Council in June 1970 that "In betting on the Communist Party we are playing Russian roulette with the future"), Savary and his party launched a series of talks with Communist representatives.[80]

Why did the Federation fail, and why has the new Socialist Party failed to complete its mission of unification? In brief, internal partisan rivalries, genuine ideological differences, the loyalty of Communist voters, and the continuing strength of Gaullism all played a part in the failure of the non-Communist Left to move beyond the stage of temporary electoral alliances.

Radicals, Popular Republicans, and Independent Conservatives

The Gaullist era has been catastrophic for three of the key parties of the Fourth Republic: the Radicals, the Popular Republican Movement (MRP), and the Independents. Together they had supplied premiers for nineteen of the Fourth Republic's twenty-seven governments.[81] Their deputies occupied 40 to 50 percent of the seats of the Fourth Republic's National Assembly. To be sure, each had had its problems. The Independent Conservatives (who called themselves independents or moderates, but never conservatives) were never a united party, even after the creation of the Centre National des Indépendants et Paysans (CNIP) in 1951. The Radicals, like the Independents, were a party of individualistic *notables,* of leaders without organized followers. Moreover, they were divided, as long they had been, over what it meant to be "of the Left" in the modern world. Pierre Mendès-France attempted to modernize the party, commit it to social reform, tighten its internal discipline, and extend its appeal. He failed and left the party, taking a number of his supporters with him. By 1956 the MRP, unlike its fellow Christian Democratic parties which built lasting government coalitions in Germany and Italy, had already disillusioned and lost over half of its five million voters of 1945–1946. In the last years of the Fourth Re-

[80] *Le Monde,* June 21–22, 1970.

[81] Including two from a splinter Radical group, the UDSR. Williams, *Crisis and Compromise,* p. 294.

public, each of these parties was further plagued by internal quarrels between those who wanted to "Keep Algeria French" and those willing to accept autonomy for Algeria. However, had it not been for de Gaulle, they might well have continued to *se débrouiller,* to muddle through.

The Radical Socialists

De Gaulle's assault on the "parties of yesteryear" — implicit in 1958 and explicit in 1962 — first almost leveled the Radical Socialist Party. Along with their Left-Center neighbors, the UDSR, they had elected 91 deputies in 1956. When the elections of November 1958 were over, they had only 41. By 1965 they were eagerly looking to a federation of the Left as their only means of survival. When that Federation collapsed in 1968, the Radical Socialist Party, isolated and reduced to a National Assembly delegation of only 14, seemed to be on its deathbed. And then a highly successful writer and editor, Jean-Jacques Servan-Schreiber, decided to rebuild this moribund party into a dynamic Third Force movement. He was elected secretary general of the party in the fall of 1969, pledging to come up with a new party program within three months. In February 1970 the party adopted a program calling for the general abolition of government subsidies to private industry and agriculture, the establishment of preschool nurseries for children from low-income families, the establishment of confiscatory inheritance taxes on large fortunes, the strengthening of municipal government, and the creation of a United States of Europe.[82] For the old Radical Socialist Party, which had never been socialist and which had ceased to be radical once the church was separated from the state in 1905, these were bold commitments.

Servan-Schreiber upset the favored Gaullist candidate in a National Assembly by-election in the city of Nancy in June 1970, thereby establishing himself as a political figure to be taken seriously.[83] The victory was essentially a personal one. Whether he can succeed in reinvigorating the Radical Party, a decade and a half after Mendès-France tried and failed, remains to be seen. Unless he is extremely successful, the result could simply help perpetuate the fragmentation of the non-Communist opposition.

[82] The program is presented and defended in Jean-Jacques Servan-Schreiber and Michel Albert, *Ciel et Terre* (Paris: Denoël, 1970).

[83] Servan-Schreiber's victory was not necessarily an indication of his potential in national politics for he benefitted from local discontent over the national government's decision to route the Paris–Strasbourg superhighway through Metz rather than through Nancy.

Independents and Popular Republicans

The Independents, most of whom initially shouted their undying faith in de Gaulle, were early winners in the Fifth Republic (with 115 seats in 1958), but eventual losers. In the legislative elections of 1962, after de Gaulle's plan for Algerian independence had turned many conservatives against him, the Gaullist wave left standing only thirty-four "Independent Republican" deputies — formally pledged to Gaullist discipline — and some two dozen unaffiliated Independent deputies. The Independent Republicans became a second major Gaullist party, alongside the UNR.

The MRP, which had run in the 1946 elections as the "party of fidelity" to de Gaulle, now found itself unable to halt the desertion of its followers to the Gaullist camp. Its group in the National Assembly dwindled from 83 in 1956 to 65 in 1958 to 36 in 1962, at which time it joined with a number of unaffiliated deputies and many of the surviving Independents to form a new parliamentary group named the *Centre Démocratique*. Popular Republicans and anti-Gaullist moderate conservatives again joined forces in support of Jean Lecanuet, the MRP candidate against de Gaulle in the presidential elections of December 1965. They had in common an interest in European unification and an aversion both to communism and to Gaullism's authoritarian style. Their collaboration continued through the legislative elections of 1967 and 1968, although the parliamentary group was renamed Progress and Modern Democracy. In the fall of 1967, contrary to the usual passion for independence among French parties, the MRP announced it was ceasing publication of its newspaper and joining the *Centre Démocratique;* the MRP would survive separately only as a political club.[84] Yet even fusion of the old Center and Center-Right could not prevent Popular Republicans from being caught in the middle in what in the 1960's increasingly was becoming a straight fight between the Gaullists on the one hand and the Federation of the Democratic and Socialist Left, allied with the Communists, on the other. As a parliamentary group, the new Center shrank from 59 members in 1962 to 41 in 1967 to a mere 33 in 1968.

For seven frantic weeks in the spring of 1969, the Center seemed still to have a chance of regaining a leading role in French politics. As President of the French Senate, Alain Poher, a little-known figure from the MRP, played an important role in the campaign which led to the defeat of de Gaulle's dual referendum proposals for reform of the Senate and regionalization of French administration. Shortly after de Gaulle's resignation in the wake of that defeat of April 27, the polls

[84] *Le Monde*, September 15, 1967.

began pointing to Poher as the man who might beat Georges Pompidou.[85] In the second and third weeks of May, a series of polls showed that Poher had the first-ballot support of 34 to 39 percent of adult Frenchmen, usually only 3 to 4 percentage points behind Pompidou. On the runoff ballot between Poher and Pompidou, his strategists argued (with supporting evidence from the early polls), additional votes from the Communists and Socialists would push Poher right into the Elysée Palace.

In fact, Poher won less than 24 percent of the vote in the first ballot on June 1st and only 42 percent in the runoff. What went wrong with the Centrist strategy? Some of the probable reasons for its failure are revealing. First was the problem of disunity. Jean Lecanuet, the Centrist candidate of 1965, lent vigorous support to Poher, as did the remnants of the Radical Party, which was now free of the Federation. But even before the first ballot, the president of the Centrist Progress and Modern Democracy group in the National Assembly, Jacques Duhamel, and a former secretary general of the MRP, Joseph Fontanet, among others, had been lured into the Gaullist camp by promises of greater flexibility in European policy and by fears of dependency upon Communist votes. Not only was the Gaullist coalition holding together after de Gaulle, contrary to Centrist expectations, but it was actively recruiting among its opponents.

Even had the Center been united, it lacked the powerful national party machinery which the Communists and Gaullists were able to mobilize in their candidates' behalf. Moreover, Poher found himself under vigorous attack not only from the Gaullists, who argued persuasively that without a parliamentary majority the Center candidate would have to call new elections and even thereafter to depend upon shifting coalitions of a Fourth Republic nature, but also from the Communists, who argued that he was at least as reactionary as Pompidou and more sympathetic to the American imperialists. Along with his lackluster television performances, these factors seem to have been largely responsible for Poher's consistent drop in the polls to an election-day low point of under 24 percent. But could the battle not still be won in the runoff? Pompidou's opponents had polled a total of 56 percent of the votes cast in the first ballot. Only one of these — businessman Louis Ducatel, the "anti-politician" candidate — asked his supporters (all 284,000 of them) to vote for Pompidou in the run-

---

[85] On the fluctuation of voter sentiment in the spring of 1969, see Alain Lancelot and Pierre Weill, "L'Evolution politique des électeurs français de février à juin 1969," *Revue Française de Science Politique*, XX: 2 (April 1970), pp. 149–181. On the campaign conducted by Poher, see, in the same issue, Jean and Monica Charlot, "Les Campagnes de Georges Pompidou et Alain Poher," pp. 224–248.

off. If one were to follow the usual American political strategy, against a clearcut conservative the reformist candidate nearest the middle should be well placed to capture a part of the middle-of-the-road voters as well as most of those to his left, who would have no place else to go. Unfortunately for Poher, the "most Left" quartile of the electorate is politically much further from Center in France than in the United States. The Socialists did indeed throw their meager following to Poher. But the Communists, the PSU, and the Trotskyist candidate, Alain Krivine (who had polled 1 percent of the vote), all asked their supporters to abstain in the runoff. Abstentions increased from 21 percent of registered voters in the first ballot to 31 percent in the second, helping to insure Poher's defeat. Internal disunity, the powerful, organized opposition of Communists and Gaullists, general fear of a return to the instability of the Fourth Republic, and the intransigence of the extreme Left all had conspired to frustrate Centrism's finest hope.

The Gaullists

When Charles de Gaulle returned to the premiership of France in June 1958, he had no intention of founding yet another political party. It was his conviction, frequently reiterated, that political parties, especially in France, deepened the divisions in a population which he, de Gaulle, was determined to unite.[86] The French parties, with their selfish and quarrelsome ways, he often had argued, were responsible in good part for the governmental weaknesses which led to the collapse of the past two republics. His contempt for political parties extended even to those which claimed to be loyal to him. Had not the MRP ministers stayed on to collaborate with the Socialists and Communists when de Gaulle resigned as premier in 1946? Had not de Gaulle's own Rally of the French People (RPF) yielded to the temptations of the parliamentary game in the mid-1950's, despite the General's strict instructions that they were to collaborate with no other parties until the constitution had been revised?

The new Gaullist party which emerged shortly before the November 1958 elections, the Union for the New Republic (UNR), was the creation of Gaullists, but not of de Gaulle, who forbade any party from

---

[86] See John S. Ambler, "The Democratic Union for the Republic: To Survive de Gaulle," *Rice University Studies,* Vol. 54: No. 3 (Summer, 1968), pp. 1–4; de Gaulle, *War Memoirs,* Vol. I, *The Call to Honor* (New York: Viking, 1955), pp. 79–80, and Vol. III, *Salvation* (New York: Simon and Schuster, 1960), pp. 272–276, 292–293, 307–330; and Roy Macridis, ed., *De Gaulle, Implacable Ally* (New York: Harper & Row, 1966), pp. 41–43.

using his name, even as an adjective.[87] Only gradually and tentatively, beginning in the fall of 1962, when the National Assembly voted no confidence in the Pompidou government, the Assembly was dissolved and new elections called, did de Gaulle begin to recognize the need for a stable party base in the Assembly.

In hopes of electing a Gaullist majority in the elections of November 1962, de Gaulle's representative (and Minister of Culture) André Malraux offered the Gaullist name and, in most cases, exclusive Gaullist candidacy, not only to the UNR candidates but also to Gaullists of the Left and to certain Independents and Popular Republicans who consented to accept the label — and the ensuing discipline — of the Association of the Fifth Republic. Following a Gaullist electoral victory, the Democratic Union of Labor (UDT), a small party of reform-minded Gaullists, quickly fused with the UNR in what, in December 1962, officially became the UNR-UDT. Most of the converted Independents, however, chose to form their own Gaullist party, the Independent Republican Party, under the leadership of Finance Minister Valéry Giscard d'Estaing.

The Fifth Republic coalition strategy was renewed in 1967, 1968, and 1969, on each occasion drawing a few political figures from other parties into the major Gaullist party, the UNR. Partly as a result of infusion of new blood, that party changed its name in 1967 to "Democratic Union for the Fifth Republic," and again in 1968 to "Union of Democrats for the Republic" (UDR). In many respects the UDR (as we shall refer to it henceforth) is a new kind of French party. Like the "catch-all" parties which have flourished in the postwar period in West Germany and Great Britain, the UDR eschews sectarianism and appeals for votes from all the important segments of French society.[88] It deplores dogmatic ideology and approaches most political problems in a pragmatic fashion. It views its major function to be the support of national leaders. These characteristics each deserve closer examination.

Gaullist Doctrine

The statements and writings of Gaullist leaders over the past two decades and more suggest that they share at least three attitudes in addi-

---

[87] The early history of the UNR is described in Jean Charlot, *L'U.N.R., Etude du Pouvoir au Sein d'un Parti Politique,* Cahiers de la Fondation Nationale des Sciences Politiques, No. 153 (Paris: A. Colin, 1967), Ch. 1; *Elections 1958,* pp. 15–19; and *L'Année Politique,* 1958, pp. 129–150.

[88] See Otto Kirchheimer, "The Transformation of Western European Party Systems," in Joseph LaPalombara and Myron Weiner, eds., *Political Parties and Political Development* (Princeton: Princeton University Press, 1966), pp. 177–200.

tion to their loyalty to de Gaulle: they are French nationalists; they believe in a strong, stable state, built around a strong executive who represents the national interest; and they consider themselves to be modern and progressive in comparison with the "prophets of the past" of the traditional parties.[89] If Gaullism means anything more than simple obedience to de Gaulle, certainly it means attachment to the General's "certaine idée de la France," to the notion of an active and independent French role in world affairs. ". . . France is not really herself unless in the front rank," wrote de Gaulle in the first paragraph of his *War Memoirs*. ". . . only vast enterprises are capable of counterbalancing the ferments of dispersal which are inherent in her people; . . . our country, as it is, surrounded by others, as they are, must aim high and hold itself straight, on pain of mortal danger. In short, to my mind, France cannot be France without greatness."[90] However divided they may be on other questions, Gaullists, including Gaullists of the Left, tend to agree that Gaullism is, at least in part, a form of nationalism.[91]

Gaullist nationalism is a very different species from the rigid, doctrinaire nationalism associated in the Third Republic with Charles Maurras and his *Action Française*. In the service of "French greatness," de Gaulle was surprisingly flexible, to the point of granting independence to most of the French empire, including Algeria, even though he was called to power largely by French Algerians and the army for the purpose of keeping Algeria French. His is what is best called "pragmatic nationalism." The Gaullist movement can be pragmatic in its choice of means, since the objective of French greatness lacks the necessary specificity to form the base for a coherent, binding ideology. As the object of a fundamental and continuing quest, nationalism is Gaullism's functional equivalent to the British Labour Party's commitment to greater social equality. For a catch-all party, the nationalist appeal has the distinct advantage of excluding no one.

Gaullists also generally agree (and for many this follows necessarily from the nationalist objective) that France needs a powerful and independent executive, capable of serving as arbiter between rival interests, as guardian of the national interest, and as a constant check upon par-

---

[89] The quoted phrase is from the editorial in *Notre République,* October 15, 1965.

[90] De Gaulle, *War Memoirs,* Vol. 1, p. 3.

[91] See, for example, Michel Debré, *Au Service de la Nation* (Paris: Stock, 1963), p. 273; Edmond Michelet, *Le Gaullisme, Passionante Aventure* (Paris: Fayard, 1962), pp. 17–19, 141; Georges Pompidou to the UNR Conseil National, as quoted in *Le Monde,* May 21, 1963; and René Capitant, "L'U.N.R. et L'U.D.T.," *Notre République,* February 4, 1966.

tisan ambitions.[92] Lastly, Gaullists distinguish themselves from traditional French conservatives in their greater insistence upon rapid economic expansion and the modernization of French political, military, and economic institutions. The UNR repeatedly announced its mission was to "construct the new France," to "lead this country toward the destinies of the twenty-first century."[93] One of the party's publications was baptized *La Nouvelle Frontière,* as evidence of a Kennedy-type commitment to getting France moving.

Gaullist leaders distinguish themselves not only by this constellation of attitudes (nationalism, modernism, and belief in a strong executive), but also by the *style* of their politics. The UNR insisted that it "is not a party, particularly not a party like the others."[94] It was rather "the union of Frenchmen and Frenchwomen, of all origins, determined to support, without the spirit of party, the action of General de Gaulle and pursue his work within the framework of the Fifth Republic."[95] The UNR and its successor, the UDR, have set out to create the image of a modern, nonideological, classless, antiparty party, one which has nothing in common with its rivals. What the country needs, said former UNR Secretary General Jacques Baumel, is a "practical approach to the great problems, a sense of the real and the concrete, to the exclusion of all ideology and of all a priori-ism."[96]

The Gaullist Electorate

With this kind of an appeal, and with the heroic figure of de Gaulle at its head until 1969, the Gaullist movement has succeeded remarkably well in drawing votes from Frenchmen of all social classes and from all geographical regions. In the legislative elections of 1958, 1962, and 1967, the UNR and UDR electorate was more representative of the population as a whole than that of any other party. It differed from the population as a whole, and usually only moderately, in that it contained a larger than average proportion of older people, women, devout Catholics, retired people, businessmen, and people from the East, West,

[92] This argument was elaborated by de Gaulle in his Bayeux speech of 1946, which the UNR adopted as fundamental doctrine. Première Assises Nationales, Bordeaux, November 13–15, 1959, "UNR, Résolutions Adoptées par les Assises," a UNR publication (Paris, 1959), p. 1.

[93] Jacques Baumel, former UNR secretary general, as quoted in *Le Monde,* February 1, 1965, and November 5, 1963, respectively.

[94] "Qu'est-ce que l'UNR-UDT?" supplement to *La Nation,* May 8, 1963.

[95] "Pour une France Moderne," supplement to *La Nation,* May 8, 1964, p. 2.

[96] Le Gaullisme et son avenir," *Nouvelle Frontière,* January 1964, p. 36.

and North.[97] For example, attitude surveys conducted prior to the November 1962 elections suggest that the UNR got slightly less than its share of votes on the first ballot from voters 21–34 years of age (28 percent of UNR voters were in this group, which made up 31 percent of the whole sample) and slightly more than its share from voters age 65 and over (20 percent to 15 percent in the whole sample).[98] The same survey showed that the UNR probably drew less than its share of workers' votes (15 percent from this group, as opposed to 20 percent so classified in the whole sample), and more than its share of retired persons (17 percent to 12 percent).[99] Survey data from December 1966 showed that 31 percent of workers polled at that time intended to vote Gaullist, as opposed to 30 percent having that intention in the whole sample.[100]

The extended, or presidential, Gaullist electorate, that majority of Frenchmen who voted for de Gaulle in the referendum of October 1962 and on the second ballot of the December 1965 presidential election, is more distinctive than the restricted, first-ballot UNR/UDR electorate. On December 17, 1965, de Gaulle drew the votes of only 49 percent of young people ages 21–34, while drawing the votes of 65 percent of voters age 65 and over.[101] He had the votes of some 67 percent of businessmen, but only 45 percent of those of workers. More striking is the preponderance of women and of devout Catholics in the extended Gaullist electorate. In a national survey on voting intentions, on the eve of the runoff in December 1965, de Gaulle had the support of 61 percent of all women in the sample who had made up their minds, and only 49 percent of men.[102] He apparently drew the votes of some 66 percent of those who considered themselves "regular practicing Catholics," 37 percent of "nonpracticing Catholics," and only 18 percent of persons declaring themselves "without religion."[103] Since in France as in Italy, women tend more often to be churchgoers than men, the factors of religion and sex are interrelated.

[97] See Ambler, "The Democratic Union for the New Republic," pp. 13–18; *Elections 1958; and Elections 1962.*

[98] *Elections 1962,* p. 230.

[99] *Ibid.,* p. 231.

[100] See Fichelet *et al.,* "Premiers Résultats," p. 14.

[101] *Sondages,* 1965, No. 4, p. 36.

[102] *Ibid.*

[103] *Sondages,* 1966, No. 2, pp. 15–19. With respect to the religious views of party leaders, a recent survey found that 90 percent of the Gaullist leaders sample attended church at least occasionally, as opposed to only 36 percent of Socialist leaders. Mark Kesselman, "The Recruitment of Rival Party Activists in France," a paper delivered to the meetings of the International Political Science Association, September 1970, p. 28.

After the Algerian war was concluded, when de Gaulle did battle with the parties his strongest opposition came from the Left; hence many women, devout Catholics and businessmen were drawn into the Gaullist camp in order to prevent a revival of the dreaded popular front government. It appears that for the first time many of these same people swung behind Gaullist candidates on the first ballot in the crisis legislative elections of June 1968, after the Gaullists had fully exploited popular fears of chaos and communism. The Gaullist parties apparently made substantial gains among women, older persons and businessmen, but none at all among workers.[104]

When de Gaulle extended the Gaullist electorate, he did so largely by drawing in the more conservative elements of French society. The trend toward a conservative Gaullist majority was even more marked in the June 1969 presidential elections, after de Gaulle's resignation. Pre-election surveys suggest that 54 percent of those who intended to vote for Pompidou on the first ballot of the June 1969 elections considered themselves to be of the "Right" or "Extreme Right," as opposed to only 36 percent of those who intended to vote for de Gaulle in the 1965 presidential elections.[105] And yet Pompidou apparently still received as many votes from the working class as did the Communist candidate Jacques Duclos, showing that the UDR was still a "catch-all" party, though of a more conservative coloring than it had been in 1958.[106]

In geographical terms Gaullism's uniqueness has been its strength in the bastions of rural traditionalism of the West (Normandy, Brittany, and the Vendée) and of the East (Alsace-Lorraine) as well as in the economically dynamic regions of northern France, where the tradition tends to be Leftist.[107] The 1968 and 1969 elections saw further geographical extension of Gaullist strength. Gaullist parliamentary candidates won at least 30 percent of the vote in all but three of France's ninety-five departments. On the first ballot of the June 1969 presidential election, Georges Pompidou won 34 percent or more of the votes in every department. Except for its decidedly Catholic bias (and it

[104] Alain Duhamel, "Le Sondage de l'I.F.O.P." *Le Monde,* June 28, 1968. Compare with "Les Elections Législatives de Mars 1967," *Sondages,* 1967, No. 3.

[105] Lancelot and Weill in *Revue Française de Science Politique,* p. 280.

[106] *Ibid.,* p. 269.

[107] *Elections 1958,* pp. 361–371; *Elections 1962,* pp. 291–428; François Goguel, "L'Election Présidentielle Française de Décembre 1965," *Revue Française de Science Politique,* XVI: 2 (April 1966), pp. 221–254; Goguel, "Les Elections Législatives des 5 et 12 Mars 1967," *Ibid.,* XVII: 3 (June 1967), pp. 446–449; and, for the June 1968 elections, the maps in *Le Monde,* June 25, 1968.

must be added that there are a number of Protestants and Jews among Gaullist leaders), the Gaullist electorate is fairly representative of the diversity of French society.

Organization

Undoubtedly many of those who flocked to the UDR in June 1968 had only an ephemeral, *faute de mieux* kind of loyalty to the Gaullist movement. There is good evidence that in 1958, at least, Frenchmen in general did not have the same lasting loyalties to political parties which contribute to stability in American politics.[108] If the Gaullists are to avoid drowning in a repetition of the flash flood which swept them into power, they must develop lasting voter loyalties as well as an organization to institutionalize their movement. On the first count, the results of opinion polls, as well as the steady growth of their electorate, suggest that they are making strong headway.[109] Georges Pompidou's striking victory in the presidential elections of June 1969, a few weeks after the defeat of de Gaulle's last referendum proposal, is clear evidence of the survival of Gaullist loyalties after de Gaulle. Pompidou's first-ballot score of 44 percent of the votes cast was almost identical to that of de Gaulle on the first ballot of the December 1965 presidential election.

On the second count — creation of a firm organization — there has also been solid progress, although the party is still almost absent in some areas. As is fitting for a party which borrows from both the Left and the Right, the UDR falls neither into the traditional category of "cadre-type party" nor into that of "mass-type party."[110] As in the cadre party, programmatic commitments are avoided, and decision-making is the affair of a rather small clique of men. Unlike the cadre party, the UDR is highly centralized and disciplined. In terms of membership, there has been no massive recruiting, such as the one which won the RPF a million members in 1948. Yet with a formal membership which grew to over eighty thousand by 1963, at a time when French party memberships generally were low, the UNR became much more of a mass organization than typical French cadre parties like the Radicals and the Independents. Only the Communist Party has more members than the present UDR. Moreover, after an initial fear of flooding the party with partisans of French Algeria, UNR

[108] Converse and Dupeux, "Politicization of the Electorate."

[109] See *Sondages*, 1963, No. 2, p. 59, compared with Deutsch, Lindon, and Weill, *Les Familles Politiques*, pp. 46–53.

[110] These categories were delineated by Duverger in *Political Parties*. They have been refined by Francis Sorauf in *Political Parties in the American System* (Boston: Little, Brown, 1964), pp. 160–162.

leaders used study circles, forums, cadre schools, women's, youth, agricultural, and student clubs, and a variety of other techniques in order to catch a larger proportion of the population in the party's organizational net.

The organization of the UDR has been aptly characterized by René Rémond as a "government party."[111] Created to organize popular and parliamentary votes in support of an existing Gaullist government, the UDR has enjoyed adequate sanctions and rewards to enforce discipline and has staved off factions, like that of the French Algeria partisans, which would commit the party to specific programs and hence perhaps embarrass the government. Like the national organization of the British Conservative Party, the UDR organization is designed not to make policy decisions, but rather to mobilize support for those who do. There are the usual elected party organs at the legislative district, department, and national levels, but, in practice, the national central committee, and especially its twenty-five-man executive bureau, working closely with cabinet members on important questions, has a far stronger voice in determining party policy than either the biennial National Congress or the six-hundred-member National Council. Like government parties everywhere, the UDR acts as a transmission belt between governors and governed; yet it tends to be a one-way communication, serving to inform and organize the electorate in support of government policies more than to express and digest demands from below. During de Gaulle's presidency, the Gaullist party — often even the UDR parliamentary group — hardly seemed to have a place in its mentor's promised "society of participation."

Independent Republicans

If the UDR has been fearful of internal dissent, the reason is partly to be found in the memory of the factionalism which helped destroy its precursor, the RPF. Indeed, factionalism remains a potential threat to the present Gaullist movement, and the most important factional threat has come from Giscard d'Estaing's Independent Republicans. At each election the Independent Republicans have increased their numbers in the National Assembly, from 30 in 1962 to 44 in 1967 to 61 in 1968. Especially after his replacement as Finance Minister in early 1966, Giscard gave clear signs that his ambitions for future leadership were lofty and his hope was that the Independent Republicans, and not the UDR, would carry the Gaullist tradition into the post-de Gaulle era.[112]

[111] Rémond, "L'Enigme de l'U.N.R.," *Esprit,* February 1963, pp. 309–311.
[112] On the Independent Republicans, see the series of articles in the *Revue Française de Science Politique,* XV: 3 (June 1965), pp. 548–555; XVI: 5 (October 1966), pp. 940–957; and XVIII: 1 (February 1968), pp. 77–93.

Giscard described his attitude toward de Gaulle as one of "yes, but," to which de Gaulle reportedly retorted, "one does not govern with buts."[113] His party followers, he explained, were "loyal but not servile partners of the UNR."[114] and he and his fellow Independent Republicans distinguished themselves from many of their UDR partners by their attachment to European political integration, to economic liberalism, and to a revival of parliamentary powers. Their taste for independence was particularly troublesome to the government between the March 1967 and June 1968 elections, when the *Giscardiens* were both discontented with the Pompidou government and crucial to its parliamentary majority. During the crisis of May–June 1968, Giscard publicly called for the formation of a new government, that is to say one without Pompidou.

The Independent Republicans lost their crucial swing position, however, after the June 1968 elections, for the UDR emerged with 292 of 485 seats, far more than an absolute majority. If a portion of the Independent Republican group behaved thereafter like disciplined Gaullists, under the leadership of Minister of the Interior Raymond Marcellin, the same could not be said of Giscard himself. In the final Gaullist referendum of April 27, 1969, Giscard publicly pronounced for a "no" vote and persuaded his party at least to leave its members free to vote as they wished. When the referendum vote came back "no" and de Gaulle resigned, Giscard set about to keep Georges Pompidou off the throne. He announced that the country needed an independent, non-Gaullist president, presumably the former Independent prime minister, Antoine Pinay. But when Pompidou's nomination seemed inevitable, Giscard swung behind him. After the elections, Giscard joined the government and reclaimed the Ministry of Finance as reward, but his loyalty to the UDR has been too sporadic to be taken for granted in the future. In the municipal elections of March 1971 Giscard and his Independent Republicans joined forces with their former brethren who have been in the opposition since the Independent party split of 1962.

Gaullists of the Left

The Gaullists of the Left represent relatively few votes. In 1958, running as an independent party, the Democratic Union of Labor (UDT), they won less than one percent of the vote and failed to elect a single deputy. Nonetheless they were important to de Gaulle as evidence that his movement was not simply a revival of French conservatism.

[113] *Le Monde,* January 12, 1967.
[114] *L'Année Politique,* 1963, p. 52.

The Gaullists of the Left long had been suspicious of what they took to be Pompidou's ultraconservative economic views. In the summer of 1967 with de Gaulle's personal intervention, they helped enact into law a compulsory profit-sharing plan, reportedly against the desires of Pompidou, the cabinet, and the bureaucracy. With de Gaulle's resignation, one faction of the Gaullist Left, led by former Minister of Justice René Capitant, cut its ties to the UDR in order to be free to attack all Gaullists who might abandon the Gaullist doctrine of "association of capital and labor" through profit-sharing and labor participation in plant management. In December 1969 the UDT was reformed and formally announced its opposition to the government. The spirit of this group is expressed by its present leader, Louis Vallon, in a book about Pompidou entitled *The Anti-De Gaulle*.[115]

Perhaps half of the prominent Left Gaullists stayed in the UDR under Pompidou. When joined with other UDR deputies of a reformist bent, they insure that Gaullism will continue to include within the official family men whose views on economic and social questions range from laissez-faire noninterventionism to democratic socialism, thus providing ample grounds for future factional dispute.

"Opening and Continuity"

Pompidou's election strategy of "opening" the Gaullist family toward the Center brought in another faction whose loyalty is still tentative. Jacques Duhamel, Joseph Fontanet, and other new Gaullist converts from the Center, in early July 1969 announced the formation of a Democracy and Progress Center (CDP), which was intended to be the "spur and initiating force" of the Gaullist majority. Like the Independent Republicans, it attached more importance than had the UDR to European unification and to the rights of the French Parliament. If one were to look for a distinction between the *Giscardiens* and this new Center Gaullist group, it might well be in the latter's greater emphasis upon social reform through governmental action.[116]

Pompidou's campaign talk of opening the Gaullist majority to new men and new ideas worried a number of Gaullist notables who were not included in the new cabinet and who shared a strong personal loyalty to de Gaulle. They formed a group within the National Assembly which came to be known as "Presence and Action of Gaullism," under the leadership of former Defense Minister Pierre Messmer. The group's announced mission was to hold the new leadership to the tried

[115] Louis Vallon, *L'Anti-De Gaulle* (Paris: Seuil, 1969).
[116] See the policy declaration of the CDP in *Le Monde,* July 5, 1969.

and true Gaullist course, particularly the continued pursuit of a foreign policy of national grandeur. The group became a thorn in the side of Prime Minister Chaban-Delmas, whose Gaullist orthodoxy some members doubted, but did little to prevent President Pompidou from establishing his firm leadership over the UDR.

In certain respects the UDR is, as it claims to be, a new type of French political party. In its blending of stability and progress, it borrows from both the Left and the Right. With the UDR as its central force, the Gaullist parliamentary majority has introduced into French politics the notion of the government party, whose primary purpose is to produce the electoral and parliamentary support necessary to allow the government to survive and to act. With regard to its electorate, Gaullism's voting strength in many of the economically most dynamic and prosperous areas of France is indication of its appeal to modernizers. Like the "catch-all" parties which dominate the politics of Great Britain and West Germany, the UDR is committed to a pragmatic striving toward economic growth and progress. Though de Gaulle rejected the vision of European political unification, in many ways he and his followers belong to the new, not the old, Europe.

This is not to say that Gaullism is wholly new and unique in the French political tradition. In its heterogeneous clientele, in its suspicion of parliaments and of intermediary bodies generally, in its reliance on the plebiscite, in its combination of stability and progress — in all of these respects Gaullism belongs to the Bonapartist tradition. Yet the analogy must not be exaggerated. Gaullists are committed to democratic rights and freedoms in a way which clearly sets them apart from nineteenth-century Bonapartists, as does their commitment to modernization. Moreover, though still passionately nationalistic, Gaullists evidence few imperialist pretentions; after all, it was de Gaulle who presided over the dismantling of the French empire.

To the dismay of its critics, the Gaullist movement has passed its first and most critical test: it has survived de Gaulle's passing. The UDR and its allies remain a diverse coalition, but little more diverse, certainly, than the British Labour Party, and far less so than the American Democratic Party. If the experience of other catch-all parties in the United States, Britain, and Germany is relevant, however, now that the grand arbiter is gone, Gaullists will be able to maintain their broad coalition only if they demonstrate a capacity for compromise, only if they facilitate the expression and adjustment of demands. Those Gaullist leaders who share de Gaulle's disdain for intermediary groups and his distaste for consensus through compromise are poorly equipped for the political broker's role. And yet those who have taken over leadership are for the most part pragmatic, deeply political men like President Georges Pompidou and especially Prime Minister Jacques Chaban-Delmas. The Gaullism of referendum and presidential fiat may yet give way to a less dramatic but more democratic Gaullism of negotiation and compromise.

Trends in the Party System

In the heat of an election campaign, André Malraux once announced that "between us [the Gaullists] and the Communists there is nothing." He was wrong, but not entirely. The two most striking developments of the French political party system since 1958 have been the emergence of a powerful Gaullist bloc and the decline of the old parties — the Independents, the MRP, the Radicals, and the SFIO — which dominated the Fourth Republic. Though created to support a single man, the Gaullist movement failed to disintegrate upon his resignation. For over twelve years its voters had built up loyalties, its leaders had acquired a vested interest in its survival, and its opponents had demonstrated their inability to unite (and hence apparently to govern). Moreover, the decline of some of the old issues, especially religion, has resulted in a more consensual society of the type which favors catch-all parties. Of the old parties, only the Communist Party, the stablest of all French parties in terms of voting strength, survives as a powerful opponent to Gaullism.

The experience of governing parties throughout the democratic world indicates that the lengthy exercise of power tends to erode the wielder's popularity. A crisis of some sort — an unpopular war, a depression, a scandal, sometimes an event beyond the powers of any party to control — sends the voters in search of new leadership. But what are the alternatives to Gaullist leadership in France? One possible alternative is still the popular front alliance, such as the one which allowed Mitterrand to give de Gaulle a close race in 1965. The poor results which that strategy produced in 1968, the weakness of the Socialist Party (and its consequent fear of Communist domination), and the lingering Stalinism in the French Communist Party evidenced by its attitude toward Czechoslovakia — all represent serious obstacles to a stable alliance between the Communist Party and the non-Communist Left.

A second possible alternative majority would link the Center and the non-Communist Left in a three-way battle against the Communists and the Gaullists. This was the strategy of Alain Poher in the presidential election of 1969. Its potential advantage is that it allows disgruntled Gaullists to vote for an opposition candidate without voting for a man supported by the Communists. The lesson of the 1969 election seems to be that a Centrist coalition can win only by attracting a number of

Gaullist and Communist voters. Herein lies the major difficulty in the Centrist strategy: the parties upon which it must be based — the Socialists, the Radicals, the non-Gaullist segment of the MRP — are the groups which are most closely identified with the Fourth Republic and those most often abandoned by the voters of the Fifth Republic. Conceivably a new leader and a revitalized party could make this strategy work, particularly if the Gaullist coalition were to find itself divided. Servan-Schreiber and his Radical Party undoubtedly would like to play such a role.

The central player in the party alliance game remains the Socialist Party. So long as that party remains divided, hesitant to choose either the Communists (and abandon the MRP and perhaps the Radicals) or the Third Force (and abandon the Communists), the Gaullists continue to appear to be the only party capable of insuring government stability.

5

Governmental Institutions: The Dual Executive

On June 16, 1946, in the vain hope of forcing the constitution-makers to write a strong presidency into the second draft constitution for the new Fourth Republic (the first draft had been recently rejected by referendum), General Charles de Gaulle took to the podium in the Norman town of Bayeux:

> In brief, the rivalry of parties in our country takes on a fundamental character that sets everything adrift and very often wrecks the superior interests of the country. This is an obvious fact which is due to our national temperament, to the accidents of our history, and to the disturbances of today, but which our institutions must take into consideration in order to preserve the respect for law, the cohesion of governments, the efficiency of administrations, and the prestige and authority of the state.[1]

Just as James Madison concluded in *The Federalist* that factions among men were inevitable in a free society, so de Gaulle determined that the divisions among French political parties were endemic. Like Madison, de Gaulle proposed to control the evil through a properly devised constitution:

> How are unity, cohesion, and discipline to be guaranteed if the executive power emanates from the very legislative power that it should balance, and if each member of the government that is collectively responsible to the entire body of representatives of the nation, were, when in the government, merely a delegate of his party? It is then the chief of State — placed above political

[1] In Macridis, ed., *De Gaulle, Implacable Ally*, p. 41.

parties, elected by an electoral college that includes Parliament but that is much broader and is composed in such a way as to make him the President of the French Union as well as President of the Republic — who should hold executive power. To the chief of State belongs the duty of reconciling the national interest with the general orientation of Parliament when it comes to choosing men to govern; to him the duty of nominating the Ministers and, first of all, of course, the Prime Minister, who must be in charge of the work and direction of the Government; to the chief of State the duty of promulgating the laws and the executive orders; . . . to him the task of presiding over the meetings of the Council of Ministers and to exercise the influence and continuity without which the nation cannot last; to him the task of acting as arbiter above political contingencies, either within the Council of Ministers or in moments of great confusion by inviting the country to express in an election its sovereign decision; to him, if the country is in danger, the obligation to act as guarantor of national independence and of the treaties that bind France.[2]

Twelve years after the Bayeux speech, de Gaulle was invested as prime minister by a desperate National Assembly and empowered to direct the drafting of yet another constitution.[3] The resulting document is a clear embodiment of the constitutional doctrine formulated at Bayeux. The principal draftsman was not de Gaulle himself, but Michel Debré, a loyal Gaullist from Resistance days onward and the Gaullist movement's leading constitutional theorist. As expressed in his speech of August 27, 1958, to the Council of State, Debré's constitutional views were similar to de Gaulle's, although not identical, as we shall see. Like de Gaulle, he believed that as a result of the partisan divisions among Frenchmen "our electoral structure prevents us from having the coherent majorities which would assure, without detailed rules, the proper functioning of the parliamentary regime."[4] The path toward governmental stability and away from "assembly government," which had crippled executive leadership in the Fourth Republic, was through correct "constitutional stipulations," *i.e.*, an independent president coupled with tight restrictions on the powers of Parliament.

[2] *Ibid.*, pp. 42–43.

[3] On the origins and drafting of the 1958 constitution, see Nicholas Wahl and Stanley Hoffmann, "The French Constitution of 1958," *American Political Science Review*, LIII: 2 (June 1959), pp. 332–382.

[4] The text, as quoted here, is in William G. Andrews, ed., *European Political Institutions*, 2nd ed. (Princeton, N.J.: Van Nostrand, 1966), pp. 44–55. Quotation from p. 50.

The constitution which Debré and his advisors drafted represents a fascinating experiment in constitutional engineering, designed to compensate for French political divisions and to create, at long last, a stable balance between executive leadership and parliamentary controls. Clearly Debré's model was British parliamentary government, with its provisions for both democratic controls and vigorous leadership. Having neither tradition nor stable parliamentary majorities to build upon, he relied upon the proper ordering of constitutional roles. One of our tasks will be to evaluate the results of this experiment.

As we examine each of the major institutions of the Fifth Republic — the president, the prime minister and his cabinet, the Parliament — it will be well to recall that most of France's constitutions have worked very differently in practice from the way their drafters originally intended. The Constitution of the Fifth Republic is no exception. These institutions are best understood in terms of an evolutionary framework of analysis, one which looks first to the negative model of the Fourth Republic, next to the intentions of the constitution-makers, next to the real workings of the institution under President de Gaulle, and last (although experience here is still very limited) to their functioning under de Gaulle's successor as president, Georges Pompidou.

The President

Presidential government was not a Gaullist innovation in France.[5] President Louis Napoleon was elected directly by the people at the beginning of the Second Republic in 1848. Adolphe Thiers was the nation's chief executive officer as the first President of the Third Republic. The prime minister was not even mentioned in the constitutional laws of 1875 upon which the republic was legally based. Yet loyal republicans could not forget that Louis Napoleon destroyed the republic with a coup d'état in December, 1851, and that Thiers' successor, Marshal MacMahon, attempted to keep conservatives in power by dissolving a republican Parliament in the *seize mai* crisis of 1877. And then there were the general fears of strong executive leadership developed through long experience with the Bourbons and the Bonapartes, as the republican leader, Waldeck-Rousseau, noted in 1883:

> We have an almost instinctive aversion to the executive branch. Our feelings about it are hedged round by a whole string of prejudices and reservations, as if we were still reacting against some

[5] On the president in earlier republics, see Pierre Avril, *Politics in France*, trans. by John Ross (Baltimore: Penguin, 1969), pp. 99–107.

past enslavement. We have been its opponents for so long that we appear to have failed to notice the not insignificant fact that in 1791 executive power was otherwise known as Louis XVI, whereas today it goes under the title of President of the Republic.[6]

Belief in a strong presidency came to be associated in France with social and political conservatism.

Following the *seize mai* crisis, the President of the Republic was gradually shunted off into a ceremonial role, leaving the real executive power (such as it was) to the prime minister. Although in the Fourth Republic the president presided over full meetings of the cabinet, appointed and promoted judges with the advice of the High Council of the Judiciary, and performed certain other duties, his only major political role was to "designate" the prime minister, who then needed to be "invested" by a majority vote in the National Assembly in order to be confirmed in his position. The first President of the Fourth Republic, the Socialist Vincent Auriol, played a vigorous role, after the fall of a cabinet, in guiding those interparty (and not infrequently intraparty) negotiations which led to the eventual emergence of a coalition government. Auriol's successor, René Coty, was important in engineering de Gaulle's acceptance as prime minister by the National Assembly in May 1958. And yet the president was destined by the constitution to remain on the fringes of power.

The founders of the Fifth Republic set out to make of the president the keystone of the new political order. The first necessary step, as de Gaulle had explained at Bayeux, was to broaden the president's electoral base. Under the Third and Fourth Republics he had been elected by the two houses of Parliament meeting in joint session. The 1958 constitution determined that he should be chosen by a large electoral college composed of the members of Parliament, all the members of France's ninety elected departmental councils and of the assemblies of the Overseas Territories, and of elected representatives of municipal councils. Like the electoral college which has elected the French Senate since 1875, this body seriously overrepresented the rural population: communities with less than 1,500 inhabitants (which together make up 33 percent of the total French population) held 51 percent of the votes in the electoral college.[7]

By late summer of 1962, de Gaulle, who narrowly escaped assassination in August, had realized that his successor's authority — and hence the survival of the Gaullist republic — would be in doubt so long as

[6] Quoted in *ibid.*, p. 47.

[7] Maurice Duverger, *Institutions Politiques et Droit Constitutionnel,* 10th ed. (Paris: Presses Universitaires de France, 1968), p. 507.

he was elected indirectly and largely by the local leaders of France. De Gaulle's unique personality and historic role lent him immense authority, however elected; his successor would need the political strength which only direct popular election could provide. Hence on October 28, 1962, in a controversial referendum of which more will be said later, the French electorate agreed to a constitutional amendment which provided for direct, popular election of the president.

From that date (as in the presidential elections of December 1965 and June 1969), a citizen can become a presidential candidate by obtaining the signatures of one hundred mayors, members of Parliament, or of the Economic and Social Council, or departmental councillors, and by posting a deposit. All candidates winning at least 5 percent of the vote receive back their deposits along with a 100,000 franc reimbursement each for campaign expenses. If no candidate wins an absolute majority of the votes cast on the first ballot, there is a runoff two weeks later, normally between the two leading candidates. If they choose, one or both of these candidates may withdraw in favor of the next leading candidate. For example, if a Gaullist were leading after the first ballot, with a Communist in second place and a Socialist in third, it is conceivable that the Communist might be persuaded to withdraw in favor of the Socialist, who might have a better chance of defeating the Gaullist.

Once elected for his seven-year term, the President of the Republic is armed with a potent arsenal of powers. Article 5 of the constitution lays out his broadest responsibilities:

> The President of the Republic shall see that the Constitution is respected. He shall ensure, by his arbitration, the regular functioning of the governmental authorities, as well as the continuance of the State. He shall be the guarantor of national independence, of the integrity of the territory, and of respect for Community agreements and treaties.

More specifically, he is granted authority, without the need for approval by any other person or body, to appoint the prime minister, to dissolve Parliament (as de Gaulle did in October 1962 and again in June 1968), to assume full emergency powers under Article 16 when the institutions of the Republic or the independence of the nation are deemed threatened (as de Gaulle did in April 1961), to ask Parliament to reconsider a law just passed, to refer a law to the Constitutional Council for a judgment on its constitutionality, and to make certain appointments. In addition, he presides over the Council of Ministers, serves as commander in chief of the armed forces, exercises the right of pardon, accredits and receives ambassadors, and decides whether or not to submit a bill to popular referendum when the Parliament or the prime minister so proposes.

Michel Debré described this presidential role as that of a "higher judge of the national interest."[8] Yet, for Debré, ". . . the President of the Republic, as it must be, has no other power than that of appealing to another power: he appeals to Parliament, he appeals to the Constitutional Council, he appeals to the electorate. But this power to appeal is fundamental."[9] For Debré the president was not intended to become embroiled in the day-to-day affairs of government, which were the domain of the prime minister and his cabinet; nor was he to be the chief policy-maker, save temporarily in time of emergency. Rather, he was to be a supreme arbiter, charged with intervening from time to time to appeal unwise decisions and to remind warring parties of the demands of the national interest.

In practice, President de Gaulle was far more than an occasional arbiter. The constitution gave him only the power to appoint the prime minister, who thereafter was responsible to Parliament. Once in office, the constitution provides that "the Government [the Prime Minister and his Cabinet] determines and directs the policy of the nation." In practice, de Gaulle easily dominated his prime ministers and removed them at will. In the spring of 1962, the loyal Debré was replaced by Georges Pompidou. In July 1968, immediately after leading the Gaullist forces to a striking victory in the June 1968 legislative elections, Pompidou in turn was replaced. Neither prime minister had been censured by Parliament.

In policy areas which de Gaulle felt to be critical — notably foreign affairs, the Algerian war, and defense policy — he alone took the important decisions. The Parliament and the nation often learned of foreign policy decisions through de Gaulle's speeches, as in the case of his September 16, 1959 offer of self-determination to Algeria, or through his press conferences, as in the case of his veto of British entry into the Common Market on January 14, 1963. Even the cabinet sometimes was not informed in advance of policy pronouncements, as in the case of his press conference statement of European policy on May 15, 1962, a statement which provoked the almost immediate resignations of five MRP ministers.[10]

In a speech to the congress of the Union for the New Republic on November 15, 1959, the President of the National Assembly (and

[8] In Andrews, *European Political Institutions*, p. 51.
[9] *Ibid.*
[10] The text of this and other press conferences are to be found in *Major Addresses, Statements and Press Conferences of General Charles de Gaulle* (New York: French Embassy Press and Information Division, 1964).

later prime minister), Jacques Chaban-Delmas, stated that decision-making power in the new republic was divided into two sectors. There was the "presidential sector," which included policy relating to defense, foreign affairs and the French Community, and a parliamentary and governmental sector, comprising all other policy areas.[11] Indeed, de Gaulle did tend to leave most economic and social problems to be resolved collectively by the cabinet, or in consultation between the prime minister and the ministers affected. And yet it gradually became apparent that the *domaine réservé,* as the presidential sector came to be known, extended to whatever questions the president decided to handle personally. Once de Gaulle had managed to end the Algerian war and to quell the threat of civil war arising out of the prospect of Algerian independence, he found time and inclination to concern himself on occasion with domestic as well as foreign policy. He took a direct hand in the handling of such diverse problems as the 1963 miners' strike, the reorganization of the Paris region, the development of color television, agricultural policy, educational reform, and currency devaluation. In the early years of his tenure as prime minister, Georges Pompidou was less the chief policy-maker described in the constitution than a chief of staff for the General.

Around the president there developed a growing team of advisors and administrative experts, akin to the Executive Office of the President in the United States, although smaller, providing the president with independent sources of information as well as the means to check up on or to circumvent the staffs of the various ministries when he so desires. One of de Gaulle's favored instruments was the interministerial committee, which deprived any one ministry of a monopoly of control over an issue and allowed de Gaulle to maintain close control over questions which interested him. Often de Gaulle simply consulted directly with the responsible minister, bypassing both the prime minister and the cabinet. In a press conference on September 9, 1965, de Gaulle reported upon his activities, speaking of himself in the third person, as he often did: "Up to now during the seven-year period, the Chief of State convened the Council of Ministers 302 times, the limited interministerial councils 420 times, received in his office the Premier 505 times, the Presidents of the Assemblies 78 times, one or another member of the Government nearly 2,000 times, the Chairmen or Rapporteurs of the Parliamentary Committees or group chairmen more than 100 times, the chief government officials, experts and union leaders about 1,500 times — . . ."[12] This is hardly the description of

[11] Cited in Duverger, *Institutions Politiques,* p. 574.
[12] Andrews, *European Political Institutions,* p. 61.

an occasional arbiter, such as the chief of state described by Debré in 1958.

Bitter experience and personal inclination combined to make de Gaulle mistrustful of parliaments and of political parties which governed them. He preferred to find support for his leadership among the masses. The implicit theory of direct democracy and the search for a unified "general will" were reminiscent of Rousseau; the instrument of the referendum was equally reminiscent of the Bonapartist plebiscite.[13] Beginning with the referendum of September 28, 1958, in which 79 percent of votes cast were affirmative, de Gaulle was able to demonstrate that the masses were behind him even when the politicians were not. The overwhelming majorities which supported his Algerian policy in the referendums of January 1, 1961, and April 8, 1962, offered clear evidence both to the army and to the numerous French Algeria partisans in Parliament that the voters were on de Gaulle's side.

The referendum of October 28, 1962, on direct, popular election of the president, offered the clearest test of de Gaulle's strength against the old "political class." The usual method of constitutional amendment, laid out in Article 89, required approval of the proposed amendment by both chambers of Parliament. At the next stage the president was authorized to complete ratification either by popular referendum or by a three-fifths majority of the voting members of both houses of Parliament meeting together. Aware that the Senate was bitterly opposed to his amendment, and that the majority in the Assembly was also reluctant to strengthen further the powers of the president, de Gaulle decided to bypass Parliament by sending the proposal directly to a popular referendum under authority of Article 11. That article allows the government and the president to submit to a referendum "any bill dealing with the organization of the governmental authorities." De Gaulle's angry critics in Parliament charged that this action was blatantly unconstitutional, since Article 11 was not intended to apply to constitutional amendments, which after all were treated in a separate section. Almost all constitutional lawyers, as well as the prestigious Council of State, agreed. And yet, with all of the old political parties aligned against de Gaulle, almost 62 percent of those voting still supported the General's position with a "yes" vote. The majority of voters were unmoved by the question of constitutionality — it was after all de Gaulle's own constitution which he was interpreting.[14] Nor

[13] See Henry Ehrmann's excellent essay, "Direct Democracy in France," *The American Political Science Review,* LVII: 4 (December 1963), pp. 883–901.
[14] *Sondages,* 1969, No. 3, p. 8.

could they see any threat to democracy in allowing the people to elect their president directly.

Although his amendment passed, de Gaulle had won only the first round. An angry Assembly majority voted a motion of censure against the Pompidou government. De Gaulle retaliated by dissolving the Assembly and calling new elections. Now it was apparent that a president desirous of exercising vigorous leadership could not afford to remain aloof from all parties; without a supporting parliamentary majority, he could not maintain his chosen prime minister in office. Hence, in a speech on November 7, 1962, de Gaulle openly entered the partisan arena with a plea for a vote against "the parties of the past" which "do not represent the nation":

> Women and men of France, on October 28 you set your seal to the condemnation of the disastrous regime of the parties and marked your determination to see the new Republic pursue its task of progress, of development and of grandeur. But, on November 18 and 25, you are going to elect the Deputies. May you see that this second consultation does not run in contradiction to the first. Despite, as the case may be, all local habits and fragmentary considerations, may you confirm, through the designation of men, the choice that you, in voting "yes", made with regard to your destiny.[15]

The response, you will recall, was the election of the first united and disciplined parliamentary majority in French republican history.

Again in 1967 and in 1968, de Gaulle asked the voters for a Gaullist majority, although never mentioning his supporting parties by name. In the latter case, however, de Gaulle originally preferred — and indeed announced — a referendum to restore his personal authority after the May–June "events." Upon the urging of Prime Minister Pompidou, he finally agreed, not without reluctance, to hold a parliamentary election instead. He delayed, but did not cancel, his preferred method of reaffirming the legitimacy of his rule: the referendum. In the referendum of April 27, 1969, he again proposed constitutional amendments to the people, one instituting a new governmental unit, the region, intermediary between the central government and the department, and a second reforming the Senate. Again the jurists and the Council of State declared the mode of amendment to be unconstitutional. Again, as in earlier referendums, de Gaulle announced in advance that if the majority vote was negative he would immediately resign. All went according to the script except for the result. With the crises apparently past,

---

[15] *Major Addresses*, p. 202.

and with Georges Pompidou ready and able to assure continuity and stability as de Gaulle's successor, the electorate apparently took to heart the student slogans of the previous spring: "Ten years is enough." A poll taken during the first week of April 1969 indicated that more people disapproved of de Gaulle for circumventing Parliament in the amendment process (38 percent) than approved (29 percent), with 33 percent voicing no opinion. Prior to the October 1962 referendum, in response to a similar question, 45 percent had approved, 32 percent disapproved, and 23 percent voiced no opinion.[16] And yet the voter's general attitudes toward de Gaulle and the government were far more important in determining his vote than his views on the content of procedure of the referendum.[17]

As shown in Table 5.1, of all the votes cast, de Gaulle's "yes" vote had totaled 79 percent in the referendum of September 1958, 62 percent in that of October 1962, and now a surprisingly low 46.8 percent in April 1969. The General promptly departed the Elysée Palace and retired to his small chateau at Colombey-les-deux-Eglises. Had de Gaulle, still shaken by the events of May, planned it this way? According to François Mauriac, this had been an "unprecedented case of suicide while in *plein bonheur*."[18] The "political suicide" theory is too facile a *post hoc* explanation for a surprising defeat. Until a few days before the vote, the pollsters, the overwhelming majority of commentators, and probably de Gaulle himself, believed the "yes" vote would prevail. The suicide theory neglects the importance which the referendum had assumed for de Gaulle as a means of reaffirming his personal authority and of obtaining a popular mandate for important policy innovations.

How was de Gaulle able to dominate the Fifth Republic so completely?[19] The major sources of his authority might be categorized under four headings. The first clearly was the historic role which he

[16] Michel Brulé, "Le Referendum du 27 avril 1969," *Sondages,* 1969: No. 3, p. 8.

[17] *Ibid.,* p. 20.

[18] Quoted by Frédéric Bon, "Le Referendum du 27 avril 1969: Suicide Politique ou Nécessité Stratégique?" *Revue Française de Science Politique,* XX: 2 (April 1970), pp. 205–223. Bon rejects the suicide theory.

[19] De Gaulle has been the subject of a large number of books. The most revealing are perhaps those he wrote himself, especially *The Edge of the Sword,* trans. Gerard Hopkins (New York: Criterion Books, 1960); *The Complete War Memoirs of Charles de Gaulle* (New York: Simon and Schuster, A Clarion Book, 1968); and *Mémoires d'Espoir* (Paris: Plon, 1970). Other notable books in English are Jean Lacouture, *DeGaulle* (New York: New American Library, 1966); Alexander Werth, *De Gaulle* (Baltimore: Penguin, 1965); and David Thomson, *Two Frenchmen: Pierre Laval and Charles de Gaulle* (London: Cresset Press, 1951).

Table 5.1
Referendum Results, 1958–1969

Date	Subject	Percentage of Abstentions	Percentage of Registered Voters		Percentage of Votes Cast	
			Yes	No	Yes	No
28 September 1958	Constitution of the Fifth Republic	15.06	66.41	17.38	79.25	20.74
8 January 1961	Self-determination for Algeria	23.51	55.91	18.37	75.26	24.73
8 April 1962	Evian agreements concluding Algeria war	24.41	64.86	6.65	90.70	9.25
28 October 1962	Presidential election by popular vote	22.76	46.44	28.76	61.75	38.24
27 April 1969	Reform of regions and of Senate	19.42	36.69	41.67	46.82	53.17

had played during the second world war. From his June 18 speech from London in 1940 to his warnings against a return to political stalemate in 1946 and 1947, de Gaulle had established himself as a hero and a prophet. Secondly, he arrived in power at a time when public opinion was disenchanted with the older parties and leaders and eager to settle the Algerian war in a rapid and orderly fashion. The breakdown of military discipline in the Week of the Barricades in January 1960, then the open military revolt in Algiers in April 1961, kept alive a sense of crisis and a willingness to accept crisis leadership. As Stanley Hoffmann has shown, the appeal to the heroic leader in times of crisis is a time-honored tradition in French politics.[20] When problems grow too large and too dangerous to be handled by routine leaders, who, in the Third and Fourth Republics, rose to office and survived there largely through evading both responsibility and decisive action, then even the deputies — those jealous guardians of assembly government — come to accept a brief interlude of strong executive leadership. Sometimes, as in the cases of Georges Clemenceau in the last years of the first world war and Pierre Mendès-France at the close of the Indochinese war, the heroic leader is a practicing politician, albeit usually a nonconformist one. In 1940 and in 1958, extremely grave crises produced leaders who came from outside the ranks of the politicians and who used their powers to change the old political order rather than to defend it.

In the past, however, the heroic leader has not long survived the passing of the crisis which brought him to power. Traditional republican fears of the strong leader have combined with the anxieties of those whose vested interests seem in jeopardy to block his survival in power. De Gaulle clung to power far longer than any other heroic leader of the past century. The prospect of relative stability in France at the time of the fatal referendum of April 27, 1969, clearly was one reason for his defeat.[21] And yet this time, unlike similar occasions in the past, the heroic leader was not followed by an old-style routine leader.

A third basis of de Gaulle's personal authority was his appeal to French nationalism. In the tradition of French heroic leaders, de Gaulle called upon his compatriots to rise above their domestic quarrels in order to fulfill their destiny as a nation. De Gaulle's policy of grandeur, his repeated rebuffs to American leadership in world affairs, his *rapprochement* with the Communist powers, and his detachment from NATO all represented departures from the more modest style of Fourth Republican foreign policy. Opinion polls consistently showed that his vigorous foreign policy was more popular than his domestic policies.

[20] Stanley Hoffman, in Edinger, ed., *Political Leadership,* pp. 108–154.
[21] Lancelot and Weill, "L'Evolution politique des électeurs français de février à juin 1969."

Most Frenchmen apparently were pleased to hear their government at last talking back to the American giant as well as to all others who slighted the dignity and interests of France.

Lastly de Gaulle's personal authority cannot be understood without reference to his peculiar theory and style of leadership. That theory is spelled out in an extraordinarily prophetic manner in a series of lectures given in 1927 and later published as *The Edge of the Sword*. De Gaulle, then a newly promoted major, was reluctantly invited to lecture at the Ecole Supérieure de Guerre through the efforts of a powerful friend and mentor, none other than Marshal Philippe Pétain his rival for French loyalties in World War II. The theory of leadership expounded in those lectures (and later practiced by de Gaulle the leader) included five basic elements: social distance, mystery, instinct, self-reliance, and the pursuit of glory.

De Gaulle told his fellow officers that

> . . . A leader of this quality is inevitably aloof, for there can be no authority without prestige, nor prestige unless he keeps his distance. Those under his command mutter in whispers about his arrogance and the demands he makes. But once action starts, criticism disappears. The man of character then draws to himself the hopes and the wills of everyone as the magnet draws iron. When the crisis comes, it is him they follow, it is he who carries the burden on his shoulders, even though they collapse under it. . . . "Arrogant and undisciplined" is what the mediocrities say of him, treating the thoroughbred with a tender mouth as they would a donkey which refuses to move, not realizing that asperity is, more often than not, the reverse side of a strong character, that you can only lean on something that offers resistance, and that resolute and inconvenient men are to be preferred to easy-going natures without initiative.[22]

True to his theory, de Gaulle as President of the Republic was intimate with few men, distant and arrogant with most, including some close advisors, sustaining the image of the undefinable superiority of the "man of character."

Along with distance goes mystery:

> All religions have their holy of holies, and no man is a hero to his valet. In the designs, the demeanor, and the mental operations of a leader there must be always a "something" which others cannot altogether fathom, which puzzles them, stirs them, and rivets their attention.[23]

[22] *The Edge of the Sword*, pp. 42–44.
[23] *Ibid.*, p. 58.

In the political art of President de Gaulle, mystery and ambiguity in political statements were used for a dual purpose: they lent drama to the utterances of their creator (for example in the vision of a united "Europe from the Atlantic to the Urals"), and they obscured the government's intentions until the time was ripe for more explicit pronouncements (as in the case of Algerian policy, where "self-determination" at first seemed compatible with "French Algeria" and eventually came to mean Algerian independence).

For de Gaulle, the man of authority seems to be born rather than made. He must be intelligent, but he must also have an instinct for leadership. As he put it, "Our intelligence can furnish us with the theoretic, general abstract knowledge of what is, but only instinct can give the practical, particular, and concrete *feel* of it."[24] It seems clear that even as a young man de Gaulle believed that he himself had the necessary instincts for leadership.

Eager to act and to take responsibility for his actions,

> When faced with the challenge of events, the man of character has recourse to himself. His instinctive response is to leave his mark on action, to take responsibility for it, to make it *his own business*. . . . It is not that he wishes to turn a blind eye to orders, or to sweep aside advice, but only that he is passionately anxious to exert his own will, to make up his own mind.[25]

In order to accomplish great deeds, even a military man may have to "take the risk of ignoring the merely routine aspects of discipline."[26] De Gaulle the president, like de Gaulle the rebellious general in 1940, again followed his own advice. He sought out information and opinions, he allowed his cabinet members to state their views, then he came to his own conclusions. It was typical that when de Gaulle conferred with John F. Kennedy in 1961, the elder statesman is reported to have told his American counterpart, "And now, *Monsieur le Président et cher ami,* I say this: Listen only to yourself."

Lastly, "Glory gives herself only to those who have always dreamed of her," as he put it in a book written in the 1930's.[27] The great leader will be an egotist, de Gaulle admits;[28] but his personal glory must be inseparably intertwined with the glory of the nation. Shortly after World War II, de Gaulle is said to have told the British Ambassador, Duff Cooper, "Every day I spend five minutes thinking how what I have to do will appear in history."

[24] *Ibid.,* p. 20.
[25] *Ibid.,* p. 41.
[26] *Ibid.,* p. 45.
[27] De Gaulle, *The Army of the Future* (London: Hutchison, 1940), p. 154.
[28] De Gaulle, *The Edge of the Sword,* p. 64.

In some countries — very likely in the United States — such a recipe for charismatic leadership would be quite ineffective. Arrogance and aloofness are hardly the qualities which one would expect to be most appealing to an American electorate. The ingredients of charisma are variable according to the cultural milieu and the historical moment. In France, where crisis leaders often have been arrogant as well as autocratic, the Gaullist formula, applied by a master politician and a master showman, proved eminently successful.

The resignation of de Gaulle and his replacement by Georges Pompidou in the elections of June 1969 demonstrated that for the first time in French republican history strong executive leadership had been institutionalized. Although a man of remarkable talents, Pompidou lacked both the General's flamboyance and his historic image. And yet in the year following his election Pompidou dominated French government almost as thoroughly as de Gaulle had done.

Foreign and defense policy remained the *domaine réservé* of the President, who worked directly with Defense Minister Michel Debré. Pompidou's long experience with domestic policy while prime minister inclined him to intervene more actively in domestic affairs than de Gaulle himself had done. One shrewd and well-informed observer suggested in early 1970 that the real *domaine réservé* was now a small one — that of certain economic and social questions — and that it belonged to Prime Minister Jacques Chaban-Delmas rather than to the President.[29] On other questions Pompidou often dealt directly with the responsible minister. Making full use of the presidential secretariat, which overflows the Elysée Palace, he concerned himself with the details of policies and their implementation in a way in which de Gaulle would never have done.

Pompidou's election slogan was "continuity and opening." Except for the 12½ percent devaluation of the franc in August 1969 (a move which de Gaulle had rejected as "ridiculous" the previous fall), and the agreement to reopen the question of the British entry into the Common Market, there were no dramatic reversals of de Gaulle's policies. Pompidou's Left-Gaullist critics charged that he was abandoning the reformist elements of Gaullism, leaving nothing but a conservative doctrine of social stability and economic prosperity within a capitalist framework. If Pompidou's first-year reforms in pursuit of greater social and economic equality were short of revolutionary (notably monthly salaries for workers and the distribution of ownership shares to Renault workers), de Gaulle's eleven-year record in that field had

[29] P. Viansson-Ponté, "Where the Action Is: Pompidou Regime — An Assessment," *Le Monde Weekly Selection,* Feb. 4, 1970.

been no more impressive. In both domestic policy and in world affairs under Pompidou, France's official voice spoke rather more softly, but the message was largely unchanged.

How can one account for Pompidou's dominant role in French government when he lacks most of the attributes which seem to account for de Gaulle's authority? A brilliant graduate of the prestigious Ecole Normale Supérieure, a former teacher of classics, a postwar aide to de Gaulle, a member of the Council of State, then a Director-General of the Rothschild Bank, and finally de Gaulle's prime minister for six years, Pompidou had proved his intelligence, his administrative talents, and, increasingly, his skill as a public speaker.[30] As prime minister his popularity gradually increased until the polls showed him almost as well regarded as de Gaulle himself. Pompidou had demonstrated as prime minister that he could be as firm and authoritarian as his mentor. And yet Pompidou had nothing comparable to de Gaulle's stature as a national hero. He was virtually a political unknown when de Gaulle appointed him prime minister in 1962.

Pompidou owed his authority not to heroic personal stature but to his direct, popular election and to his control of a parliamentary majority. In the first ballot of the June 1969 elections, running against six opponents, he drew 44 percent of the vote — two-tenths of one percent more than de Gaulle himself had drawn in the first ballot of the December 1965 presidential elections. On the second runoff ballot Pompidou drew 58 percent of the vote, or 3 percent more than de Gaulle had won on December 19, 1965, although in 1965 the Communist Party had backed Mitterrand and in 1969 it asked its supporters to abstain rather than to support either Pompidou or Alain Poher.

Despite the 31 percent abstention rate (over twice as high as in 1965), Pompidou could claim to be the only man in government to have been chosen in a nation-wide election — chosen to speak for all of the people. In France, as in other democracies, a man with such credentials, when he so desires, naturally tends to dominate appointed officials, including his own appointee, the prime minister.

Equally important was the nearly three-to-one Gaullist majority in the National Assembly elected in 1968. The survival instinct prompted Gaullists to hang together on critical votes in order to preserve the Gaullist regime; hanging together meant rallying behind their leader, who clearly was Georges Pompidou. The loyal core of the Gaullist majority was the UDR, a party which Pompidou had helped to build. So long as the President continued to enjoy the support of a solid par-

[30] Pompidou's accomplishments are described in a lively and highly flattering manner by Merry Bromberger, *Le Destin Secret de Georges Pompidou* (Paris: Fayard, 1965).

liamentary majority, the hybrid, double-executive constitution would continue to function in practice as a presidential government.

The Government

Under the Fourth Republic as under the Third the absence of any stable, cohesive parliamentary majority required that all governments be coalition governments. Each minister, each "secretary of state" (the French Undersecretary) was chosen with an eye not only to his talents but also to the votes in Parliament which his selection would rally behind the government. On the average of once every six months the government (as the prime minister, his ministers, and undersecretaries are called in Europe) would be defeated in a parliamentary vote or resign in anticipation of such a vote. There would ensue a frantic period of negotiations, during which the president might have to call a half dozen or more candidates to form a government before he found one willing and able to find the magic formula.

Given the size of the semi-permanent opposition within the National Assembly, both on the Left (the Communist Party after 1947) and on the Right (the Gaullists, then the Poujadists), the trick was to offer sufficient promises and guarantees to rally the support of some two-thirds of those seated from the Left-Center to the Right-Center in the Assembly Chamber. After the collapse in 1947 of the tripartite coalition of Communists, Socialists, and MRP, the task called for a conciliator, a political broker, preferably from a small and weak party, like the Radicals, who could reassure everyone and threaten no one. The now legendary example of this type of leader was Henri Queuille, a country doctor and small-town mayor from Southern France, who served in twenty prewar cabinets and then headed three postwar governments as prime minister. A perceptive Swiss journalist described him accurately:

> The apocalyptic struggle between Thorez and de Gaulle was won by *le petit père* Queuille because his strength lay in the very field where the immediate difficulties lay; namely the field of parliamentary routine. He had no strong views on all the controversial questions which divided the parties, that of economic controls, for instance, or nationalization, or foreign policy, or the right to strike, but he knew how to handle an apparently ungovernable Parliament consisting of many minorities all bitterly hostile to one another, and he modestly and quietly solved the problem of government stability, which depended on a dozen vacillating votes.[31]

[31] Herbert Luethy, *France Against Herself* (New York: Meridian Books, 1955), p. 167.

His theory of leadership was that of the interwar British prime minister, Stanley Baldwin: "the art of statesmanship is to postpone issues until they are no longer relevant."[32]

Queuille's cabinets, like most of those of the Fourth Republic, included Socialists, Popular Republicans, Radicals, and Independents. In theory, the government was collectively responsible for its actions; in practice the rivalries between parties within the cabinet, and between factions of parties, were almost as bitter as those in the National Assembly as a whole. *Immobilisme* was usually the safest course for a government which hoped to survive. Integrated policy planning was virtually impossible.

The men called to be prime ministers under the Fourth Republic were not all temporizers by nature; Antoine Pinay, a conservative, and Edgar Faure, a Radical, for example, were vigorous men of action. It was the system which forced them to trim their sails to the shifting parliamentary winds. The major exeption to this style of leadership by conciliation was Pierre Mendès-France, who had been an outspoken critic of "le système," and who was called to be prime minister in a crisis period in June 1954 following the French defeat in the Indochinese battle of Dien Bien Phu.[33] The Parliament put up with Mendès-France's unorthodox behavior (he chose his own cabinet, without consulting the party leaders, and appealed directly to the people over Parliament's head) only so long as a sense of crisis prevailed. Once the Indochinese war had been ended, once the regime again seemed secure, his support in Parliament eroded away with each move he took, whether it was toward independence for Tunisia, abandonment of the European Defense Community plan, rearmament of West Germany under the London and Paris agreements, or attack upon the alcohol interest. In February 1955, seven and a half months after his appointment, Mendès-France was overthrown by a hostile majority in the National Assembly, including twenty dissident members of his own Radical Party, as well as the Communists, Independents, and the MRP.

Many of the causes of governmental instability in the Fourth Republic have been mentioned in earlier chapters. In the realm of habits and attitudes, stability was undermined by ideological pressure from party activists outside Parliament (which inhibited compromises within Parliament), traditional republican suspicion of the executive, and sheer careerism. Objective circumstances such as the absence of a stable majority, either in the electorate or the Parliament, and the presence of powerful antiregime parties within the Assembly were also important.

---

[32] Williams, *Crisis and Compromise*, p. 39. This book offers the best analysis available of the Fourth Republic.

[33] His story is told by Alexander Werth, *Lost Statesman: The Strange History of Pierre Mendès-France* (New York: Abelard-Schuman, 1958).

When the Gaullists came to power in 1958, with government stability and vigorous executive leadership in high positions on their list of priorities, careful attention was given to avoiding prolongation of what de Gaulle once called "the games, the poisons and the delights of the System."[34] Again, as in the case of the presidency, the assumption that there would be no stable parliamentary majority in France led the constitution-makers to arm the government with an arsenal of constitutional weapons against the Assembly and to "depoliticize" it as much as possible, that is (following a line of thought long common among nationalists and conservatives) to take it out of the hands of the parties. The constitution provides that the prime minister shall assume his powers immediately upon being appointed by the president, without need for a favorable parliamentary vote. The Parliament can reject him, but only by initiating a vote of censure.

In practice the first two governments formed after the new constitution went into effect — that of Debré in 1959 and that of Pompidou in 1962 — did present themselves and their programs to the National Assembly with a request for a vote of confidence. Yet the next three governments formed — those of Pompidou after the March 1967 elections, Couve de Murville after the June 1968 elections, and Chaban-Delmas in June 1969 — did not ask for votes of confidence, demonstrating that in practice as in law the government may take power without an expression of parliamentary approval. When a Left Federation deputy complained in July 1968 that "this eminently democratic parliamentary tradition has disappeared in recent times," the government spokesman replied that the direct, popular election of the president "has considerably modified the balance of power, as everyone knows."[35] In other words, the government's first responsibility was to the president, not to Parliament. Once in power, as will be seen when we discuss Parliament, the government enjoys a number of constitutional defenses which Fourth Republic governments did not have.

The "depoliticization" of the government was to be accomplished in two ways. The first was the provision in the constitution (Article 23) that "The office of member of government shall be incompatible with the exercise of any parliamentary mandate, with the holding of any office at the national level in business, professional or labor organizations, and with any public employment or professional activity." In contrast to most parliamentary governments, but in keeping with the practice in presidential systems, if a minister is chosen from Parliament, he must resign his seat there before joining the government. The "or-

[34] On May 6, 1953, quoted in *L'Année Politique*, 1953, p. 476.
[35] *Journal Officiel, Débats, Assemblée Nationale*, July 17, 1968, pp. 2261 and 2270.

ganic law" which spells out this article provides that each candidate to Parliament must select a *suppléant*, or alternate, to run with him. If the candidate is elected, and if he is asked to join the government, he must resign his seat in Parliament within thirty days. His seat in Parliament is then taken by the alternate.

It appears that this reform is based upon a partial misunderstanding of the hated *système* of the Fourth Republic. In his speech of August 27, 1958, to the Council of State, Michel Debré explained that "The ministerial function has become a rank insignia, a star, or rather a longevity stripe such as soldiers have, and which give recognition for a campaign. There are politicians who are distinguished by the number of hash-marks they wear on their sleeves! . . . The rule of incompatibility has become a sort of necessity to end that which has come to be called the 'portfolio race,' a game fatal for the State."[36] The theory was that members of Parliament in the old system were free to vote against a government in hopes of gaining a ministerial post in the successor government, knowing that if that government were defeated in turn they could always return to their parliamentary seats. Ministers, on the other hand, were free to conspire against their own governments, in hope of landing a more important post (perhaps the prime minister's) in the next government. The latter point was valid; as for the former, a recent study of voting patterns in the National Assembly during the Fourth Republic demonstrates clearly that potential ministers (the *ministrables*) voted to support the cabinet *more often* than did other deputies. The unwritten rules of the game seemed to call for support of the government, unless that government itself breaks the rules, as did Mendès-France in appealing for public support.[37]

The ease of movement back and forth between the Parliament and the government under the Fourth Republic may well have encouraged ministers to take a less serious attitude toward the fall of a government than they might otherwise have done. And yet the incompatibility rule in itself does not appear to have changed the situation greatly. A former Gaullist minister, Bernard Chenot, wrote:

> In any case the clause requiring separation of the parliamentary mandate and the ministerial function has had little effect: the parliamentary minister remains, in general, his district's man, attentive to signs from the shadow who is filling in for him, present each week in his fief, consolidating his local standing by becoming a local mayor or a member of the departmental council.[38]

[36] Andrews, *European Political Institutions*, p. 49.

[37] MacRae, *Parliament, Parties, and Society in France, 1946–1958*, p. 8 and *passim*.

[38] Bernard Chenot, *Etre Ministre* (Paris: Plon, 1967), p. 13.

The minister of the Fifth Republic, like his predecessor of the Fourth, continues to curry his (former) constituents' favor in preparation for the time when he again will need their votes.

When government posts change hands, it has come to be common practice for the alternate who had taken the departing minister's seat in parliament to resign, thus allowing the minister to run for his old seat in a by-election, if he so desires. For example, eleven members of de Gaulle's last government were not given posts in the government appointed in June 1969 by President Pompidou and Prime Minister Jacques Chaban-Delmas. Some, like André Malraux, the Minister of Culture, did not choose to enter Parliament. The alternates who had replaced Edgar Faure, Pierre Messmer, Jean Chamant, Pierre Dumas, and Joël Le Theule promptly resigned, allowing these men to regain their old seats in by-elections. The alternate who had replaced outgoing Prime Minister Maurice Couve de Murville refused to resign. In the face of what was seen as stubborn and unseemly behavior on the alternate's part, a Gaullist of long standing, Pierre Clostermann, then gave up his seat in the district of Yvelines, near Paris, in order to accommodate the former prime minister, who was inept enough as a campaigner to lose in the ensuing election. As in many instances in past years, custom is in fact undoing the effect of the incompatibility clause. By 1970 there was talk in Gaullist circles of removing that clause by constitutional amendment.

A second means chosen to "depoliticize" the government — one which proved ultimately to be as ineffective as the first — was the appointment of a large number of high civil servants and other experts from outside the ranks of Parliament. As shown in Table 5.2, in the early years of the Fifth Republic, over a third of the members of the government were chosen from outside Parliament. For ministries dealing with his presidential sector of policy, de Gaulle preferred reliable civil servants. A career diplomat, Maurice Couve de Murville, served as Minister of Foreign Affairs from 1958 until 1968. The Ministry of Defense was filled by one "technocrat," Pierre Guillaumat, from 1959–60, then by another, Pierre Messmer, until de Gaulle's resignation in April 1969. In the early years civil servants also reigned over the Ministries of Health, Housing, Industry and Commerce, Education, and (except for a few weeks) Interior.

As Table 5.2 reveals, the composition of the cabinet has evolved in two ways. First, it became progressively more Gaullist until the election of Pompidou as president. The Socialists were gone by 1959 and the MRP by 1962. After the 1967 elections, the government included 21 members who had joined or affiliated with the UNR group in the National Assembly (not all had run as UNR candidates), 3 from the

Table 5.2

The Political Composition of Selected Cabinets, 1958–1969

	De Gaulle July 7 1958*	Debré Jan. 5 1959	Apr. 15 1962	Pompidou Dec. 3 1962	April 7 1967	Couve de Murville July 13 1968	Chaban-Delmas June 22 1969
UNR/UDR	3	6	9	15	21	26	29
Independents	3	5	3	—	—	—	—
Independent Republicans	—	—	—	—	—	—	—
MRP	3	3	5	3	3	4	7
Progress and Modern Democracy (Centrists)	—	—	—	—	—	—	3
Radicals	2	1	1	1	—	—	—
Socialists	3	—	—	—	—	—	—
Miscellaneous	1	2	—	—	—	—	—
Non-parliamentarians	9	10	11	7	5	1	—
Total	24	27	29	26	29	31	39

The governments represented are those formed after an election or after a change of prime ministers. Cabinet personnel was shifted on many other occasions. Figures include the prime minister, full ministers, and undersecretaries (*secrétaires d'état*). Party affiliations are determined by the parliamentary party group which the minister joined or attached himself to (*apparenté*) after the most recent legislative election.

* De Gaulle first formed a government on June 1, 1958. It was filled out with additional appointments on June 9 and July 7.

Source: calculated from information in *L'Année Politique*, 1958, 1959, 1962, 1967, 1968, and 1969.

Gaullist Independent Republican group, and a handful of "technocrats" who either had not run for Parliament or who had not been elected. Only after the resignation of de Gaulle, when 3 Centrist leaders were appointed in keeping with Pompidou's policy of new "openings," was the cabinet again opened to men affiliated with other parties. The outsiders drawn into the fold in June 1969 (Minister of Justice René Pleven, Minister of Agriculture Jacques Duhamel, and Minister of Labor Joseph Fontanet, all from the centrist Progress and Modern Democracy group) numbered only 3 in an unusually large government of 39. All except those 3 had joined one of the Gaullist groups in the National Assembly before being obliged by the incompatibility rule to resign their seats thirty days after being appointed to the government.

A second clear trend in cabinet composition was toward exclusive recruitment from among members of the National Assembly. The technocrats did not all disappear by any means; they simply were asked to run for Parliament. This trend began to appear in 1962, especially after the National Assembly's vote of censure in October and the ensuing legislative elections demonstrated to de Gaulle the importance of parliamentary support. In the legislative elections of March 1967, 26 of 28 members of the government ran for Parliament. Pompidou himself was elected deputy from Cajarc, in his native district of Cantal. The government formed in April 1967 included only 5 nonparliamentarians, two of these being Maurice Couve de Murville and Pierre Messmer, who had run for Parliament and lost. After the June 1968 elections only 1 nonparliamentarian remained in the government: André Malraux; following his retirement, the new government formed under Prime Minister Chaban-Delmas in June 1969 was made up exclusively of members elected to Parliament in 1968. Some of these ministers had never actually served in Parliament, having resigned after each of the past two elections to return to the cabinet. However, the inclusion in Prime Minister Chaban-Delmas' first cabinet of 20 undersecretaries, rather than the usual half dozen or less, all chosen from one of the two Gaullist parliamentary groups, suggests that future government leadership once again may be recruited exclusively from Parliament, then trained and tested in subordinate government positions. Such is the pattern of recruitment in Great Britain.

The recognized need for political support both in Parliament and in the country as a whole has persuaded Gaullist leaders to depart from the early ideal of a depoliticized cabinet and to move in the direction of British-style party government, in which ministers are expected to be Gaullist politicians and members of Parliament. Once again the old question, "How much support will he bring to the Government?" is relevant in choosing ministers.

Powers and Mode of Functioning

The Constitution of the Fifth Republic, as we have seen, provides that "the government shall determine and direct the policy of the nation." (Article 20) The government's role in practice was better defined by de Gaulle in his press conference of January 3, 1964, when he described the cabinet as ". . . appointed by the Head of State, sitting around him for the determination and application of policy and directing the administration."[39] Legally the Council of Ministers *must* be consulted before government bills are submitted to Parliament, before certain decrees are issued, before the government asks parliament for a vote of confidence, and before a state of seige is declared. Before 1958, most important decisions were in fact taken by all ministers and "secretaries of state" (the undersecretaries) meeting as the "cabinet" under the chairmanship of the prime minister. The formal Council of Ministers, attended only by full ministers and presided over by the president, normally did little more than ratify those decisions. De Gaulle revived the Council of Ministers as the primary deliberative body and invited all members of the government — secretaries of state included — to be present. President Pompidou maintained the Council of Ministers as the primary forum for policy discussion, although given the size of the Chaban-Delmas government (39 members) most secretaries of state ceased being invited to attend. The "cabinet" now rarely meets without the president, except occasionally to discuss implementation of policies.

Within the Council of Ministers, the president clearly is in command, calling for information and opinions, posing questions, and determining the manner in which a decision will be reached. Debate is often lively and occasionally heated, as in the several long meetings on the educational reforms of 1968.

Once the decision has been taken whether by group action or by presidential fiat, the cabinet, as in Britain, is collectively responsible for it. No longer are ministers able, as they were before 1958, to disagree publicly with a government decision. Their choice is either to support it in public or to resign. "No one is forced to be a minister nor to remain one," de Gaulle sometimes said.[40] Resignations have been few — less than one a year on the average, mostly by non-Gaullists — for ministers are aware that they hardly will change a policy or bring down a government by leaving. Moreover, unless his alternate is willing to return his seat in parliament (and a dissident minister may not be cer-

[39] Andrews, *European Political Institutions,* p. 57.
[40] Chenot, *Etre Ministre,* p. 22.

tain of this), he may have no place to go. One departed minister asked the President's office for help in finding an appointive post in government. The answer came back "He is looking for a job, but I gave him one. Why didn't he keep it?"[41]

The Prime Minister

Within the cabinet, the prime minister exercises important powers, even though he tends to be overshadowed by the president in the Fifth Republic's dual executive.[42] It is the prime minister, and not the president, who runs the day-to-day affairs of government. It is he who coordinates administration of government programs, prepares drafts of important administration decrees which need cabinet approval and issues lesser decrees personally, helps to resolve conflicts between ministries, plans the development and integration of the government's legislative proposals, and handles relations between the government and Parliament. In these and other tasks he is aided by a large staff composed of his personal *cabinet,* made up of political aides as well as high civil servants on loan, the General Secretariat, and a number of attached services with varying degrees of autonomy.[43] The latter, which change from time to time, normally include the General Directorate of Administration and Civil Service, which oversees civil service personnel, the Atomic Energy Commission, the Planning Commission, and a number of others. Some of these may be placed under a "Minister (or Secretary of State) attached to the Prime Minister."

Since the creation of the Fifth Republic, political commentators have been noting the dual executive is an open invitation to rivalry and conflict. So far the president's political strength and his ability in fact, if not in law, to change prime ministers have precluded open conflict. When Michel Debré and de Gaulle differed over Algerian policy, Debré deferred to his master after dragging his feet for a time. When Pompidou's popularity increased to a point where he might be able to

[41] *Ibid.,* p. 23.

[42] The head of government usually was called the "President of the Council of Ministers" until 1958. The title "Prime Minister" (*Premier Ministre*) was formally introduced in the Constitution of the Fifth Republic, after it had been noted that in fact the President of the Republic had always served as formal President of the Council of Ministers. The frequent American term, "Premier" is only half of the title "Premier Ministre," and has never been used by the French. The title "Prime Minister" will be used here even for the Third and Fourth Republics.

[43] The prime minister's office is described by F. Ridley and J. Blondel, *Public Administration in France* (New York: Barnes & Noble, 1965), pp. 75–84.

stand up to de Gaulle, the President replaced him. After de Gaulle resigned, renewing speculation about whether the new president, Georges Pompidou, or the prime minister, Jacques Chaban-Delmas, would lead, events quickly demonstrated that the President would be head of the Gaullist movement and effective head of the government as well as head of state.

So long as the same majority controls both presidency and Parliament, the president seems able to impose his leadership. As a popularly elected leader and the legal President of the Council of Ministers, armed with a veto in such matters as important appointments and decrees, dissolution of Parliament, and recourse to emergency powers, the president has far more high cards than his executive consort.[44] Should the Parliament turn hostile to the president, however, a very serious constitutional crisis might arise.

So far the effective powers of the prime minister have varied over time, according to the inclinations of the president. It appears that they reached their highest level in the later years of President Pompidou's prime ministership, when de Gaulle seemed to be preparing him to ascend the throne "after de Gaulle." The low point may have come when Pompidou was replaced in 1968 by Maurice Couve de Murville, who was accustomed as foreign minister to implementing a policy determined from above. Yet whatever the president's attitude, the prime minister plays an important role in integrating the activities of the government. A former minister reports that when the ministries differ on a plan of action, "The arbitrations of Matignon [the prime minister's official residence] are accepted, and sometimes even solicited and, in general, respected."[45] Unless, of course, the losing party chooses to appeal from Matignon to the Elysée, where the president and his staff act as the ultimate court of appeals.

The Ministers

Like the prime minister, each of the principal ministers has his own *cabinet,* a small group of aides who assist him in controlling his own ministry (no mean task) as well as in dealing with other ministries and with the Parliament. Under the Fourth Republic many of these aides were politicians, often from the minister's home district. The Fifth

---

[44] Maurice Duverger, a leading French political scientist, concludes that "the fact that the President of the Republic presides over the Council of Ministers makes him a veritable head of Government." *Institutions Politiques et Droit Constitutionnel,* p. 571. This text is an excellent source on the nature and functioning of French constitutions, past and present.

[45] Chenot, *Etre Ministre,* p. 23.

Republic has tended to favor high civil servants on loan from one of the prestigious *grand corps* — the Council of State, the Court of Accounts, the Inspectorate of Finance, or the prefectorial corps. The trend is a reflection of the lessened importance of political relations for the minister of the Fifth Republic and the increased importance of expert assistance.

On the average, despite the rapid turnover in leadership in a few ministries, notably Education and Agriculture, the ministers of the Fifth Republic can expect to remain at their posts longer than did those of the Third and Fourth Republics. The minister now also is relieved of some of the parliamentary pressures which limited the flexibility of members of the government before 1958. And yet, he is in some respects less independent than his predecessors. The prime minister's powers of control and coordination are exercised more vigorously than before. The Ministry of Finance, which maintains a *contrôleur* — a regular in-house spy — in each ministry, is still powerful enough to destroy a minister's pet proposal. If Finance does not scotch it, the president may; and his staff keeps close tabs on what is happening within the ministries. The question may be taken out of the ministry's hands and given over to an interministerial committee, with the president himself as chairman. Of course the president also may be a powerful ally, as he was for Education Minister Edgar Faure in 1968–69.

The expansion of the powers of the president and the government since 1958 has been won at the expense first of Parliament and, to a lesser degree, of the administration. The nature and relative permanence of this victory will be the subject of the two following chapters.

6

Parliament

The former conservative prime minister and veteran politician, Paul Reynaud, spoke for a longstanding French republican tradition when he rose in the National Assembly during the October 1962 debate preceding the vote of censure and proclaimed, "For us republicans France is here and nowhere else." Whatever minor merits the leaders of France's traditional parties may have seen in 1958 in de Gaulle's vision of a "rationalized parliament," by the fall of 1962 they had concluded that parliamentary government as they had known it was dying. Indeed, the passage in October 1962 of de Gaulle's amendment for direct election of the president and the subsequent election of a Gaullist parliamentary majority the following November completed its demise. De Gaulle had completed a task which he had begun in 1944: he had destroyed "assembly government."

What Reynaud and others of the Third and Fourth Republics were reluctant to recognize was that the French National Assembly had become a rarity in the world of democratic nations. It had remained a dominating political body in an age of declining legislatures, when the once powerful British House of Commons had been reduced by party discipline to a council of legislative revision and a talk shop for the opposition. Almost everywhere the scope and complexity of governmental activities were expanding faster than parliamentary means of control. Total war, then cold war had enhanced the importance of the chief diplomat and commander in chief, at the expense of the legislature. Mass media focused upon prime ministers and ministers — or their opposition counterparts — to the point where many Englishmen and Germans hardly knew or were interested in the names of their local members of Parliament. Even in the United States, where the legislative tradition was strong, this seemed increasingly to be an age of executive leadership.

By 1958 the general public as well as the Gaullists were disenchanted with Parliament's traditional role. Many of the characteristics of Parliament under the Fourth Republic have been described. The rapid succession of governments, the parliamentary jealousy of executive leadership, the ideological quarrels, intermixed with political opportunism, the vulnerability to minority pressures, the endemic diseases of procrastination and evasion of responsibility — all of these tended to discredit assembly government.[1] Four months before the fall of the Fourth Republic, a national poll conducted by the French Institute of Public Opinion suggested that most citizens were unhappy with their deputies, as well as with the political system as a whole, which they judged to work less well than those of England, the United States, and West Germany.[2] As one student of French public opinion has shown, the French had achieved a near consensus by 1958: they overwhelmingly disapproved of the performances of Parliament and the political parties.[3] In an IFOP poll conducted in August 1958, 94 percent of those respondents who offered an opinion agreed that "parliamentary morals" had been bad during the Fourth Republic; in January 1959, 63 percent of respondents offering an opinion felt that the National Assembly would have little or no importance in the Fifth Republic.[4]

Government-Parliament Relations

Parliamentary Sessions

In drawing up the Constitution of 1958, Michel Debré, the chief constitution-maker, relied upon formal rules to guarantee executive leadership, assuming that the dependable parliamentary majorities which assure stable government in Great Britain were beyond France's reach. This constitution limited Parliament to two regular annual sessions, one of a maximum of 80 days, beginning on October 2, and a second of a maximum of 90 days beginning on April 2. No longer would the government be harassed by a Parliament in semi-permanent

[1] For a brief history of the Fourth Republic, see above, Chapter 1, pp. 10–13. On the "gamesmanship" aspects of the Fourth Republic, see Chapter 3, pp. 64–66, and Chapter 5, pp. 137–138. The electoral and party systems of the Fourth Republic are described in Chapter 4.

[2] *Sondages,* 1958, No. 3, pp. 46, 51, 53, and 65.

[3] Fougeyrollas, *La Conscience Politique dans la France Contemporaine,* Ch. 3.

[4] *Le Référendum de Septembre et les Elections de Novembre 1958,* Cahiers de la Fondation Nationale des Sciences Politiques, No. 109 (Paris: A. Colin, 1960), pp. 278–279.

session; unless the government and the president chose to call a special session, Parliament henceforth would meet for less than six months each year.

The two exceptions allowed by the constitution to this six-month maximum were both strictly limited by Gaullist interpretation. Article 16 provides that if the president assumes emergency powers, Parliament must remain in session so long as the powers continue in force. In practice, when de Gaulle assumed emergency powers in April 1961, in response to the military revolt in Algiers, Parliament remained in session (except for an unconstitutional, but highly traditional, one month summer vacation); yet de Gaulle would permit it neither to pass legislation nor to consider a motion of censure against the government.[5]

Parliament is also allowed to call a special session by means of a petition signed by a majority of the members of the National Assembly. When such a petition bearing more than the required number of signatures was submitted to President de Gaulle in March 1960, however, he refused to convene the Assembly. He argued that the petition had been inspired by agricultural pressure groups which had no legal right to force a special session; indeed, to capitulate to them would be "contrary to the character of our new institutions." Moreover, he explained (contrary to Michel Debré's interpretation in August 1958), that the president has the power to accept or reject a petition for a special session as he sees fit.[6] As on so many occasions during his eleven years in office, de Gaulle assumed that it was his responsibility to defend the "national interest" against the presumably narrow and self-interested perspectives of the nation's legislators.

The Scope of Parliamentary Authority

A second new restriction placed upon Parliament was the limitation of the scope of its authority. In the past there had been no effective limitations upon the legislative powers of Parliament. However, in Article 38 of the 1958 Constitution, Parliament found its legislative powers restricted to specified questions which together constitute the domain of law; in all areas outside that domain the government alone can take regulatory action by decree. On certain questions, including civil rights, the determination of crimes and misdemeanors, taxes, electoral laws, and the nationalization of industries, Parliament is authorized to establish fairly detailed "rules." On other questions, such as "the

[5] Duverger, *Institutions Politique*, p. 540.
[6] The text of de Gaulle's letter to the President of the Assembly is found in *L'Année Politique, 1960*, p. 640.

general organization of national defense," the administration of local communities, education, property rights, and national economic planning, Parliament may establish only "the fundamental principles," leaving the details to be filled in by executive decrees. The government enjoys complete freedom on all questions which are not dealt with specifically, such as the creation or elimination of government ministries.

The effect of this limitation, which is enforced by the Constitutional Council (which will be discussed later), has been to reduce drastically the number of private member's bills that often are designed to protect the interests of an individual or group within a member's constituency. In his excellent book on the French Parliament, Philip Williams noted, "Indeed, it is a sign of the triviality of members' preoccupations in the Fourth Republic that nine-tenths of the bills introduced in its last year, and half those passed, would have fallen into the domain of regulations."[7] If one effect has been to free Parliament from consideration of trivia, another clearly has been to contribute to the shift in balance of the power from Parliament to the executive.

Executive Controls over the Legislative Process

More important than the restrictions upon parliamentary legislative powers is the impressive array of controls which the government has over Parliament. Among the most important are the following.

1. The government controls the agenda of Parliament; it may determine what shall be discussed and when. As a result, bills which originate in Parliament rather than with the government have little chance of being debated. In 1957, 71 of the 198 laws passed had originated in Parliament; in 1959, only 1 out of 52 passed could claim a parliamentary origin.[8] Parliamentary bills fared only slightly better in succeeding years.

2. When debate on a bill opens on the floor of either chamber of Parliament, it is the government's original version, with only those amendments which the government has agreed to, which are the subject of debate, rather than a bill rewritten in committee, as was often the case before 1958. If the minister in charge fears that one or more parts of a bill may be defeated if voted upon separately, he may require a "package vote" (*vote bloqué*) on the entire, unamended bill. The package vote was used 23 times during the first legislature (1958–62)

[7] Philip Williams, *The French Parliament: Politics in the Fifth Republic* (New York: Praeger, 1968), p. 57.

[8] Pierre Avril, *Le Régime Politique de la Ve République* (Paris: Librairie Générale de Droit et de Jurisprudence, 1964), pp. 43–44.

and 66 times during the second (1962–66), even though the Gaullists enjoyed a solid majority in the National Assembly after 1962.[9]

3. When the National Assembly and the Senate fail to agree on a bill, the government may call a conference committee of seven members from each house. Should the chambers continue to disagree, the government may either allow the Senate to block the Assembly version (if it disagrees with that version), or it may ask the Assembly to pass its version again, at which time the bill is enacted over the Senate's veto. Hence, when the Senate is friendly to the government (as it rarely has been), the government may use it to block the Assembly; when the Assembly is more friendly, the government may easily bypass the Senate, as it has done on numerous occasions.

4. As in the Fourth Republic, the government may make the acceptance of a bill a matter of confidence, forcing the deputies either to approve the government or to bring it down, with the dissolution of the National Assembly an almost certain consequence. Contrary to the practice of earlier Republics, the bill which is declared a matter of confidence is considered passed automatically, without a vote, unless a motion of censure bearing the signatures of 10 percent of the deputies is submitted within twenty-four hours and then passed by an absolute majority of the Assembly members. Putting the Senate bypass together with the confidence vote provisions of the constitution, the government was able to push through its nuclear striking force program in the early 1960's without a favorable vote in either house. A motion of censure may be posed at any time in the National Assembly, although the signators may not sign another censure petition during the same three-month session of Parliament. The government is not responsible to the Senate in the sense that it cannot be overthrown by a Senate vote.

5. In budgetary matters the government has two new means of protection. The new constitution stipulates that, as in England, only the government may introduce bills which would either raise public expenditures or cut government revenue, i.e., the great majority of significant bills. In the early years of the Fifth Republic this new article was hauled out repeatedly by the government as reason for rejecting even amendments such as one which would have raised certain railroad workers' pensions and cut the Transportation Ministry budget to provide the funds. By 1964, however, in a debate on revision of the pensions code, the government minister was willing to accept a number of amendments, most of which would cost the government money.[10]

Second, in order to avoid the prolongation of budget debates which

---

[9] Pierre Avril, *Le Gouvernement de la France* (Paris: Editions Universitaires, 1969), p. 49n.

[10] Williams, *The French Parliament,* p. 82.

under the Fourth Republic habitually delayed passage of the budget until well after it theoretically was to go into effect, the constitution provides that the budget may be put into effect by government ordinance if it is not voted within 70 days. Since 1959 Parliament has regularly adopted the budget before Christmas, "a feat never achieved in the previous thirty years."[11]

6. Should the executive branch wish to enact laws without sending them through Parliament, rather than regulations on details for which it needs no authorization, it has three possible courses of action. First there is the popular referendum, authorized by Article 11 in the case of "any bill dealing with the organization of the governmental authorities, entailing approval of a Community agreement, or providing for authorization to ratify a treaty that, without being contrary to the Constitution, might affect the functioning of institutions." Since the proposal for a referendum may come either from the government *or* from Parliament, the president may follow this procedure without the approval of Parliament. As has been noted, even constitutional amendments may be enacted in this manner.

Second, "When the institutions of the Republic, the independence of the nation, the integrity of its territory, or the fulfillment of its international commitments are threatened in a grave and immediate manner and when the regular functioning of the constitutional governmental authorities is interrupted," the president may assume emergency powers under Article 16 and "take the measures commanded by these circumstances, after official consultation with the Premier, the Presidents of the assemblies and the Constitutional Council." On the one occasion when this article was applied, in April 1961, when a quartet of generals seized Algiers and threatened to "liberate" the French mainland, de Gaulle retained his emergency powers for over five months — long after the immediate threat had ended. The eighteen legislative ordinances issued under authority of Article 16 deal with a variety of subjects, as well as with the immediate crisis.[12]

The third and most common method by which the executive makes laws is the delegation of powers under Article 38. The National Assembly of the Third Republic had made a practice of handling crises by delegating power to the government to issue "decree-laws." This practice was outlawed in the Constitution of the Fourth Republic, but revived nonetheless under the form of "framework laws," in which Parliament set only very rough outlines, to be filled in by executive

[11] *Ibid.*, p. 78.
[12] This episode is the subject of Martin Harrison's "The French Experiment of Exceptional Powers: 1961," *Journal of Politics*, XXV: 2 (1963), pp. 139–158.

decrees. The Constitution of 1958 once again legalized the decree-law, henceforth to be called an ordinance. Parliament has only to define a subject and establish the time period during which the government is to wield law-making powers in that realm. By a date determined in the enabling act, the government must submit to Parliament all ordinances issued under the delegated authority.

In the course of the first two legislatures, from 1959–67, the government was delegated law-making authority under Article 38 on seven different occasions. On two occasions the subject was related to the Algerian war; three enabling acts concerned adaptations in her economic life required by France's membership in the Common Market; one dealt with French Somaliland; and the last was the famed "social scourges" act intended essentially to enable the government to deal with the related problems of alcoholism and home distillers. In each case the government formally complied with the constitution by submitting its ordinances to Parliament, then, through control of the parliamentary agenda, refused to allow the legislative bodies to debate them. The many friends of the home distillers in the National Assembly struggled vainly for four years to force a debate on the "social scourges" ordinances before giving up in despair.[13] The government's attitude on this question created resentment on the part of a number of deputies, including some on the majority benches. The resentment was heightened in the spring of 1967 when the government decided not to bother easing its program of social welfare reforms through a newly elected National Assembly, in which the government had only a narrow majority. Instead, it elected to ram through the enabling act of June 22, 1967, by making it a matter of confidence.[14] Then the executive branch could legislate at its ease. When the ordinances enacted under this authority were submitted to Parliament, however, the government agreed for the first time to parliamentary consideration of them and a number were amended upon the recommendations of parliamentary committees. The government may have wished to show its good will in this matter; a more important motive may have been the government's own desire to amend some of the ordinances, after its law-making authority had expired.[15]

Impressive as these restriction are, the exile of the once-proud Parlia-

---

[13] The interesting story of that bill is told briefly in Williams, *The French Parliament*, pp. 85–89.
[14] Edgard Pisani resigned from the cabinet in protest over this decision. See his explanation, "Sur Une Démission," *Le Monde*, May 13, 1967.
[15] Léo Hamon and Jacques Manesse, "Chronique constitutionnelle et parlementaire française, *Revue du Droit Public et de la Science Politique*, (Sept.–Oct. 1969), pp. 922–924.

ment to the outer fringes of power in the Fifth Republic was achieved as much by political as by constitutional means. Had the government not enjoyed the support of at least a passive majority in the National Assembly, its satchel full of constitutional powers over Parliament could not have saved it from being defeated by a motion of censure. If 50 percent of the members of the Assembly are hostile to the government, 5 motions of censure could be posed each session, or 1 approximately every 2 weeks. The requirement that a vote of censure rally 50 percent of all members of the Assembly behind it in order to defeat the government was carried over from the Fourth Republic, where it was little used. What prevented a successful vote of censure before October 1962 (8 were attempted, including 4 on the nuclear striking force) was the fear that censure would bring a dissolution of the Assembly and then an election in which the deputy would have to explain to his constituents why he had opposed the popular de Gaulle. Indeed, that fear was confirmed in the elections of November 1962, when Gaullist candidates drove from office many of those deputies who had voted censure. Henceforth, the Gaullists enjoyed solid majority control in the Assembly; party discipline now ensured a favorable vote for virtually any measure which the President and the cabinet might propose.

The National Assembly

Party Strength

In the fall of 1958, when 67 percent of all respondents in a national poll indicated that they wanted "new men" in Parliament, it was natural enough that the legislative elections of November 1958 should have produced a turnover of parliamentary personnel greater than any other in this century save that of 1945.[16] The National Assembly which emerged from those elections included only 131 holdovers out of 465 deputies from France proper. The most dramatic political consequences of that turnover were, as shown in Table 4.1 on p. 73, the decimation of the Communist delegation and the emergence of a powerful Gaullist group. The Communists dropped from 150 in 1956 to a mere 10 — well below the minimum of 30 needed to form an official group and to gain representation on standing committees. The Gaullist UNR com-

[16] Mattei Dogan, "Changement de régime et changement de personnel," in *Le Référendum de Septembre et les Elections de Novembre 1958,* Cahiers de la Fondation Nationale des Sciences Politiques, No. 109 (Paris: A. Colin, 1960), p. 278.

manded 204 of the 578 seats in the Assembly (including deputies from Algeria and from Overseas France). That first legislature of the Fifth Republic was stacked with partisans of French Algeria. They dominated the 115-man Independent group, made up a powerful faction within the divided UNR group, and found spokesmen in all the other parties except the Communist. As de Gaulle moved further and further in the direction of Algerian independence, he provoked bitter opposition from those deputies, including a number in the UNR, who felt that the Fifth Republic had been created, and that they had been elected, for the purpose of keeping Algeria French.

The Assembly elected in 1962 was more Gaullist than the first. The 71 deputies from Algeria had been removed by presidential ordinance immediately after Algeria became independent in July 1962. The anti-Gaullist Independents had been virtually eliminated from the Assembly; the remnants were too few to form a party group and so they joined the new Democratic Center group with the MRP. The Communists and Socialists had begun a revival which was to continue in the 1967 election, but were not yet strong enough to pose any threat to Gaullist control. With the Algerian war concluded and with the more tactful Pompidou prime minister in place of Debré, who was known for his brusqueness, the Gaullist majority dutifully (though not always happily) delivered its votes to the government. The government now gave more attention to majority deputies than it had customarily done in the first legislature, especially when they presented their amendments behind the scenes, as in parliamentary committees or party study groups or through the parliamentary party's elected officials.[17]

Far more than in the past, Assembly votes became clear majority-opposition confrontations.[18] On foreign policy votes, however, the unity of the opposition disappeared; a censure motion introduced by the Socialists attacking de Gaulle's NATO policy in April 1966 failed to attract the support of the Communists, who more often sided with de Gaulle than with the more "pro-American" Socialists on foreign policy matters.

The third legislature, which served a short fifteen months, from March 1967 to June 1968, included more Communists (73) and more

[17] Jean Charlot, L'U.N.R., Etude du Pouvoir au Sein d'un Parti Politique, Cahiers de la Fondation Nationale des Sciences Politiques, No. 153 (Paris: A. Colin, 1967), pp. 143–184; Williams, The French Parliament, pp. 102–109.

[18] This trend is documented by David Wood, "Majority vs. Opposition in the National Assembly, 1956–1965: A Guttman Scale Analysis," American Political Science Review, LXII: 1 (March 1968), pp. 88–109.

Socialists and Radicals (121 in the new Left Federation group) than any other since 1958. The bare Gaullist majority left Giscard d'Estaing and his Independent Republicans in a strategic swing position. Giscard was openly critical when the government decided to bypass Parliament on social security reforms by demanding an extensive delegation of power. Giscard's discontent with the meager powers left to Parliament by the government was shared, more and more openly, by UNR deputies. By the end of the spring 1967 session of Parliament, Prime Minister Pompidou was complaining of the "intolerable" and "inadmissible" attitude of some majority deputies.[19] And yet the opposition parties were too fundamentally divided, as the events of May 1968 dramatized, to take advantage of the majority's weakness.

The fourth legislature, elected in June 1968 after the spring riots, was so lopsidedly Gaullist that the government had no need to worry of being brought down by a vote of censure. The Gaullist parties between them held almost three-fourths of the seats. The opposition parties were too weak even to take themselves seriously. Moreover the government succeeded in luring three members of the Centrist group, Progress and Modern Democracy, into the cabinet, thus splitting one of the three opposition groups in the National Assembly. And yet, as we shall see, the government's parliamentary army grew increasingly restive in its assigned role of providing a solid majority of votes for whatever the government decided to do.

Occupational Backgrounds

These shifts in party strengths brought with them subtle changes in the occupational backgrounds of the deputies. As in the Third and Fourth Republics, deputies in the Fifth are drawn from a wide variety of professions.[20] With the decline of the Socialist and especially the Communist Parties, however, the portion of deputies who had been industrial or white collar workers declined from 22 percent in 1956 to 6.5 percent in 1958, before rising (with the Communist Party) to 13 percent in 1967.[21] Farmers, who had made up 13.5 percent of the Assembly's membership in 1936 and 11.5 percent in 1958, declined in number to only 7 percent in 1967. Seats once occupied by Independents and MRP deputies, a number of whom were farmers, were taken

[19] *Le Monde,* June 30, 1967.
[20] The backgrounds of deputies in the Third and Fourth Republics are examined by Mattei Dogan, in Dwaine Marvick, ed., *Political Decision-Makers.*
[21] Williams, *The French Parliament,* p. 34.

by Gaullists, of whom only 6 percent were farmers in 1962.[22] The proportion of teachers also declined from 15 percent in 1956 to 10 percent in 1958 and 1962, before recovering to 14 percent in 1967, as the Socialist Party, the traditional party of schoolteachers, regained some of its lost seats.

The Gaullist wave brought into the Assembly an increase in the number of high civil servants (9 percent in 1962, as against 4 percent in 1956) and medical doctors (12 percent in 1962, as against 5 percent in 1956), along with a slight decline in the number of lawyers (11 percent in 1962, down from 13 percent in 1956 and 20 percent in 1936).[23] The Gaullist deputies also included more businessmen than most other groups, and particularly more managerial personnel, who increased from 5 percent of all deputies in 1956 to 9 percent in 1962, before declining temporarily to 6 percent in 1967.[24]

Organization

The affairs of the National Assembly as an institution are administered by an elected *bureau,* headed by the President of the Assembly. The president is not a neutral, nonpartisan figure on the model of the British House of Commons. For the first ten years and more of the Fifth Republic's life, a former minister and Gaullist leader, Jacques Chaban-Delmas, served as the Assembly's president, before ascending to the prime ministership. Chaban-Delmas' loyalties clearly lay with de Gaulle and the Gaullist movement; and yet on occasion he could be a vigorous defender of the rights of Parliament, as in mid-1961, when he announced in the Assembly that the government was behaving as "an autocrat arrogating itself full powers the better to abuse them, especially by preventing, through its control of the agenda, the discussion of any private member's bill and indeed of any subject desired by the representatives of the nation."[25] Chaban's successor in 1969, Achille Peretti, continued to play the dual role of loyal Gaullist and defender of parliamentary interests.[26]

[22] See the breakdown by occupation and party affiliation in Mattei Dogan, "Note sur le nouveau personnel parlementaire," *Le Référendum d'Octobre et les Elections de Novembre 1962,* p. 431.

[23] Williams, *The French Parliament,* p. 34.

[24] *Ibid.*

[25] *Journal Officiel, Débats, Assemblée Nationale,* July 6, 1961, p. 1480, as quoted in Williams, *The French Parliament,* p. 62.

[26] See his end-of-session statement, in which he pleads for an end to the government's practice of dumping legislation on Parliament in the closing weeks of a session, *Le Monde,* July 2, 1970.

Much of the organization of the Assembly's work is accomplished through the parliamentary parties, or "groups" as they are called, which may or may not coincide with organized parties outside Parliament. The party group presidents are members of the "Conference of Presidents," which works with the government (whose business takes priority) in fixing the agenda and organizing debates. The groups also select their representatives on the Assembly's standing committees, where seats are allotted in proportion to the size of the various party groups. A deputy who belongs to no party, or to one with fewer than thirty seats, must attach himself to an existing party group or take a chance on getting one of the few left-over committee positions.

Committees

Among the many features of traditional French parliamentary life which the Gaullist law-givers of 1958 were determined to reform was the dominant role of legislative committees. In the Fourth Republic, as in the Third, the Assembly committees were virtual counterministries, sufficiently powerful and knowledgeable to kill or to maim the government's legislative proposals and to keep the ministers in mortal fear for their political lives.[27] It is a sound general rule that a contemporary legislature is unlikely to wield much power unless it has permanent, specialized committees, capable of developing expert knowledge and of following a problem over time. The impotence of the House of Commons is attributable in part to its large, unspecialized committees, which may consider a defense bill one week and a meat packing bill the next.

The 1958 Constitution permits permanent, specialized committees, but only 6 of them. The result, in accordance with an Assembly decision to put almost every deputy on a committee, has been the emergence of 4 committees of 60 members each (Foreign Affairs; Finance, Economy, and Economic Planning; National Defense and Armed Forces; and Constitutional Laws, Legislation, and General Administration) and 2 committees of 120 members each (Cultural, Family and Social Affairs and Production and Exchange).[28] In prac-

---

[27] On the role of committees in the Third Republic, see R. K. Gooch, *The French Parliamentary Committee System* (Hamden, Conn.: Archon Books, 1969), a reprint of the 1935 original; and on the Fourth Republic, Williams, *Crisis and Compromise,* Ch. 18.

[28] On legislative committees in the Fifth Republic, see Eliane Guichard-Ayoub, Charles Roig, and Jean Grangé, *Etudes sur le Parlement de la Ve République* (Paris: Presses Universitaires de France, 1965), pp. 60–62 and 94–99; Pierre Avril, *Le Régime Politique de la Ve République,* pp. 45–51; and Williams, *The French Parliament,* pp. 62–65.

tice these committees are not as unwieldy as they appear, for many committee members attend meetings only when a bill of interest to them is under consideration. As in the past, the committees often chew up government bills. Also as in the past, the Defense Committee tends to defend the army's interests, the Production Committee is attentive to farm prices and hostile to higher farm taxes, etc.; and yet the larger size and broader jurisdiction of the new committees have made it more difficult for pressure groups to control them as effectively as they often did in the Third and Fourth Republics. Once the committee report is ready, the government frequently accepts some of the proposed amendments, then pushes its amended version through the Assembly with the aid of party discipline, which is more effective on the floor than in committee.

The Constitution of 1958 also permits the creation of special committees for the purpose of examining a particular bill, presumably one which cuts across the jurisdictions of the standing committees. Michel Debré would have preferred to abolish the standing committees and rely exclusively upon these special, *ad hoc* committees. In practice the standing committees have resisted this means of by-passing their jurisdiction; after some unsatisfactory experiences with special committees (one created in June 1961, and stacked with friends of the farmers, wanted the government to pay for the disposal of milk surpluses, at no cost to the farmer), even the government has usually preferred to deal with the standing committees. In an attempt to speed up the legislative process through increased use of special committees, the Assembly altered its rules of procedure in March 1970 to facilitate their creation.[29]

Question Period

Another of Michel Debré's borrowings from the British House of Commons was the question period, a time in which deputies may probe into the policies and actions of the various ministries. The purpose was to be constructive communication between the branches. No longer was the discussion to be concluded with a vote, in which the government might be felled, as in the "interpellation" sessions of earlier Parliaments. This British transplant, like a number of others, failed to take root. The question period was set for Friday afternoon, when most deputies are already heading to their home districts for the weekend. Most questions have dealt with local complaints which hold

[29] Claude Emeri and Jean-Louis Seurin, "Chronique constitutionnelle et parlementaire française," *Revue de Droit Public et de la Science Politique,* May–June 1970, pp. 659–662, 697–700.

little interest for anyone except the questioner and his constituents. With no vote in prospect, even when limited discussion is allowed (as on the "oral questions with debate") the exchange is deprived of the drama necessary to interest either the Assembly or the public. Often a minister will appear to read answers for other absent ministers whose departmental activities are largely a mystery to him. On one often-described Friday afternoon, André Malraux found himself reading the prepared answers of his fellow ministers before an audience of eight deputies, five of whom walked out before he was finished.[30] Attendance at question periods rarely exceeds fifteen to twenty deputies. The opposition parties seem to have neither the means nor the will to make use of the question period as a way of confronting the government on major issues, as does the British opposition. The power of the Gaullist-dominated Conference of Presidents to select the questions to be answered seriously inhibits the use of the question period for opposition purposes.

In March 1970 a new type of oral question was authorized: the question of current interest (*question d'actualité*), to which the government must reply at the first question period following its submission, if the Conference of Presidents so decides.[31] This is one more attempt to infuse life into an institution which has not notably improved either communication between the executive and legislative branches or legislative control over the government. The question period has been more successful in the Senate, where legislative powers are less important and hence less distracting.

Habits vs. the Law

Of the members of the National Assembly elected in 1958, 62 percent had never before been members of the French Parliament. It seemed an ideal time to break the old habits of the French deputies. And yet many of these old habits soon reappeared, breaking through the confines of the new rules. In the old Assembly a few "box carriers" (*boîtiers*) cast hundreds of ballots for absent deputies, often leaving public records of four or five hundred votes cast when only a few dozen deputies had actually been present. Henceforth, according to the constitution and the organic laws which spelled it out, the vote was to be "personal"; a proxy vote was allowed only when illness or some other rare emergency kept the deputy away from the floor. In fact the old boxes did not last long, for voting by paper ballot was replaced in late

[30] November 22, 1963. Williams, *The French Parliament*, p. 48.
[31] Emeri and Seurin, "Chronique constitutionelle et parlementaire," pp. 673–675 and 743–744.

1959 by an electronic system whereby the deputy must turn his personal key in an apparatus built into his desk in order to vote. Within months, however, at the time of an Assembly vote one could see a number of friends and party whips dashing from empty desk to empty desk casting votes with the keys which absent deputies obligingly left in their desks.

The founders of the Fifth Republic attempted to reduce absenteeism by another, more Draconian means. A deputy was to forfeit a third of his pay if he missed over a third of the roll-call votes and two-thirds if he missed over half. In fact, after the first few months these fines were a dead letter, buried by the same sense of camaraderie and mutual protection which has always characterized the National Assembly.

It would be inaccurate to conclude that the Assembly has been reduced to a simple rubber stamp. Its protests have led to the modification of many government bills, including such important ones as the adoption reform bill of 1966 and the higher education reforms of 1968–69. Most often, however, the government has conceded only on the minor issues, then, if necessary, brought out its heavy artillery — the package vote, delegated powers, and party discipline — to force through its major proposals, unchanged. Deputies on all sides of the chamber have come to feel that their Assembly is a farce, that it matters little whether they even attend. Absenteeism has risen to alarming proportions. Gaullists deputies, as well as others, have spoken out bitterly against the package vote, the resort to delegated powers, and the end-of-session barrage of bills which the government typically rams through Parliament with little time for their consideration. Despite President Pompidou's reassurances that the government would treat Parliament with more respect, his first year in office offered little sign of change.[32]

The heirs to an old and proud French parliamentary tradition have not adapted easily to the modest role of the British M.P. The government, in its impatience and its fear of reviving old parliamentary practices, often has run roughshod over Parliament, bending de Gaulle's constitution to suit its purposes. As a result, the pendulum has swung heavily from assembly government to executive domination. As its legislative function has declined, Parliament has been slow to develop other important functions. The divided opposition parties do not offer a cogent and consistent critique of government policy, which is one of the House of Common's major functions; nor have the committees and

[32] See *Le Monde,* June 28–29, 1970 (on the UDR's discontent with Prime Minister Chaban-Delmas) and July 2, 1970 (on end-of-session complaints in Parliament).

the question period developed into effective means of overseeing the behavior of the government ministries. The National Assembly remains an institution in search of a mission.

The Senate

When a host of angry Senators accused de Gaulle of wishing to destroy the Senate prior to the referendum of April 27, 1969, the General could reply that he had defended that body against the parties of the Left, who wished to abolish it entirely in 1946,[33] he had restored its powers and prestige in 1958 by giving it a role nearly equal to the Assembly's in the legislative process; he had placed its president first in line to succeed the President of the Republic should that office fall vacant; he had extended the term of the 283 senators from seven to nine years (with a third elected every three years). And yet, despite Gaullist hopes of using the Senate as a support against the Assembly, the upper chamber soon became a refuge for leaders of the old parties, a veritable fortress retreat of the old political order.

The Gaullist response was to bypass the Senate and allow a second Assembly vote to decide a question, as the constitution permits, when the two chambers cannot agree or when the government refuses to accept their compromise. Since the government is responsible only to the Assembly, and not the Senate, the upper chamber could not force the government to resign even with a unanimous vote of no confidence. A feud developed between the Senate's President, Gaston Monnerville (a Radical, originally from French Africa) and de Gaulle after Monnerville accused the President of criminal misuse of his powers over the constitutional amendment for direct election of the president in October 1962. Thereafter, full ministers boycotted the Senate, sending undersecretaries to defend their legislative proposals.

The Senate largely escaped the Gaullist political landslides of 1958 and 1962 because of the indirect manner of its election. It is chosen by an electoral college, 97 percent of whose members (over 100,000) are representatives of municipal councils. Another 3 percent (some 3,000) are chosen by departmental General Councils. The members of the National Assembly are also electors, although they make up only half of one percent of the total. The non-Gaullist parties have held their own much better at the local level — and hence in the Senate — than in the National Assembly.

Not only is the Senate weighted toward the older parties, it is also

[33] See the text of de Gaulle's televised interview in *Le Monde,* April 12, 1969.

chosen by a predominately rural constituency. Communes with less than 1,500 inhabitants made up approximately 29 percent of the French population in 1958; in that year they had 53 percent of the votes in the senatorial electoral college.[34]

As the irrelevance of the Senate came to be widely recognized — despite the frequently high quality of debate in that chamber — the suggestion was raised, on the Left as well as in Gaullist circles, that the Senate be replaced by or combined with the existing Economic and Social Council. That Council is composed of representatives of farmers, industrial workers, white-collar workers, businessmen, and a variety of other economic and social categories. Of its 200 members 140 are selected by professional associations and the remaining 60 directly by the government. The Council must be consulted by the government on important social and economic programs, although its advice may be ignored. Although it sometimes influences government decisions behind the scenes, its political role ever since its creation in 1946 has been marginal.[35]

In February 1969, de Gaulle announced that he was calling a referendum to approve the creation of new regional governmental units and the reform of the Senate. The new Senate was to combine representatives of local governments with representatives of professional associations; hence, it would bring a new perspective to the legislative process. The new President of the Senate, Alain Poher, did vigorous battle with de Gaulle in defense of the old Senate, which he feared would be reduced to a mere consultative body in its new form. When the referendum proposals were defeated, causing de Gaulle to resign, the interim President of the Republic was, of course, none other than the President of the Senate, Alain Poher.

The replacement of Gaston Monnerville by Alain Poher as President of the Senate in 1968 began a process of reconciliation between the Senate and the government that continued after de Gaulle's resignation. Full ministers, including Prime Minister Chaban-Delmas himself, once again appeared on the floor of the Senate. On November 21, 1969, contrary to a tradition dating from the Third Republic, the government introduced a financial bill in the Senate rather than in the Assem-

[34] Guichard-Ayoub, Roig, and Grangé, *Etudes sur le Parlement de la Ve République*, pp. 1–41. The Senate is, as Maurice Duverger describes it, France's "Chamber of Agriculture." Duverger, *Institutions Politiques*, pp. 590–593.

[35] The Social and Economic Council has been studied by J. E. S. Hayward, who finds that its influence has varied over time, reaching a high point in the early years of the Fifth Republic. See his *Private Interests and Public Policy: The Experience of the French Economic and Social Council* (London: Longmans, 1966).

bly. Nonetheless, the Senate's mode of election and political composition seems certain to chain the upper house to its secondary role within a Parliament which as a whole plays only a secondary role in France's new political order.

The Constitutional Council

How were the restrictions set by the Constitution of 1958 upon the scope of Parliament's law-making authority to be enforced? In the past, Parliament, ever jealous of its sovereignty, had been, in effect, the sole and final judge of its own powers. The Senate and the President of the Republic had the right to appeal to the Constitutional Committee, but made virtually no use of it. The constitution-builders of 1958 believed that since both Parliament and the government were interested parties, as well as natural rivals, neither should be entrusted to interpret and enforce the constitution. The solution chosen was to create an independent Constitutional Council, empowered to decide jurisdictional disputes between Parliament and the government as does the American Supreme Court in similar disputes between the federal government and the states. The new Constitutional Council was more powerful than the Constitutional Committee under the Fourth Republic, which was asked for only one ruling in its entire history.[36] Yet the new council's jurisdiction is far narrower than that of the United States Supreme Court, for except in election disputes, the ordinary citizen cannot appeal to the Council; only the president, the prime minister, and the presidents of the two houses of Parliament may refer cases to it for judgment.

The Constitutional Council is composed of three members appointed by the President of the Republic, three by the President of the Senate, three by the President of the National Assembly, all for non-renewable nine-year terms, plus all former Presidents of the Republic. It judges the regularity of elections, with the power to determine the winner or to call a new election in case of a dispute. It must be consulted before and during the president's assumption of emergency powers under Article 16. It alone judges when the president has become physically incapacitated and can be replaced. Finally, the council judges the constitutionality of laws and treaties. The standing orders of each house of Parliament must be submitted for the council's judgment as to their constitutionality, as must all organic laws (those which spell out portions of the constitution).

The Constitutional Council often has been accused of being a politi-

---

[36] Williams, *Crisis and Compromise,* pp. 305–306.

cal arm of the government. Indeed five of the original members appointed in 1959 had belonged to one of the Gaullist parties.[37] In the fall of 1962, when Gaston Monnerville, as President of the Senate, asked the council to rule on the constitutionality of de Gaulle's decision to bypass Parliament in amending the constitution, the council replied that it had no jurisdiction; ruling after the referendum, the council held that the voters in a "direct expression of national sovereignty," had already settled the matter by approving the amendment.[38] In the first few years of the Fifth Republic, the council's decisions concerning the interpretation of Article 34 on the scope of Parliament's law-making powers most often favored the government's restrictive point of view. Over the next decade, however, the council frequently ruled against the government. On 23 occasions during the second legislature (1962–67) the government sought a ruling that a law passed by the Parliament of the Fifth Republic was outside the domain of the law and could be altered by government ordinance. In 10 of these cases the government won, but it lost completely on 3 and partially on another 8, with the council declaring itself incompetent to rule on the remaining two.[39] On one occasion in the course of the third legislature (1968–69), the Senate proposed that veterans of the Algerian war be accorded the standing and privileges of war veterans, along with veterans of the two world wars. The Minister of Veterans Affairs replied that such a bill was not within the constitutionally-defined domain of law and hence could be enacted only by government ordinance. Upon appeal from the President of the Senate, the Constitutional Council declared in favor of the Senate, on the grounds that the subject involved the obligations imposed by national defense upon the citizenry and hence was within the domain of law.[40] If the Constitutional Council exercises considerably less than full and independent powers of judicial review, it nonetheless is more than a government rubber stamp.

How well did Michel Debré and his collaborators succeed in their attempt of 1958 to design a rationalized Parliament? Certainly the

---

[37] Duverger, *Institutions Politiques,* p. 662.

[38] This decision has been offered as proof that the council is not independent. De Gaulle might well have rejected or neutralized a negative council decision. Maurice Duverger has argued, however, that the council's position is correct; Article 17 of the organic law of Nov. 7, 1968, gives the council jurisdiction only over laws "adopted by Parliament" (*Ibid.,* pp. 654–655). This argument is debatable, for Article 59 of the constitution specifically authorizes the council to "ensure the regularity of referendum procedures."

[39] François Goguel, "Bilan du travail législatif 1962–1966," *Projet* (March 1967), p. 289.

[40] Hamon and Manesse in *Revue du Droit Public,* pp. 920–921.

new order was better able to take vigorous action when the circumstances seemed to warrant. For example, anti-inflation programs were more consistently applied than in past years. The home distillers, who were politically almost untouchable under the Fourth Republic, were subject to stringent restrictions by the Fifth. And yet the institutions of the Fifth Republic did not evolve according to the plan. Having acquired impressive constitutional powers over Parliament, after 1962 the government found itself with the kind of solid parliamentary majority for whose assumed absence the powers were designed to compensate. Thereafter, the Gaullists held permanent control of all committee chairmanships in the Assembly and dominated the Conference of Presidents. When the Senate refused to comply with the government's wishes, it found itself overridden time and again on the second reading in the Gaullist-dominated Assembly. The combination of constitutional authority with Gaullist discipline placed the government in a position to control the Assembly's every move. The opposition became demoralized and almost ceased trying to offer a systematic challenge. The result was that Parliament no longer could serve as an effective channel of communication between the people and their government. When legal channels are closed off, politically conscious and aggrieved citizens are likely to turn to the streets. The rash of tractor blockades, strikes, and militant protests from many quarters in recent years may be related to the weakness of communication lines from the bottom up in the Gaullist regime.

7

Governmental Institutions: The Administration

The Administrative Machine: Chained or Unchained?

One of the most interesting paradoxes of French society is the existence in this land of individualists of one of the largest and most powerful state bureaucracies of the Western world.[1] In the mid-1960's, the national government employed over 1,200,000 persons, not counting the military, civilian employees in the military services, or those employed in the nationalized industries. The United States, with almost four times as many people, had only some 1,600,000, again excluding members and employees of the armed services. Even in Britain, two decades after the Labour Party began to create its version of the welfare state, the British national civil service numbered under a million members. Many of the employees who are paid by local government in Britain and the United States — schoolteachers, for example — are employees of the national government in France. Local and state governments employ some eight million people in the United States, a million and a half in Britain, but less than 400,000 in France.

Under the Third and Fourth Republics the high officials in this giant bureaucratic machine frequently were regarded as experienced and reliable crewmen who held the ship of state on course while the ministers played their games of musical chairs on the top deck. Since

---

[1] The best general description of French administration in English is Ridley and Blondel, *Public Administration in France*. In French, see Gérard Belorgey, *Le Gouvernement et l'Administration de la France* (Paris: A. Colin, 1967). For a critique of the traditional, legalistic studies of French administration (including Belorgey's), and for a survey of recent empirical studies on the subject, see Ezra Suleiman, "The French Bureaucracy and its Students: Towards the Desanctification of the State," *World Politics,* XXIII: 1 (October 1970), pp. 121–170.

1958 many of the critics of the Gaullist Republic have complained that the bureaucrats and the technocrats are even more powerful and less effectively in check than before. High civil servants no longer have to content themselves with exercising power behind the scene; a number of them have been selected to be ministers themselves. As for the rest, the annoyance of parliamentary investigations and controls have been all but eliminated. Are we to conclude that the administration is the ultimate wielder of governmental power in France? Is this, as the cliché holds, a country "which is not governed, but administered"? An examination first of the evidence favoring this interpretation then of the evidence suggesting qualifications will help to delineate the administration's effective power.

The Importance of the French Civil Service

The first and most obvious of the advantages of France's centralized administration, from the Battle of Waterloo to May 13, 1958, was its stability. Had there been no well-developed state bureaucracy, France's many changes of political leadership would have been more traumatic. One must be careful not to exaggerate either this stability of the bureaucrats or the instability of the politicians. In some ministries, for example the Ministry of Foreign Affairs under the Fourth Republic, ministers held their positions far longer than prime ministers. The outgoing minister not infrequently was asked to stay on under the new prime minister. And yet, in the period from September 1944 to May 1958, the average number of ministers serving in each of the fifteen permanent ministries was close to thirteen. A number of these men served more than once.[2] Often when regimes changed, as in 1848, 1940, and 1945, there was a heavy turnover of high-level administrative personnel.[3] However, even when high civil servants were purged or transferred, the structure of administration remained largely intact, along with the traditional ways of doing things. Frequently rapid turnover in executive leadership and stalemate in Parliament left policy vacuums which the administration filled. For example, economic planning and the development of atomic energy were policy fields largely controlled by civil servants under the Fourth Republic.[4]

[2] The turnover was lowest in Foreign Affairs (7 ministers) and the Postal Ministry (8), and highest in Finance (19), Defense (18), and Veterans Affairs (19). Calculated from Appendix III in Williams, *Crisis and Compromise*, p. 497.

[3] Suleiman, "French Bureaucracy," pp. 128–129.

[4] See Ch. 2 above and Lawrence Scheinman, *Atomic Energy Policy in France under the Fourth Republic* (Princeton: Princeton University Press, 1965), pp. 204–215.

The bureaucracy's powers of *freinage,* or applying the brakes, are more apparent than its powers of innovation. Even in the Fifth Republic it takes a confident and determined minister to buck the traditions and personal preferences of the ministry's high civil servants. Many a project can be lost, or at least long postponed, when high civil servants in the labyrinthian recesses of the powerful Ministry of Finance elect to use delaying tactics.

A second advantage to power-seekers within the administration is the centralized character of the apparatus of government. This is not to say that the bureaucrats are all in Paris. On the contrary, the great majority of them are scattered in field offices, subprefectures, and prefectures all over France. Some three thousand towns and villages can boast the presence of a state road engineer.[5] With well-developed branch offices throughout the country, the ministries have less need of cooperation from local officials than do their American counterparts. For instance, despite efforts to decentralize administration of the educational system, most decisions about what French children must learn and in what sequence are taken in Paris and implemented without encountering such obstacles as America's state legislatures and independent school districts. As we shall see, local governments at the municipal and departmental levels have such limited taxing powers that they need grants from the national government for most of the things they do. Even when the mayor and his council have funds, they normally must obtain the approval of the departmental prefect, or at least the subprefect (both of whom are civil servants within the Ministry of Interior), before they can spend the money to construct a building or develop a park.

Yet another advantage of the French administrative system is the quality of personnel attracted into its higher ranks and the enormous prestige which they enjoy, both of which undoubtedly are related to the important powers which high civil servants exercise. From the "civil administrator" class A and the "administration attaché" class B to the clerical and typist classes C and D, the French civil service offers respectable employment.[6] Many a French mother dreams that her son may one day find a career with the government. The humble may dream of a secure job with a pension in the clerical ranks. The ambitious dare to hope for a position in one of the *grand corps* of high civil servants, particularly in the Council of State, the prefectoral corps, or

---

[5] Ridley and Blondel, *Public Administration in France,* p. 29.

[6] Judging from the declining number of candidates for lower echelon civil service positions, it appears that the security of government employment is less attractive in a prosperous economic era. See Michel Crozier, "Crise et Renouveau dans l'Administration Française," *Sociologie du Travail* 8: 3 (Jul.–Sep. 1966), p. 241.

the Inspectorate of Finance. The fortunate few who reach these lofty heights can be assured that if they tire of public service private industry will be eager to hire them.

Among the several schools which prepare high civil servants, two stand out: The Ecole Polytechnique and the Ecole Nationale l'Administration. If a boy is bright, oriented toward technical studies and perhaps in need of a free university education, he may spend two or more years after secondary school studying science and mathematics and then join the two thousand or more candidates who compete by examination for the hundred and fifty places in the beginning class at the Ecole Polytechnique. Founded by Napoleon in 1795 to produce army engineers and artillerymen, the Ecole Polytechnique, while remaining a military school, has become in practice a major supplier of engineers and administrators both for government and for private industry. Only a handful of the annual graduates now make a career in the army. Those who graduate in the top quarter of their class usually are offered positions in one of the technical corps of the civil service, then sent for further training to the School of Mines or the School of Bridges and Highways. Ultimately they may make their way into high administrative positions even outside the technical services. Most of the rest, after a compulsory tour of military duty, find their way into private industry.

If a boy prefers a nontechnical education and can afford a university education, he may aim for admission to the National School of Administration, which is known as ENA. First he normally completes three years in one of nine institutes of political studies, preferably the one in Paris, which supplies the largest number of successful ENA candidates. If he is one of the fortunate few who are admitted, he is assured a place in the civil service. Yet only if he graduates high in his class from ENA will he have the opportunity to enter one of the *grand corps* of high civil servants. The select of the select who are admitted to the corps of the Council of State or the Inspectorate of Finance may find themselves detached to a variety of ministries and even to the private staffs of ministers. They belong to a prestigious reservoir of talent from which men are drawn for positions of responsibility throughout the administration. Some two-thirds of the Inspectors of Finance and one-third of the Councillors of State normally are detached for service outside their corps at any given time.[7] ENA graduates who are not near the top of their class must be content with less prestigious corps or with membership in the nonspecialized corps of civil administrators.

In the generation since ENA's creation in 1945, its graduates have spread throughout the higher echelons at the civil service. Their ad-

[7] Suleiman, "French Bureaucracy," p. 147n.

mirers speak of ENA's major contribution to the excellence of French administration as well as to the art of public administration. Their detractors, noting their predominantly bourgeois origins and the old school ties which bind them, warn against the oligarchy of the technocrats. In 1967 two Leftist ENA graduates joined the critics by writing a book entitled *The ENArchy or the Mandarins of Bourgeois Society*.[8] Indeed, the family backgrounds of ENA students are predominantly bourgeois. Over two-thirds of the candidates admitted in 1959 were sons of high civil servants, professional men, or managerial personnel.[9] And yet while half of all ENA students are recruited at large, primarily from among recent university graduates, the other half must be recruited from among class B civil servants — the equivalent of Britain's executive class. In 1959 over half of those admitted to ENA in this category were sons of middle and lower ranking civil servants and white-collar workers. Whatever their social origins, by the late 1960's ENA graduates formed a highly influential elite in the French civil service.

The French administrator also benefits from a tradition of state intervention in social and economic affairs which lingers from the predemocratic era of Bourbons and Bonapartes, and which retains some of the old flavor of benevolent despotism. Even in a democratic age, it seems that French administrators often have felt that there is a rational solution to most problems and that the trained and experienced administrator is most likely to find it.[10] Assured that he is "the cream of the cream," supported by a long tradition of state intervention, ensconced near the heights of a powerfully centralized bureaucracy, the French high civil servant is, indeed, almost as impressive a figure as the mandarin of ancient China (who also was recruited by examination).

Limitations upon Bureaucratic Power

Fortunately, from the democrat's point of view, French civil servants do not form a monolithic block, nor are they the only wielders of power in the French political system. The first and most obvious limitation upon their power as a class is their lack of unity. The administrative class may have little in common with class B civil servants, whose social and educational backgrounds tend to be more modest, not to speak of the gap in background and outlook between the princes at the top and classes C and D, who face constant reminders of their lowly status in

---

[8] Jacques Mandrin (a pseudonym), *L'Enarchie ou les Mandarins de la Société Bourgeoise* (Paris: Editions de la Table Ronde, 1967).

[9] Ridley and Blondel, *Public Administration in France*, p. 38.

[10] On this point see Michel Crozier, *La Société Bloquée* (Paris: Seuil, 1970), pp. 83–85.

a very hierarchical structure. Within the administrative class, the *grand corps* are distinct from the rest and distinct from each other. The "old boy" networks which link former *Polytechniciens* and former ENA students are largely separate. ENA was created after World War II to help unify an administrative class which previously had been recruited by the separate ministries and divided into hundreds of corps. In fact the most prestigious corps were left intact. Members of the corps of the *Conseil d'Etat,* the prefectoral corps, and the Inspectorate of Finance continued to monopolize most of the highest administrative posts. A man who is not admitted into one of the *grands corps* upon entry into the civil service normally is excluded from them for life, just as members of the executive class have little access to the administrative class, save through ENA. Jealousies and divisions between strata of civil servants are still very much a part of life in the French bureaucracy.

More important, administrators tend to identify with the ministry or office in which they are posted. Prefects become spokesmen for the interests of "their" departments. Administrators in the Ministry of Agriculture tend to favor spending more money to help the farmers, while those in the Ministry of Finance typically resist proposed increments in government expenditures. Old school ties among high civil servants help to smooth relationships between ministries, but they do not supress interministerial rivalries. Even within a single ministry, there frequently is conflict between the chief civil servant (the *Directeur*) and those civil servants who belong to the minister's personal staff, or *cabinet*.

Even if French high civil servants were able to present a united front, their powers of innovation would be curtailed. Dramatic new programs normally require new funds, which only Parliament can provide, and the implementation of a plan, as opposed to its elaboration by study groups, requires political leadership as well as the cooperation of the groups to be affected. Indeed, as an intricate bureaucratic structure, housing a myriad vested interests, the administration tends to be better at conserving than at changing.[11] Change invariably threatens the vested interest of some office or category of the administration, which very likely can find interested groups outside the bureaucracy to join in defense of the status quo. It is significant that Jean Monnet, the leading figure in the development of French economic planning, was brought into the civil service from the outside as were the scientists who guided French atomic energy development in the Fourth Republic. French high civil servants can be effective innovators, as they were in the late 1950's and early 1960's in designing the new institutions which

[11] See Crozier, *La Société Bloquée,* Ch. 5.

gave the Paris region both more local services and better region-wide planning; yet they function most effectively in this role when prodded and supported by a strong government.

The Gaullists, with their commitment to a strong and stable executive, as well as to the modernization of French society, have offered high civil servants more opportunity to implement their dreams than did the governments of the Fourth Republic. And yet if the innovative potential of the administration has expanded, so too have the powers of the prime minister and his cabinet to exercise political control over their civil servant subordinates. Although some ministers are more successful than others in establishing political controls, in general the governments of the Fifth Republic are better able to maintain steady pressure for the implementation of their policies than were those of the Fourth Republic. The waiting game now is one which the government may hope to win.

The bureaucracy protects itself against many misuses of administrative powers through an elaborate system of administrative courts, which are distinct from the regular courts. An aggrieved citizen may take his complaint to one of these tribunals — in certain cases to the highest of these, the Council of State — in search of relief or compensation. When an official is deemed to have surpassed his legal powers, the administrative courts are authorized to annul his ruling. When an aggrieved citizen is judged to have suffered damages as a result of a wrongful act by a government official, the administrative courts can order the government to compensate him. Although created by the government and staffed by high civil servants, the Council of State has developed a tradition of independence which is respected by both Parliament and the executive.

Yet another check upon bureaucratic powers is provided by the political, social, and economic organizations with which the administrator deals. Recent research has shown that the prefect needs the help of the mayors in his department in order to carry out the development programs which will mark him as a dynamic administrator in the eyes of his superiors. The mayors feel they are in equal need of the prefect for help in obtaining financial grants; yet each may prefer to picture the other as a rival — the prefect in order to explain his failures in terms of the backwardness of the local mayors, and the mayor in order to impress his constituents with the great obstacles which he must overcome in order to defend their legitimate interests.[12] The symbiotic

[12] In English, see Mark Kesselman's excellent article, "Over-institutionalization and Political Constraint: The Case of France," *Comparative Politics* III: 1 (October 1970), pp. 21–44. In French, see Jean-Pierre Worms, "Le Préfet et ses Notables," *Sociologie du Travail*, 8: 3 (Jul.–Sep. 1966), pp. 249–275.

relationship between these two officials has the effect of inhibiting bold reforms in local government. Similar dependencies upon groups whose cooperation is needed — be they farmers, shopkeepers, or big corporations — tend to restrain the independence of the civil administrator in many branches of government.

Before we turn to a final summary of the national bureaucracy in France, it would be well to look more systematically at what the French call "local administration" and its relationship to the central administration.

French Local Government

In contrast to the varied patterns of local government in the United States, the French commune and department present a picture of striking uniformity.[13] Whether the mayor happens to be a Communist, as in Le Havre, or a Gaullist, as in Bordeaux, communal government functions in very much the same way. It could hardly be otherwise, given the extensive central controls which Paris has exercised over the whole of France since well before the Revolution.

France's centralized administrative apparatus was first created by the Bourbon monarchy, then restructured and tightened by Napoleon. Although republicans gave verbal deference to the concept of "local liberties," once the central government was safely in republican hands, the Third Republic (like the First before it) contented itself with requiring election of local councils and mayors, then leaving these officials with minimal independence. The republican taste for equality and for uniformity, combined with memories of locally based rebellion against the First Republic, dissuaded reformers from tampering with the centralized character of the French state.

From the Napoleonic era to the present, the communes (now some 38,000 of them) and the departments (which number 95 in France proper) have been the primary units of local government. Two intermediary units within the department — the cantons and the *arrondissements* — are little used except as election districts. The commune elects a municipal council, which in turn selects one of its members as mayor. As the capital, and especially one with a tradition of launching revolutions, Paris is not allowed a mayor, but is administered by the Prefect of Police and the Prefect of the Seine, both responsible to the

[13] Good general descriptions of French local government are to be found in: Brian Chapman, *Introduction to French Local Government* (London: Allen and Unwin, 1953); Ridley and Blondel, *Public Administration in France;* and Herré Detton, *L'Administration régionale et locale en France* (Paris: Presses Universitaires de France, 1964). Local politics are described and analyzed in Kesselman, *The Ambiguous Consensus.*

national government. The department is also allowed an elected general council, although the prefect — the executive officer and usually the guiding force in the department — is a civil servant appointed by the Minister of the Interior. The department is the basic administrative unit for the various ministries of the central government. With varying success, the prefect attempts to coordinate all governmental activities within the department. The prefect's role is a dual one: he represents Paris, yet acts as well as chief executive of the general council. This duality of roles — state administrator and representative of the local population — is characteristic of mayors and local councils as well. It is significant that on ceremonial occasions the mayor invariably drapes himself in the tricolor sash — the symbol of his role as representative of the French Republic — rather than in the local coat of arms. He and his council are required by national law to implement public assistance programs, maintain schools, support a local police force and fire department, and provide certain other services, all subject to the supervision and approval of the prefect. Even though the communes are required to build and maintain schools, they have no control over curriculum or over the appointment of teachers. Should the municipal government fail to perform these services in accordance with the law, the prefect may make changes in the local budget and raise taxes to meet added costs. When a mayor and his council cannot agree on a budget, the prefect, with the support of the Ministry of Interior, not infrequently dissolves the council and calls new elections.

Once a commune has provided the compulsory services, it may choose to maintain libraries, a slaughterhouse, parks, nurseries, savings banks, pawnbroking shops, and innumerable other activities, so long as the departmental prefect approves and the national Council of State (on appeal) rules that the service is in the local interest. The critical limitation on the extension of municipal activities is financial rather than legal. The 1962 census revealed that with the continuing migration away from rural areas 24,000 of the 38,000 communes had populations of under 500. Even when joined in intercommunal syndicates, most of these communes are too poor even to provide basic services without subsidies from higher echelons. The taxes which the many small communes of France are authorized to raise produce such meager revenue that even running water was unavailable in many rural communes until well after the second world war.

Despite the limited powers and means of local self-government, elective offices are highly prized as steppingstones by politicians who hope eventually to be elected to the National Assembly, and as local political bases for even the most eminent of national politicians. Under both the Fourth and Fifth Republics, almost two-thirds of all members of the National Assembly have been at the same time members of municipal or departmental councils or both.[14] Prime Minister Georges Pompidou was following an established tradition in March 1965 when he ran for and was elected to the municipal council of the town of Cajarc in central France. In a country where so much is determined in Paris, his local supporters, like those of other prominent political figures, undoubtedly feel better protected with one of their own men sitting near the seat of power. Far from supressing the expression of local sentiments, centralization has produced a Parliament full of spokesmen for the parochial interests of the townships and departments of France.

Along with stability goes a sense of cooperation and compromise which has been notably stronger at the local than at the national level. In the larger communes, interparty competition for office is still fairly sharp. In smaller communes the mayor typically is a "community father" type who seeks to maintain harmony in his town. Often he does so by taking an "above politics" stance and appealing to all parties to join him in defending the community's interests against the national government. Following the municipal elections of 1965, 32 percent of the 37,764 mayors selected by municipal councils had run on a non-partisan, "defense of local interests" ticket.[15] A recent "Practical Guide for the Municipal Orator" suggests a model speech which includes the phrase: "separated by ideas, perhaps, but always united in action, we will promote together the greatest good for our communities."[16]

In the smaller communes, and to a degree even in the larger ones, there is pressure to moderate partisan conflict in the interests of unity. The apparent consensus and the spirit of compromise in local politics are shallow, however. They are possible because most of the divisive political issues, from economic policy to church schools, are decided at the national level. Were local governments to be vested with greater policy-making powers, communal unity would be threatened. Power-lessness (save in a negative, defensive sense) may be the price of unity in French local politics. Centralization of decision-making, however, severely limits the experience of Frenchmen in local self-government.[17]

[14] *Le Référendum de Septembre et les Elections de Novembre 1958,* Cahiers de la Fondation Nationale des Sciences Politiques, No. 109 (Paris: A. Colin, 1960), pp. 259–260.

[15] Jeannine Verdès-Leroux, "Charactéristiques des maires des communes de plus de 2,000 habitants," *Revue Française de Science Politique,* XX: 5 (October 1970), pp. 975–976.

[16] Quoted in Kesselman, *The Ambiguous Consensus,* p. 160.

[17] This, of course, was one of de Tocqueville's most serious charges against French administration in his time (see *The Old Regime and the Revolution*). The theme is explored again by Alfred Grosser in "France: Nothing but Opposition."

Especially in smaller cities and towns, the Gaullists have had very limited success in persuading the voters to replace established officials. After a decade of national rule, the Gaullists held less than 10 percent of all local offices. In cities of over 30,000 population, where Gaullist strength in local politics is greater than in small towns, a very generous Ministry of Interior classification claimed pro-Gaullist "majority" victories in only 78 of 192 cities in the municipal elections of 1965 and 73 of 192 in those of 1971.[18]

Since 1958 the Gaullist government has made numerous efforts to reform the finances and organization of local government, with only limited success. It has encouraged communes to merge with their neighbors to form stronger and wealthier units. Only 1 percent of the 38,000 communes have done so. The national government has encouraged the formation of urban districts and of rural, multi-purpose "syndicates" to provide common services (such as water, fire protection, garbage collection, road maintenance, etc.) to several neighboring communes. By July 1966, 454 urban communes had grouped together in 67 urban districts and 5,780 rural communes had joined 581 multipurpose syndicates, not counting the older and more numerous single-purpose syndicates.[19] Although significant, these reforms have been resisted and often thwarted by local officials and administrators who fear that change will mean loss of personal and local control. The national government has considered, then delayed, plans for comprehensive reform of local government on the grounds that local resistance is too powerful.[20]

At the regional level, economic planners long have felt the need for an administrative unit larger than the department. In 1964, twenty-one regions, some of which, like Burgundy, Brittany, and Auvergne, were christened with the names of the historical provinces of France, were set up under the administration of a regional prefect, invested with important administrative and economic powers, who serves also as prefect of one of the member departments. The regional prefect is advised by a Regional Commission of Economic Development (CODER), which includes representatives of elected local authorities, organized local interests, and others appointed by the government. The region appears to have achieved a permanent place in French administration, although it has yet to fulfill its initial promise. The government's intent was for the region to take an important place in the development and implemen-

---

[18] Kesselman, "Over-institutionalization and Political Constraint," pp. 22–29, and *Le Monde,* March 23, 1971.

[19] Jean-Claude Groshens, "Les Problèmes Actuels de l'Administration Locale en France," *La Revue Administrative,* No. 118 (Jul.–Aug. 1967), pp. 381–382.

[20] Kesselman, "Over-institutionalization and Political Constraint," pp. 13–15; and Jean-Pierre Worms, "Le Prefet."

tation of the four-year national plans for economic development. As in the case of municipal government reforms, however, the plan has met resistance from local office holders and departmental administrators, who fear that their status and the defense of local interests might be jeopardized by regionalization.[21] De Gaulle's proposal to develop new representative institutions at the regional level was delayed when the referendum including that plan was rejected by the voters in April 1969.

Despite the many limitations upon the independence of the French national bureaucracy, one cannot understand the French political system without knowing something of the pervasiveness and conservative effects of an "over-institutionalized" administration.[22] It is an administration which has been much admired by foreign observers for its expertness, its efficiency, the excellence of its personnel, and the extent of its authority. Among the French themselves, the years since 1958 have seen increasing disillusionment with the state bureaucracy. Politicians on the Left were the first to charge that under de Gaulle technocracy had won out over democracy. As the attack became more general, the presumed arrogance, the closed character, and the over-centralization of the bureaucracy became common topics of political debate.

By the late 1960's, a number of Gaullist leaders had joined the critics and were calling for administrative reform. No less an authority than Prime Minister Jacques Chaban-Delmas told the National Assembly in September 1969 that a "tentacular" and "inefficient" state administration is a major obstacle to the development of a modern, participant society in France. It is "tentacular because, through the unlimited extension of its responsibilities, it has little by little placed the whole of French society under its wing."[23] Local governments, public corporations, and even private firms are stifled by excessive government controls, he continued, even though their own demands for protection and subsidies have contributed substantially to the creation of the octopus. The solution, the Prime Minister argued, is to "redefine the role of the State. It must do its job better in the future, but stop there and not seek to do that of others. It must give or restore true autonomy and hence effective responsibility to local governments, to universities and to nationalized industries."[24] The goal, for the Prime Minister, is greater local

---

[21] Pierre Grémion, "Résistance au Changement: le Cas des Institutions Régionales," *Sociologie du Travail,* 8: 3 (Jul.–Sept. 1966), pp. 276–295.

[22] The term is Kesselman's.

[23] *Journal Officiel, Débats, Assemblée Nationale,* Séance du 16 septembre 1969, p. 2251.

[24] *Ibid.,* p. 2253.

participation and responsibility in decision-making. The government must be decentralized, and not simply in the sense of giving local offices of national ministries more autonomy. Offices which are not critical should be abolished, loosening the tentacles of the octopus to encourage local initiative.

Is Chaban-Delmas correct when he describes the centralized bureaucracy as a primary obstacle to participatory democracy? Quite probably it has had some such effect over the years; yet at present the nature of the causal relationship between bureaucratic decision-making and self-government is more complex. We have noted the reluctance of Frenchmen to participate in civic organizations and the existence of political cleavages which hamper collective decision-making. It seems likely that one of the major reasons for the extension of bureaucratic controls has been the unwillingness and inability of local governments and private organizations to handle the problems of a modernizing society. The chain of causality would appear to be circular — bureaucratic solutions inhibiting the development of citizen skills in collective decision-making, with the result that again and again the bureaucracy must be called in.

It is not surprising that the Prime Minister's vision of a "new society," a more participant society, was not uniformly well received. For Gaullist deputies local control means opposition party control in most French communes. For local officials and national bureaucrats reform means possible loss of personal status and danger to local interests. The centralized institutions which administer France are deeply rooted in her history and culture. They are supported by a network of vested interests. They will not submit to the reformer without a battle.

8

Policy Processes

In France, as in other major Western democracies, the answer to the question "who governs?" is not simple. The principal actors in the French policy-making process, including those outside as well as inside government, vary in two important ways. First, the principal policy-makers have changed over time; those interest groups and governmental institutions which were powerful under the Third and Fourth Republics often have had markedly less influence under the Fifth. Second, the chief decision-makers change as the topic changes. When the subject is foreign policy and the Republic in question is the Fifth, one can confidently presume the President of the Republic is playing the lead role. When the subject is agriculture or education, then interest groups, parliamentary committees, ministers, and bureaucrats all may influence the final outcome, at any given time. Both these sources of variance — time and subject — deserve attention.

The Third and Fourth Republics

The instability of coalition governments in the Third and Fourth Republics gave power to the bureaucrats, who continued to carry out established policies; to the Parliament, whose committees regularly rewrote government bills; to the parties, which controlled Parliament; and to various interest groups, which could turn their supporters against uncooperative deputies. One classic example of the power of certain kinds of interest groups in the Third and Fourth Republics is the battle of the alcohol lobby for state subsidies.

The Politics of Alcohol

During World War I the French government decided to encourage the production of sugar beets, which could be converted into alcohol, a product drastically needed for the manufacture of gunpowder.[1] Once the war was over, the government was persuaded by sugar beet and wine growers to buy up the surplus of alcohol resulting from the increase in the production of sugar beets and wine and the decline in the demand for alcohol. Eventually, a government agency, the *Service des Alcoöls,* established a monopoly over the alcohol market. Beginning in 1923, in an attempt to get rid of the mounting alcohol surplus, the government required oil refineries to add a specified proportion of alcohol to gasoline. The guaranteed purchase of alcohol was abandoned by the Vichy government but restored by the Fourth Republic in response to the demands of alcohol producers of various sorts. By fiscal year 1953–54, the government was buying some 105 million gallons of alcohol per year at a cost of $139,000,000. Most of this was sold at a fraction of its cost. For example, the alcohol which refineries once again were required to add to gasoline after 1952 cost 100 francs per liter, as opposed to 14 francs per liter for the gasoline which it displaced. The motorist's reward for helping to subsidize the *carburant national* was poorer mileage, inferior engine performance, and an accumulation of sludge in his engine.

The success of the alcohol lobby can be explained largely by two factors: the strength of the major producers' organizations and the dependence of the government parties upon farm votes. The General Confederation of Beet Growers (CGB) represented 150,000 farmers, many of them prosperous. The National Syndicate of Home Distillers (SNBC) could claim to represent some three million farmers who had a traditional right to distill modest amounts of tax-free liquor, presumably for home consumption. Another million and a half winegrowers (whose surplus wine often was distilled) also had an interest in continuation of alcohol subsidies. The Beet Growers Confederation and the Home Distillers Syndicate had firm friends on the Agriculture and Beverages Committees of the National Assembly (which were overloaded with deputies from farm districts), and often in the Ministry of Agriculture as well. The Syndicate, with its impressive numbers (in sixty-one departments at least a quarter of the adult males were home distillers), gave its stamp of approval only to parliamentary candidates who pledged to defend its interests.

Any government which dared restrict the existing privileges of alcohol producers was certain to have a battle on its hands. Prime Minister

[1] The following description of the alcohol lobby draws heavily upon Bernard Brown's "Alcohol and Politics in France," *American Political Science Review,* L1: 4 (December 1957), pp. 976–994. See also Charles K. Warner, *The Winegrowers of France and the Government since 1875* (New York: Columbia University Press, 1960), especially Chs. 6–9.

René Mayer tried to economize on government expenditures in early 1953 by reducing the alcohol subsidy. He was labeled "the assassin of French agriculture" by the alcohol lobby, then overthrown by a vote of no confidence in the National Assembly, a vote in which the defection of deputies from farm districts played a major part. Prime Minister Pierre Mendès-France launched a more serious assault on the alcohol problem in January 1955, with the issuance of a series of decrees intended, among other things, to reduce the number of home distillers, tighten the licensing of liquor sales, and limit the production of sugar beet alcohol. He was accused of being a tool of the "trusts" and of attempting "to destroy the middle class and to enslave the peasantry he so despises."[2] His campaign to reduce the alarmingly high rate of alcohol consumption was met with charges that he had sold out to Coca Cola. According to spokesmen for the alcohol lobby, it was unpatriotic to favor soft drinks over wine or spirits and unhealthy as well. The *Moniteur Vinicole* (a winegrowers' newspaper) later warned that "To drink water may be dangerous. Fight against cancer by drinking alcohol."[3] The National Assembly bowed to the demands of the alcohol lobby and each year voted to postpone the implementation of the anti-alcohol decrees.

A poll conducted by the French Institute of Public Opinion indicated that in early 1955 some 81 percent of adult Frenchmen approved the anti-alcohol decrees. Why was such a popular program thwarted? Simply because the flimsy governments of the Fourth Republic normally could not survive without votes from Peasant, Independent, Popular Republican, and Radical Party deputies elected from agricultural districts. A determined minority within the range of parties which normally supported governments could exercise an inordinate amount of power. In most cases party discipline was too weak to permit leaders to prevent defections.[4] It was not until the Fifth Republic, and then only through the exercise of delegated powers, that the government was able to restrict the privileges of the home distillers.[5]

In the main, prior to 1958 interest groups had more success in de-

[2] Quoted in Brown, "Alcohol and Politics," p. 992.

[3] Quoted in *ibid.*, p. 984.

[4] It should be noted that the belief that farm votes can be bought or lost with farm programs has given farmers influence beyond their numbers even in Britain, where disciplined political parties once were thought to minimize interest group pressures. See Roland Pennock, "Responsible Government, Separated Powers, and Special Interests: Agricultural Subsidies in Britain and America," *American Political Science Review,* LVI: 3 (September 1962), pp. 621–633.

[5] For a brief case study of the "Social Scourges" bill of 1960, see Williams, *The French Parliament,* pp. 85–89.

fending the status quo than in forcing policy changes which might benefit them.[6] The dispersion of power in the French political system of the Third and Fourth Republics provided many defensive strongholds (the parties, the legislative committees, the bureaucracy), but obstructed the formation of positive majorities. The effective defense of vested interests was illustrated (and caricatured) many years ago by Robert de Jouvenel in his description of a hypothetical piano tax.

> The Minister of Finance proposed the establishment of a tax on pianos. It was an urgent reform; it was needed in order to balance the budget. It was, moreover, a democratic measure. In sum, everyone was agreed to vote for it. "However," the socialists remarked, "we must exempt professional musicians." "And also dancing instructors," answered the radicals, who represent the middle classes. Others chimed in "Let's exempt parents with three living children." "And families which have a son in the service." "Those who have spent ten years in the colonies." "Members of the teaching profession." "Wine merchants."
>
> Finally the tax on pianos was passed by an enormous majority. Unfortunately there was no one left to pay it. . . .[7]

Despite occasional important accomplishments such as the pioneering moves toward the Common Market, the Fourth Republic, like the Third, indulged in its share of "piano tax" legislation.

The Fifth Republic

Changes in the policy-making process after 1958 markedly altered the role of interest groups.[8] The dramatic decline in the influence of political parties (including parties supporting the government) in the decision-making process almost closed off effective interest group access via this route. The weakened position of Parliament and the reduction

[6] The most complete analysis of French pressure group activities is Jean Meynaud's *Les Groupes de Pression en France,* Cahiers de la Fondation Nationale des Sciences Politiques, No. 95 (Paris: A. Colin, 1958). See also, by the same author and in the same series, *Nouvelles Etudes sur les Groupes de Pression en France,* No. 118 (Paris: A. Colin, 1961). In English, on Fourth Republic pressure group activities, see Georges Lavau, "Political Pressures by Interest Groups in France," in Henry Ehrmann, ed., *Interest Groups on Four Continents* (Pittsburgh: University of Pittsburg Press, 1958).

[7] De Jouvenel, *La République des Camarades,* pp. 86–87.

[8] On interest groups in the Fifth Republic, see Bernard Brown, "Pressure Politics in the Fifth Republic," *Journal of Politics,* XXV: 3 (August 1963), pp. 509–525.

in the number of its committees deprived some interest groups of other privileged points of access. The Agriculture, Beverages, and Education Committees disappeared, along with many others, the first two being absorbed into the Production Committee and Education into the Cultural and Social Affairs Committee. The large new committees were more difficult for an interest group to control than had been the case with the smaller ones of the Fourth Republic. The important policy decisions now were made largely in the executive branch.

Within the executive branch, de Gaulle was known to be hostile to special interests. When he refused to call a special session of Parliament on agriculture, as requested in March 1960 by the required number of deputies, he explained,

> . . . it seems beyond question to me that their claims, as formu-
> lated, result largely from urgent demands on the part of the
> leaders of a professional group. Now, whatever may be the repre-
> sentativeness of this group as regards the particular economic
> interests which it defends, it is nonetheless — according to the
> law — bereft of all authority and of all political responsibility.[9]

Indeed, the feeling on the part of trade unions and some farm associations of being denied access to the decision-making process probably
was one reason for the rash of strikes and farmer demonstrations in the
1960's.

Yet, apart from those issues which the president has handled directly,
it is by no means certain that organized interests generally have been
less influential in the Fifth than in the Fourth Republic. The most
effective interest groups have been those with expert staffs and close
relations with the civil servants who draft bills. Those industrial,
financial, and agricultural organizations upon which the administration
long has depended for information and cooperation now find themselves closer to the center of power.[10] With the possibilities for reform,
French administrators, like their British counterparts, need the cooperation of the major organized interests in order to avoid obstruction to
their plans for the modernization of a concerted economy.[11] From the
interest group's point of view, once a plan has cleared the executive

[9] As quoted in Bernard Brown and James Christoph, eds., *Cases in Comparative Politics* (Boston: Little, Brown, 1969), p. 125.

[10] On the close relationship between the administration and organized
interests, see Henry Ehrmann, "French Bureaucracy and Organized Interests," *Administrative Science Quarterly*, V: 4 (March 1961), pp. 534–555.

[11] On the British case, see Chapter 12, "The New Group Politics," in
Samuel Beer, *British Politics in the Collectivist Age* (New York: Knopf,
1965).

branch, it is very likely to be enacted with few important amendments. A study of an agricultural law enacted in 1962 indicates that it was written almost entirely by the Minister of Agriculture and the civil service, in collaboration with farm organizations.[12]

In brief, organized interests have taken cognizance of the shift in the center of decision-making from Parliament to the executive and have turned their focus primarily upon the administration. The big losers have been those interests, like organized labor, which have neither strong support in Parliament nor ready access to the administration.

The varieties of decision-making styles in the Fifth Republic are best exemplified by case studies. The two which follow illustrate two of the most significant patterns.

The Creation of the Atomic Striking Force in 1960

Perhaps the clearest manifestation of de Gaulle's quest for the restoration of France's once-eminent role in world affairs was his creation of the French atomic striking force, the much-debated *force de frappe*. Since the prewar years, when he had openly criticized France's Maginot Line strategy of national defense, de Gaulle had been a proponent of powerful offensive weaponry. Had not the fatal Munich Conference of 1938 proved the diplomatic impotence of nations whose armies were unprepared to move beyond their own national borders? Had not the six-week war of the spring of 1940 proved that a defensive army was inadequate even at defense? In the 1930's the key weapons of offense had been the tank and the airplane. In the postwar period the ultimate weapon unmistakably was the atomic bomb, coupled with the means to deliver it. Without an atomic striking force, de Gaulle reasoned, France was doomed to perpetual dependence upon the United States.

De Gaulle happened to re-emerge as head of the French government at the time when French scientists and technicians were very close to the development of an atomic bomb. The development process had been gradual, largely unpublicized, and under the direction of the French Atomic Energy Commission (CEA) rather than of the cabinet or the National Assembly.[13] In late 1954 Prime Minister Pierre Mendès-France discussed the potential for a military atomic program

[12] Gaston Rimareix and Yves Tavernier, "L'Elaboration et le Vote de la Loi Complémentaire à la Loi d'Orientation Agricole," *Revue Française de Science Politique,* XIII: 2 (June 1963), pp. 389–425.

[13] For an excellent analysis of the political aspects of the development process, see Scheinman, *Atomic Energy Policy in France under the Fourth Republic.*

and then, without issuing formal orders, acquiesced in the expansion of weapon-oriented nuclear research. More than three years later, only a month before the Algiers revolt of May 13, 1958 which felled the Fourth Republic, Prime Minister Félix Gaillard signed an order calling for the development of an atomic bomb to be completed and tested by early 1960. Even before de Gaulle returned to assume political leadership, a prime minister and a substantial number of deputies had concluded that if France's voice again was to carry weight in international circles, if her security was to be guaranteed by something more certain than the United States' will to intervene (perhaps at the risk of devastation of American cities), France needed atomic weapons.[14]

In the course of the Fourth Republic, de Gaulle's supporters often had spoken out favoring the development of atomic weapons. Once in power, they "forged the reluctant preparations of the Fourth Republic into the political and military banner of the Fifth."[15] France blasted its way into the nuclear club on schedule with the detonation of an atomic device deep in the Sahara on February 13, 1960. The following summer, in closed sessions with the Finance and Defense Committees of the National Assembly, the government unveiled its plan for the development of a French nuclear striking force. Initially the bomb was to be carried by the French-made Mirage IV fighter-bomber. Land-based ballistic missiles, then missile submarines, would be added to the arsenal.

In late September 1960, shortly before the National Assembly was to reconvene for its fall session, the Assembly's National Defense Committee issued a statement which foretold the political battle to come. The committee asked the government, "Could a part or the whole of this program be carried out within a European framework, drawing upon the support of N.A.T.O.?"[16] In the same vein, party meetings held in early October by the Radicals and the MRP voiced doubts about the wisdom of creating an all-French *force de frappe.* Maurice Faure asked the Radical Congress, "What is this deterrent force, which will not deter our enemies from attacking us, but which will dissuade our friends from coming to our aid?"[17] Among party spokesmen only the UNR Central Committee came to the defense of the *force de frappe,* as expected, describing it as "the indispensable instrument of our defense, the condition of our independence, the essential element of our action in favor of peace."[18]

[14] *Ibid.,* pp. 186–191.
[15] *Ibid.,* p. 195.
[16] *L'Année Politique, 1960,* p. 93.
[17] *Ibid.,* p. 100.
[18] *Ibid.*

In the second week of October, the *force de frappe* proposal was considered by the Defense, Finance, and Foreign Affairs Committees in the National Assembly and by the parallel committees in the Senate. The proposal was approved, after amendment, by narrow majorities in the Assembly's Defense and Finance Committees. The Assembly's Foreign Affairs Committee was unable to agree either on the government's proposal or on a satisfactory alternative. In the Senate committees, the government proposal had fewer supporters.

On October 18, the National Assembly began its first-reading debate on the *force de frappe* plan. The *rapporteur* for the Finance Committee warned that the plan would be costly and would jeopardize the fulfillment of France's commitments to NATO. Joël Le Theule, the Gaullist *rapporteur* for the National Defense Committee, supported the plan but cautioned against neglect of the modernization of conventional forces.[19] The general debate which ensued revealed the variety and extent of opposition to the government's proposal. Four major types of opposition emerged. The first came from the Communist group, now down to a mere ten deputies, which undoubtedly viewed the *force de frappe* as another threat to the peace-loving Soviet Union. The "Europeans" in the National Assembly — those deputies most dedicated to the unification of Europe — formed a more important opposition. Most of the MRP and Socialist deputies and a scattering from other parties believed that if there were to be an atomic striking force, it ought to be a multinational European force. A third objection came from French Algeria partisans, who felt that France ought to win the Algerian war before expending its resources on hardware which would be of no help in quelling the smoldering revolution across the Mediterranean. Lastly, a number of deputies doubted that the government's plan would produce a force of anything more than symbolic importance. For example, René Schmitt of the Socialist Party told the National Assembly on October 18, "I consider the choice which has been made with regard to the Mirage IV to be profoundly regrettable. The operation will be costly and ineffective. Under these conditions the *force de frappe* is only an expression of a megalomania to which it is time to put an end."[20]

In the hallways of the Palais Bourbon, a rumor began circulating: a motion to send the *force de frappe* proposal back to committee had been signed by a number of members of the majority as well as by many opposition deputies. The MRP and the Independents — both supporters of the government up to this point — apparently could not be counted on for support on this issue, unless the government was will-

[19] *L'Année Politique, 1960,* p. 106.
[20] *Ibid.*

ing to make major concessions. Without these groups, the government did not have a majority in the National Assembly. At that point, on October 19, acting with the authorization of the cabinet, Prime Minister Debré announced that he was making the *force de frappe* plan "a matter of confidence." Under Article 49 of the constitution, a bill so designated is considered approved, without a vote, unless a motion of censure is filed within twenty-four hours and then passed by an absolute majority of the members of the National Assembly. As expected, a motion of censure was duly filed bearing 68 signatures: 23 Socialists, 17 Radicals, 6 Centrists, 19 Independents, and 3 members of the "Unity of the Republic" (a French Algeria group).

On October 25 the censure motion was debated, then voted upon. Of 578 deputies, 207 voted to censure the government. Those voting for censure were the 10 Communists, 44 of 45 Socialists, the 18 Radicals, 13 of 24 Centrists, 21 of 58 Popular Republicans, 62 of 122 Independents, 26 of 32 Unity of the Republic members, and 13 of 32 unaffiliated deputies. Only the UNR deputies remained loyal to a man. The 207 votes for censure were far more than the 109 and 122 anti-government votes recorded on the two previous motions of censure under the Fifth Republic. And yet why did the government resort to the confidence vote procedure if only 207 of 578 deputies were against the measure? The answer seems to be that in an ordinary vote the government would not have had a majority. However, because many Independents and MRP deputies had been elected in 1958 as supporters of de Gaulle, the government knew that despite their opposition to the *force de frappe,* they would hesitate to vote censure, knowing it would mean dissolution of the Assembly, followed by new elections in which they would have to explain to their constituents why they had opposed the popular de Gaulle.

The bill went to the Senate, where opposition was even stronger than in the Assembly. The first reading in the Senate terminated with the defeat of the bill. As is customary, it then went to a conference committee composed of both senators and deputies. When this committee failed to reach an agreement, the bill was returned to the National Assembly for a second reading.

The second reading in the Assembly was almost a repetition of the first. Again the government invoked Article 49 and declared the bill a matter of confidence. Again a motion of censure was filed. Undoubtedly many deputies shared the sentiments of François Valentin, President of the National Defense Committee, who told Debré, before an applauding National Assembly, "You are preventing the Assembly from voting on the bill itself. You have the legal right, but in such a case the letter of the law kills. It kills the true character of the law which is to express the general will." If the government is to behave in this manner, he continued, "What is left for Parliament?"[21] Nonetheless, this second motion of censure finally drew only 214 votes, distributed very much as before.

Back went the bill for a second reading in the Senate, where it was soundly defeated a second time. Now, after the bill had been "passed" twice in the National Assembly and defeated twice in the Senate, the government exercised its option under Article 45 to let the Assembly decide. After two rehearsals, everyone knew exactly what was expected. As soon as the spokesmen for the relevant Assembly committees had reported a third time, Prime Minister Debré declared that the *force de frappe* bill again would be a matter of confidence. A third motion of censure promptly was filed. On December 6, 1960, after a ritualistic debate of only forty-five minutes in length, the vote was taken. Two hundred and fifteen deputies — essentially the same as in the two prior censure votes — voted to censure the government. Since this total fell far short of a majority of members of the National Assembly, the *force de frappe* bill was declared passed.

Here is perhaps the most striking case of executive law-making in the short history of the Fifth Republic. The government bill was forced through, unamended, without a favorable vote in either house. In an Assembly debate on November 22, 1960, François Valentin recalled that when the constitution of the Fifth Republic was being drafted he asked whether Article 49 would allow the government to pass a law without its being approved by either house. He reports being told by a person who was "highly qualified" "that this was only an academic exercise and that a government which had neither obtained a favorable vote in the Assembly nor prevented a hostile vote in the Senate could neither morally nor politically promulgate the law."[22] However, by 1960 de Gaulle and Debré believed that they could — indeed that they must — promulgate such a law. Although the *force de frappe* continued to be surrounded by controversy, it became a permanent, though relatively modest, item in the French budget.

The Higher Education Orientation Law of 1968

The barricades had only recently been cleared from the streets of Paris, and order had not fully been restored when, in July 1968, the new Minister of Education, Edgar Faure, announced an "agonizing reappraisal" of French educational policy and "a democratization of instruc-

[21] Quoted in *ibid.*, p. 120.
[22] Valentin, as quoted in *L'Année Politique, 1960*, p. 121.

tion from kindergarten to the university." The reformist tone of the minister's remarks to the National Assembly prompted Robert Poujade, secretary general of the UDR, to warn that "You must not submit to the law of those who wish to impose their arbitrary will."[23] Indeed, when Faure produced his plan for higher education in October 1968, a number of Gaullist leaders wondered whether the student rebels had not won, despite the Gaullist election victory in June. Defying a tradition of highly centralized administration of 160 years standing, universities were to be given extensive autonomy in determining what they would teach and how. At each level, from the newly designated "units of education and research" up to the Ministry of Education, most policies, except for those concerning examinations, were to be set by elected administrative councils in which as many as 50 percent of the members would be students.

When brought before the cabinet, the proposal reportedly drew vigorous criticism from Foreign Minister Michel Debré, whose commitment to the concept of a strong, centralized state is well known. De Gaulle cut off his first prime minister with the remark that Debré apparently thought "the Education Minister is crazy — which I don't think he is."[24] At the outset, a majority of the members of the cabinet opposed the Faure reforms. Faure prevailed in good part because de Gaulle supported him; the President was determined to make educational reform one pillar of his new program for a more decentralized and more participatory society.

By the time the proposals formally reached the National Assembly in late September, the Assembly's Cultural Affairs Committee (whose president was a former Minister of Education, Alain Peyrefitte) had already studied them and decided that some amendments were needed. Students should be required by law to vote in the elections of their council representatives, in order to avoid domination of those elections by "activist minorities." Moreover, the law should be redrafted to provide that a clear half of the administrative council members should be permanent faculty members, excluding teaching assistants, who might identify too closely with student views.

The opening of general debate in the National Assembly revealed that a number of prominent Gaullist deputies had serious reservations about the reform bill. Christian Fouchet, another former Gaullist Minister of Education, warned that the plan risked reducing the faculty to "a body subject to the students." Alexandre Sanguinetti feared that

[23] Unless otherwise noted, the quotations which follow are to be found either in *L'Année Politique, 1968,* or in the *Journal Officiel, Assemblée Nationale, Débats,* July–October 1968.
[24] *New York Times,* September 21, 1968.

by weakening the central government's control over education, the bill would "open a breach in the state." Other backbench Gaullists objected that the plan would introduce politics into the universities and give power to students who had only recently demonstrated their irresponsibility. Faure met these objections with a skillful blend of firmness in defense of the major elements of his plan and flexibility as to details of implementation. He appealed to the opposition parties not to turn their backs on a vitally needed reform, then shored up his support in the Gaullist ranks with appropriate quotations from de Gaulle and warm praise for Georges Pompidou. Faure accepted a number of amendments, including one guaranteeing permanent faculty members half of the council seats and another reducing the number of student seats on a council if fewer than 60 percent of the students should turn out to vote. Prime Minister Couve de Murville closed the debate with a plea that the "first great political vote of the legislature" be marked by "the solidarity which unites us when it is a question of essentials." Without invoking the blocked vote, the government obtained National Assembly approval of the Faure education orientation law on October 10, 1968 by the impressive vote of 441–0, with 33 Communists and 6 UDR deputies abstaining.

Two weeks later the Senate took up the bill for debate. Again the strongest criticism came from the Gaullist benches. Victor Golvan warned that under this law "Certain schools will become revolutionary bastions against the will of the majority of students. . . . We will vote for this plan, but our fears are great because of the present climate." Former presidential candidate Pierre Marcilhacy pointed out to the Education Minister that "It is your friends who are criticizing you, and it is your opponents — of whom I am one — who are supporting you most firmly." Again, however, the government's appeals for unity were heard. The final vote was 260 for and none against; only 18 Communists abstained, and even they publicly recognized the "positive aspects" of the reform.

Reforms which would have had little chance of adoption a year earlier were now passed without a single opposing vote in either house. The student riots of May 1968 had persuaded virtually everyone that educational reforms of some sort were necessary. Edgar Faure had led the fight with spirit and acumen. The Prime Minister had thrown his full weight behind the plan. Finally, and most important for the hesitant Gaullist legislators, it was clear that de Gaulle wanted the Faure reforms enacted.

As any knowledgeable student of democratic policy-making could have predicted, the battle was not over. Laws do not implement themselves, especially when they involve the reconstruction of traditional institutions and pose threats to vested interests. For revolutionary students, piecemeal reform was unacceptable. The reforms had no sooner been adopted than the National Union of French Students (UNEF) announced that "UNEF will fight the new reform as it fought the Fouchet reform. For us it is not a question of seeking to improve the university. The battle will recommence as soon as classes begin and students return." In fact, elections of student representatives on administrative councils were held, and on the average over half of all students participated in them, enough to show that UNEF, which had called for a boycott, was not in control. The inclusion of students in the administrative councils may well have weakened the hand of student radicals in 1968–69, but the mixed councils were by no means a universal success. Late in 1969, one of the student organizations which had participated in the elections, the National Federation of French Students (FNEF), decided to withdraw its 750 student members of administrative councils on the grounds that "the orientation law is destined to remain an empty skeleton." It blamed the superficiality and incoherence of the reforms as well as a "rigid and sterile" administration.[25] On the conservative side, in the winter and early spring of 1969, a number of local Gaullist "Committees for Defense of the Republic" fought a running battle with Faure over his purported indulgence of student revolutionaries.

Within the academic world, the separate and specialized *Facultés* of the University of Paris put up strong resistance to the creation of those closer-knit, multidisciplinary universities which Faure's reform plan required. Related reforms in secondary education also met strong resistance from the association of holders of the prestigious *agrégation* diploma (who resisted plans to break their monopoly over the best-paid teaching posts), from the Association for the Defense of Latin (which deplored plans to reduce the usual five-year Latin requirement in *lycées*), and from parents of university-bound secondary school students (who feared that the planned mixture of college preparatory with general education students at the junior high school level would lower the quality of education). Faure's successor as Minister of Education, Olivier Guichard, complained in December 1969 that each proposed reform seemed to spark a new "war of religion."[26]

Guichard himself had been the subject of controversy when Faure was dropped as Minister of Education after Pompidou's election as President of the Republic in June 1969. Although Guichard pledged to carry out Faure's reform plans, reformists charged that he had been

[25] *Le Monde,* December 4, 1969.
[26] *Le Monde,* December 3, 1969.

appointed to kill them, or at least to delay them to death. His appointment was widely interpreted to mean that change would be more cautious and gradual in the future. Guichard did not bury the Faure reforms; yet in the face of severe budget limitations and organized conservative opposition, it was apparent that their implementation would be a long and difficult affair.

The orientation law of 1968, like many major French reforms, was possible because of a conjuncture of two factors: a crisis situation and strong, if temporary, leadership. Like other French institutions, the French educational structure posed strong resistance to change, resistance which was destined to continue for years after the orientation act became law.

The Reserved Domain of the President

These case studies and the descriptions in earlier chapters of major political institutions provide some of the materials necessary to answer the question of who makes policy in the French Fifth Republic. The first and most obvious answer, although a partial one, is that French government since 1958 has been presidential government. The decision to create the *force de frappe* is an extreme example of a general pattern of presidential dominance in foreign and defense policy decisions. Within the executive branch, the prime minister leaves initiative in the foreign policy field almost entirely to the president. The foreign minister's effective role is not to make policy, but to advise the president and to implement his decisions. Of course the president must rely heavily upon experts and advisers. When he wishes, however, he may maintain direct control over the elaboration of policy proposals simply by referring them to the Interministerial Committee for Foreign Affairs, which is responsible to the president rather than to the foreign minister. He may insure that his views are well represented in that committee by selecting high civil servants and members of his staff to meet with it.

As for Parliament, it has had a very limited role indeed in the formulation of French policy concerning Algeria, the Atlantic Alliance, and the more political aspects of Common Market development. De Gaulle's major foreign policy decisions such as withdrawal from NATO and rejection of British entry into the Common Market, were made without parliamentary approval, often without parliamentary debate on the subject. When he felt the need for a formal expression of popular support for his policies during his move toward a policy of Algerian independence, he twice chose to appeal over Parliament to the people themselves. Parliament's role in foreign affairs has been no more important under President Pompidou than it was under his predecessor. The

French decision to re-open Common Market negotiations with Great Britain was as exclusively an executive decision as was de Gaulle's earlier decision to terminate them.

As we have seen, the president's "reserved domain" is not necessarily limited to foreign and defense policy. In August 1962, after miraculously surviving an ambush in which his automobile was hit by some 150 bullets, de Gaulle decided that the constitution should be amended, by referendum, to provide for direct election of the president. He informed the cabinet, announced his decision to the nation, ignored the advice of the Council of State and the Constitutional Council that amendment by referendum without parliamentary approval was unconstitutional, and sent the referendum directly to the voters. His proposal was approved, against the vigorous opposition of both chambers of Parliament and all non-Gaullist parties.[27] From 1962 de Gaulle and his successor have intervened actively in a number of domestic policy areas, including educational reform, agricultural policy, and currency devaluation.

Since 1958 the president has enjoyed unprecedented constitutional powers. Since 1962 he has been the accepted leader of a stable Gaullist majority in the National Assembly. Since 1965 he has been the popularly elected representative of the French national electorate. In combination, these sources of authority concentrate enormous powers in his hands. And yet the French president is no dictator. The referendum of April 1969 on de Gaulle's proposals for constitutional amendments concerning the Senate and regionalization offers clear evidence of the limitations upon presidential power. It was the rejection of these proposals by the voters which forced de Gaulle's final resignation, in accordance with his prereferendum pledge. This defeat is sufficient reminder that presidential dominance, even in the "reserved domain," ultimately depends on the President's ability to command popular majorities in referendums or in legislative elections.

In any complex society the problems of governance are too numerous and too complicated to be handled by a single man. In a democratic political system the leader has the additional problem of maintaining majority support among the voters and within Parliament. Often he must be willing to collaborate, to share power. Hence in most domestic policy areas, a number of political actors participate in the French decision-making process. Here the enactment of the Faure educational reforms is more typical of the process than is the creation of the *force de frappe*. The prime minister, the cabinet, the other ministers, high

---

[27] For a good case study of the 1962 constitutional amendment, see Bernard Brown, "The Decision to Elect the President by Popular Vote," in Brown and Christoph, *Cases in Comparative Politics*, pp. 148–181.

civil servants, Parliament, the majority parties within Parliament, and organized interests all may contribute to the shaping of policy.

The Role of the Prime Minister

The prime minister's role is not an easy one. He is appointed by the president, but must answer to Parliament, which may vote him out of office. According to the constitution, it is the responsibility of his government to "determine and direct the policy of the nation"; in practice, as we have seen, he does indeed "direct" the policy of the nation, but he "determines" it only insofar as the president permits him to.

After the resignation of de Gaulle, there was speculation that henceforth the prime minister might share power more equally with the president. Indeed the new prime minister, Jacques Chaban-Delmas, a politician with both ability and flair, spoke like a genuine leader. In the early fall of 1969, he proposed to the National Assembly a bold plan for a "new society," one which was to be less class-ridden and less highly centralized. President Pompidou remained silent on the subject. Gradually it became clear that the President was less impressed with the need for urgent social and political reform than was the Prime Minister. When asked in a news conference in July 1970, why he had never used the term "new society," the President replied, "Since I didn't invent the expression, I don't see why I would use it." He denied that there was any "basic disagreement" between himself and the Prime Minister, but added, "In any case, if there is a nuance to our thinking, I will say perhaps — this is due to my training or even to my function — that I attach more importance to man in society than to the form of the society itself."[28] The "nuance" of difference between the two executive heads very likely was responsible for the painful slowness with which specific proposals on the "new society" emerged from the executive branch.

The Prime Minister did not abandon his campaign. In speech after speech he deplored the obstacles to greater equality and to broader popular participation in France's "stalemate society," and outlined his vision of the "new society." Concrete achievements such as profit-sharing at Renault, monthly salaries for workers, effective government encouragement of cooperation between national unions and employers associations, and tentative steps toward administrative decentralization, all suggest that the spirit of reform espoused by Chaban-Delmas has not been entirely stifled. In favorable response to the Prime Minister's words and actions in his first eighteen months in office, 63 percent of

[28] *Press Conference of Georges Pompidou, President of the French Republic, at the Elysée Palace, July 2, 1970* (New York: Ambassade de France, Service de Presse et d'Information, n.d.), p. 3.

those Frenchmen polled in December 1970 declared themselves satisfied with Chaban-Delmas as prime minister, as opposed to only 45 percent satisfied in July 1969. The 63 percent satisfaction score was only two percentage points behind the President's score.[29]

The president clearly remains the dominant partner, without whose tacit approval no important policy could be chosen. And yet in the field of domestic policy, the prime minister may play an important role in initiating and shaping the proposals which become policy. The lack of clear differentiation between the role of the president and that of the prime minister is a natural source of conflict between the two men. Should the president's majority in Parliament weaken, or should he ever lose that majority, the potential for conflict would be increased enormously. The president appoints the prime minister, but legally can neither fire him nor keep him in office against the wishes of a majority in Parliament. He may dissolve Parliament and call new elections, but then must either live with the new majority or resign. As for a recalcitrant prime minister, the president can of course request his resignation but cannot force it. The president could stalemate the operations of the government and make it very difficult for the prime minister to hold on, however, simply by refusing to sign all government ordinances and decrees.

In practice the president's acknowledged position as head of a majority party has prevented the emergence of such problems. Future presidents may not always be so fortunate.

The Roles of Ministers and Civil Servants

Ministers other than the prime minister also play important roles in the policy-formulating process, both individually within their own jurisdictions, and collectively as members of the Council of Ministers, which must be consulted before bills are sent to Parliament for enactment. The heads of major ministries, for example the minister of finance, whose ministry must clear all measures which will increase public expenditures, and the minister of the interior, who supervises regional and local government for the whole of France, are men of considerable power. It was Edgar Faure, minister of education, who, with the help of his staff, devised the reform plan which survived minor amendments to become the Higher Education Orientation Act of 1968. The chief architect of the anti-inflation policies of the Fifth Republic has been Valéry Giscard d'Estaing, twice minister of finance.

In these as in many other domestic policy areas, the president has merely supported policies formulated by his ministers. And yet his

[29] IFOP polls, as reported in *Le Monde,* January 1, 1971.

support, however passive, has been critical to the minister's success. Both Faure and Giscard d'Estaing left important marks on French policy, so long as the president added his authority to theirs. When it no longer served the president's interests to keep them, they were replaced. (Giscard left the Ministry of Finance in January 1966, but returned to head it once more in July 1969.)

When one moves from the level of major policy to the level of day-to-day management of government affairs, the president ceases to be a principal actor. Here the prime minister is the chief coordinator, the ministers are the chief administrators, and the high civil servants are frequently the powers behind the throne. Since laws do not implement themselves, the administration is forever preparing decrees and ordinances to flesh out the skeleton of the law. In a very real sense the civil servants who prepare these ordinances are contributing to the policy-making process, just as they do when drafting legislative proposals.

It takes a confident and knowledgeable minister to change procedures and policies which his high civil servants view as the proper and customary manner of doing things. Yet with persistence and political support from above, the politicians can prevail. One interesting example is to be found in the history of the Debré law of 1959, which offered varying levels of government financial aid to private schools in return for varying degrees of state control.[30] A Ministry of Education known for its secular tradition was forced to accept and to administer a program of state aid for religious schools. In the process the minister himself, a high civil servant with socialist leanings, André Boulloche, resigned in protest. After the law was enacted, a resistant civil service rejected a high proportion of the early requests for aid "contracts." Eventually, however, the vast majority of private schools were granted support. Given the strength and the persistence of the government, the civil servants could neither block the bill's passage nor for long sabotage its implementation. French civil servants clearly play an important (and often conservative) role in the policy-making process; but their power and independence in the Fifth Republic must not be exaggerated.

The Role of Parliament

Humble as its present role may be in historical perspective, Parliament still helps to shape domestic legislation. The government often accepts parliamentary amendments to its bills, although rarely on the

[30] For a case study of the Debré law, see Bernard Brown, "The Decision to Subsidize Private Schools," in Brown and Christoph, *Cases in Comparative Politics,* pp. 113–147.

central features of the proposal. Parliamentary amendments, sometimes offered in committee and sometimes on the floor, helped to shape not only the Faure educational reforms but also, for example, the Debré law of 1959 on private schools, the value-added tax law of 1963, which helped to simplify France's complex fiscal system, and the adoptions law of 1966, which strengthened the legal rights of adoptive parents.[31] On occasion, particularly since de Gaulle's resignation, even the Senate makes its amendments stick. For example, the "anti-wreckers" bill of 1970, which makes participants liable for damages incurred in riots and demonstrations, was amended by the Senate. A joint Senate-Assembly conference committee then reached a compromise which satisfied Senate objections and also met with the approval of the Assembly.

Even on occasions when Parliament seems to be exerting little influence, behind the scenes the UDR caucus and the leaders of the Gaullist parties may be raising objections which the government will meet before sending a bill to Parliament. Obviously the president and the prime minister must maintain their parliamentary majority. It is the job of the minister for relations with Parliament to rally that majority in support of government bills. In the main, the minister for relations with Parliament serves as a kind of high ranking whip. Like the whips of the British House of Commons, however, he also reports to the government upon signs of discontent among the ranks. Even in Gaullist France, over the long run the government is limited in its actions by what its supporters will accept.

Members of Parliament play another traditional role quite apart from the enactment of major laws. In the Fifth Republic, as in its predecessors, each deputy, each senator acts as an ambassador for his constituency. He is expected to lobby such ministries as Interior, Education, Construction, and Agriculture in support of the applications for national funds submitted by local governments in his district, on whose councils he may also serve. The member of Parliament also is viewed by his constituents as an ombudsman, a one-man grievance committee whose job it is to defend the interests of individuals and groups within his constituency in their battles with the national administration. Among the costs of this ambassadorial role is the heavy burden of tasks which it places upon the members of Parliament and the time spent by various ministries dealing with numerous requests for special consideration. The major benefit is a slight humanization of the relationship between the citizen and the national machinery for policy-making and administration.

[31] On the tax bill of 1963 and the adoptions bill of 1966, see Williams, *The French Parliament,* pp. 93–97.

The Role of Interest Groups

So far we have reviewed the policy-makers *within* the institutions of government. These institutions, of course, do not exist in a vacuum. In France, as in all democratic political systems, the government normally prefers to enlist the cooperation of major groups which will be affected by a law. If, for example, farmers generally are bitterly hostile to an agricultural reform, the government may be faced with two unpalatable alternatives: to abandon implementation of the law or to use coercion and risk producing violent demonstrations and the loss of farmers' votes. Even if the government chooses to use coercion, the means available to it in a free society may well be insufficient to force compliance.[32]

A relevant case in point is the miners' strike in 1963 in France's nationalized coal industry. On March 1, 1963 three major unions announced a strike. The government quickly issued a requisition decree, signed by de Gaulle, ordering all miners to stay on the job. The miners, angered by the government's tough response, stayed out of the mines for more than a month. The government at first announced that there would be no negotiations until work resumed. It refrained, however, from dispatching troops or police to break the strike. By late March, de Gaulle and the government were ready not only to negotiate, but to offer major concessions, including a substantial wage increase. On April 3 an agreement was reached with the unions. Two days later the workers returned to the mines. Even for the proud de Gaulle, backing down seemed preferable to the violence and political discredit which would have been among the costs of attempting to enforce the government's order.

Accommodation with interest groups may be reached in France in one or both of two ways. The government may view Parliament as the voice of the citizenry and may accept amendments to its bills when a sizeable number of deputies and senators insist that these are necessary for the protection of particular social and economic groups in society. It appears, for example, that the Parliamentary Association for Free Schools, an organization of members of Parliament sympathetic to Catholic schools, played a significant role in softening state controls over private schools in the Debré law of 1959, thus making the law more acceptable to the church.

A more straightforward means of seeking the support of interested parties is by simply enlisting the cooperation of major organized interests when a bill is being drafted. This seems to have been the pro-

[32] On this point see Beer, *British Politics in the Collectivist Age,* Ch. 12.

cedure followed in drafting the agricultural act of 1962. In order to facilitate this type of collaboration, there are hundreds of permanent advisory councils, many with interest group representatives as members, scattered through the ministries. If the officials of the Ministry of Agriculture wish their advice, representatives of the National Federation of Farmers' Association (FNSEA), as well as those of many other farm organizations, will be readily available. The National Federation of Education (FEN), representing public school teachers, is well represented on the National Council of Education, the chief advisory body in the Ministry of Education. The National Council of French Management (CNPF) selects representatives to a variety of advisory councils in the Planning Commission and in the ministries which deal with industry and finance. Dozens of other organizations are similarly represented.

According to one version of pluralistic democratic theory, a democracy functions most effectively when policy is made through a process of continual compromise and conciliation among the various interests in society. Two criticisms of this theory are often voiced: first that the "public interest" may not always be the lowest common denominator of interest group demands; second, that some sections of society are invariably slighted because of their lack of organization, resources, or access to the policy-making process. Gaullist France is invulnerable to the first criticism. De Gaulle and his successors have tended to view interest groups as suspect and to insist, contrary to the democratic pluralist argument, that only political leaders can define the public interest. And yet interest groups do influence policy in France. Since they do, the second criticism is relevant. Indeed, there are underrepresented elements, chief among them being the working class, which has few spokesmen in Parliament and very limited influence in the ministries. The fault is only partially the Gaullists'. With the exception of the Communists (who often have refused to be drawn into the deliberations of a bourgeois government), the working class has been underorganized and divided, both in partisan politics and in labor organization. In consequence the voices of the business community are less often contradicted than would be the case were labor as united and as willing to participate in the policy process as in Great Britain.

It is clear that the executive branch has gained the upper hand in the Fifth Republic. The dominance of the president in foreign affairs is striking in comparison with earlier French Republics. Comparatively speaking, however, the President of the United States and the Prime Minister of Great Britain control the foreign policies of their countries almost as completely as does the President of France. In the formulation of domestic policy, the participants are more numerous, although ultimate power in this field is far more concentrated in the hands of the chief executive in France than in the United States and probably more so than in Britain, where a tradition of compromise and conciliation softens the impression of one-man government by the prime minister.

The ability of minority interests to block reforms certainly has been weakened, although by no means destroyed, under the Fifth Republic. Parliament has been tamed, but not permanently crippled. It is well to bear in mind that the primary foundation of executive power in France is majority support, both in the National Assembly and in the electorate. Should that support weaken or fail, executive power would weaken or collapse along with it.

9

French Foreign Policy

The historic tendency toward disequilibrium between liberty and authority in internal French politics finds its counterpart in the realm of foreign policy in an abiding disparity between the goals established and obligations assumed by the regime on the one hand, and the resources at France's disposal to meet these objectives on the other. Between the first and second world wars the responsibility for overseeing the peace of Europe in the face of an increasingly nationalistic and more powerful German state fell largely to France. In the Fourth Republic, despite a progressively enlightened colonial policy with respect to Africa south of the Sahara, French leadership set itself against the current of decolonization in Indochina and Algeria at the eventual cost of the Republic itself. Under the tutelage of General de Gaulle the Fifth Republic consciously pursued a policy designed to reassert France, a middle-range power in the framework of the current international system, as a nation of the first rank with the status and prestige — if not the power and capability — of the continental superpowers of the mid-twentieth century. Thus, for the past fifty years, either voluntarily or as a consequence of the force of circumstance, France like Sisyphus has been engaged in a struggle against its environment.

The Continuity of French Foreign Policy

France's postwar international conduct is not as unique as some would claim. The contrast between postwar British and French foreign policy for example is more apparent than real. Britain, no less than France, sought to postpone, if not avoid, coming to grips with the implications of an international system that was significantly different from the one which existed before the second world war. Their respective moments of truth came at different times and in different contexts, but the lessons for both were essentially the same. The failure of

French policy toward Germany in the late 1940's bore first witness to the illusoriness of her assumptions and expectations, but it was in the arena of colonial policy that the magnitude of postwar change and ferment was brought home to the French nation. Britain's inherent weaknesses were less evident at the outset of the postwar era and took a longer time to surface. But even when they did, Britain made little effort to scale down her global aspirations and pretensions to great power status to the level of her limited resources. Indeed, in one sense France proved to be the more adaptive former great power for although she was engulfed in colonial wars for a long time after the Liberation, she ultimately did shed her colonial garb and concentrated her attention on Europe. Britain meanwhile continued and continues to divide its efforts and loyalties among the three worlds to which Winston Churchill once said Britain belonged: the Commonwealth, the Atlantic, and Europe.

It should also be emphasized that despite the appearance of radical change in the foreign policies of the Fourth and Fifth Republics, the continuities between these two regimes tend to be greater than their differences. One persistent feature of both Republics is the effort to increase France's role and influence, regionally and globally, although significant differences emerge in the selection of means to this end. Another is the failure of either regime to bring objectives and resources into equilibrium. The Fourth Republic tried to develop new forms of interstate relationships in order to improve French capabilities; the Fifth Republic looked with suspicion and even hostility on integrative schemes and focused its efforts on fostering domestic stability, promoting economic and monetary strength, and restoring classic patterns of diplomacy in order to sustain the drive toward national destiny. Both regimes saw France as a major power, and both set out to recover as much as possible of what had been lost. Thus one discovers many common threads in French postwar policy toward the Atlantic Alliance, Eastern Europe, the Soviet Union, black Africa and even to some degree, European unification. We are, of course, speaking of propensities rather than absolutes, and both in terms of style and intention differences are to be found. What is important is to recognize these differences for what they are and not to ascribe false meaning to them.

Several factors have contributed to this continuity. First, the Fourth Republic was interposed between two Gaullist regimes. In the twenty-five years between the Liberation and de Gaulle's resignation from the presidency in April 1969, foreign policy was under his direct guidance for more than twelve years and under his influence — through public interventions and the presence of supporters both in Parliament and, from 1954 in government — for even longer than that. It was characteristic of the Fourth Republic that while it sought to adapt French policy to the changing realities of the international environment and while it made some dramatic and far-reaching decisions, it never really undertook a thoroughgoing reassessment of the basic premises of French foreign policy. During the interregnum de Gaulle too adapted in some measure to changing circumstances. Consequently, when he resumed power in 1958 he found little difficulty in maintaining the broad outline of existing French diplomacy.

Second, relatively few if any among the French elite and articulators of public opinion were disposed to challenge the provisional government's insistence on postwar French rights and on international recognition of French status and rank to which de Gaulle ascribed so much importance. The humiliation of "defeat-occupation-collaboration-liberation" had had a profoundly debilitating effect on public morale for which the resistance movement could only partially compensate. Calls for national unity and renewal based on France's historic position and rights and on her participation (however modest or technical) in victory over Germany were a welcome antidote. The symbolic importance of international recognition of French claims in Europe and in her empire outweighed any concern that there was an existing, and perhaps growing, asymmetry between the policies being formulated and French capacity to sustain them. De Gaulle's call to *grandeur* tapped the wellsprings of deep-seated traditions, feelings, and beliefs, and it is not surprising that subsequent political leaders were reluctant to stray too far from that course. As Raymond Aron reminds us, the political leaders who succeeded de Gaulle in 1946 "contrary to all legendary accounts, took over without abandoning the policy of greatness."[1]

Third there was the political system of the Fourth Republic itself. Weak and unstable coalition governments representing temporary alliances, often brought together only for the purpose of resolving a particular crisis, were not inclined, let alone equipped, to make dramatic foreign policy decisions. To the extent that survival was their goal, procrastination or avoidance of making choices was an essential practice. The improbability of being able to reach consensus on alternatives to existing policies led many cabinets to avoid grappling with foreign policy issues unless and until they reached crisis proportions, usually because of external pressures. Alternatively, foreign policy questions might be introduced precisely in order to undermine an existing precarious consensus. Consequently, in the Fourth Republic foreign policy occasionally was caught up in the domestic game of politics. These

[1] Raymond Aron, *France, Steadfast and Changing* (Cambridge, Mass.: Harvard University Press, 1960), p. 148.

factors minimized the possibilities for long-term planning or for consistency in the execution of foreign policy, and it is often pointed out that even the relative stability of leadership at the level of Minister of Foreign Affairs (only seven persons held this post during the Fourth Republic) was insufficient to offset the enervating effects of the overall political system. Needless to say this had decisively negative effects on France's international image.

The Role of the President

The arena of foreign policy was paramount for General de Gaulle, and this for reasons revealed in the opening sentences of his memoirs: "France is not truly herself except in the first rank; . . . only vast enterprises are capable of counterbalancing the ferments of dispersal which are inherent in her people."[2] Thus, on the one hand, destiny compels France to international prominence, and, on the other, a nation like France requires a strong and dynamic foreign policy to overcome inherent internal discord. One is reminded of Ortega y Gasset's observation that "the great nations have been made not from within but from without. A successful international policy, a policy of high emprise, is the only thing that creates a fruitful internal policy."[3] For Ortega, nations were built around vast enterprises; for de Gaulle, the latter were necessary to maintain the nation against the pull of centrifugal forces. The interdependence between foreign policy and the domestic political system is thus established: a decisive, coherent, and consistent foreign policy requires a strong and stable political system; a policy of national ambition helps to reinforce the stability of political institutions.

Constitutional engineering may be a first step toward fulfillment of the goal of stability and effectiveness, but analysis of the constitutional document does not contribute significantly to our understanding of the nature and operation of foreign policy in the Fifth Republic. Although presidential powers were augmented in a number of respects — dissolution, referenda, emergency powers — presidential prerogatives in the foreign policy field were only marginally increased over those held in earlier political regimes. One of the few significant changes was the restitution to the president of the right, held by him in the Third Republic, to negotiate international treaties. In the Fourth Republic the president only had the right to be informed of such negotiations. As we saw earlier, the constitution vests responsibility for determining and conducting the policy of the nation (foreign as well as domestic) in the

[2] De Gaulle, *War Memoirs,* Vol. I, p. 3.

[3] José Ortega y Gasset, *Invertebrate Spain,* trans. Mildred Adams (New York: W. W. Norton, 1937), p. 29.

government (article 20) and responsibility for national defense in the hands of the prime minister (article 21). Yet nowhere is the political activity of the president more manifest than in matters of external policy and national defense.

To de Gaulle these matters were too important to be left to the politicians. Justification for such conduct could be found in abstract principle if not in the written word of the constitution. The provision in article 5 that the president "shall be the guarantor of the independence of the nation, of its territorial integrity, of its treaties," is the foundation of this interpretation. As de Gaulle stated in 1962 in support of his referendum on the manner of electing the president:

> The keystone of our system is the new institution of a President designated by the French people to be the head of the state and the guide of France. Far from . . . being obligated as in the past to remain within a role of counsel and representation, the constitution vests him with distinguished responsibility for the destiny of France and of the Republic.[4]

Elaborating on the means and powers at the disposal of the president, de Gaulle noted that "these powers . . . lead the President to inspire, guide and animate national action. It happens that he has to conduct it directly, as I did, for example, throughout the Algerian affair."[5] The statement on Algerian policy could have been applied to every sphere of foreign policy activity.

The effects of the concentration of foreign policy activity in the presidency were felt everywhere — in government, in Parliament, and in the administration. In the case of the government it meant the transfer of initiative and policy formulation from itself to the president. This does not mean that the cabinet was totally without influence but such influence as it did exert was spasmodic and marginal. One of the few instances where de Gaulle appeared to be challenged successfully from within his government was on the question of his war on the dollar, and it resulted not in a change of direction, but in a modification of the tone of policy. The time devoted by Parliament to foreign policy questions is no less than that spent by the Fourth Republic, but time is a poor measure of influence.[6] Parliament can hold the government ac-

---

[4] *Major Addresses, Statements and Press Conferences of General Charles de Gaulle, May, 1958 to Jan. 1964* (French Embassy, Press and Information Division), p. 191. Hereinafter cited as *Major Addresses*.

[5] *Ibid.*

[6] On the question of Parliament's role in foreign relations, see Jean Baillou and Pierre Pelletier, *Les Affaires Etrangères* (Paris: Presses Universitaires de France, 1962), especially pp. 290–315.

countable for its acts but it has no access to the president in the realm of political responsibility. Bringing down a government as executor of presidential policy carries with it the risk of dissolution at the hand of the president. Thus, Parliament is condemned to a more or less academic role in the realm of foreign policy making. As for the administration, such discretion as it had been able to exercise in weak and unstable governments evaporated in the presence of the Gaullist regime. The Ministry of Foreign Affairs has been much more the executor than the formulator of policy — a trend which had been in evidence for some time, but for different reasons, under the preceding regime. On the other hand, the existence of coherent and continuous government has enabled that ministry and others with responsibility in the realm of foreign affairs to operate with greater efficiency and effectiveness.

The Aims of French Foreign Policy

Three themes pervade postwar French foreign policy: security, status, and independence. National and international conditions and the temperament of leadership have led to different emphasis at different times. However, these three themes have persisted since the Liberation, and most governments have sought to maximize all three. The desire to avoid making a definitive choice among them led to a certain ambivalence of policy and occasionally to contradictory claims and situations. The most important substantive policies of postwar France — Franco-German relations, European unification, Atlantic Alliance, relations with the Soviet bloc, the *force de frappe* and colonial relations — can be subsumed under one or more of these categories.

Security is the first concern of any nation. For liberated France it was an obsession. Three times in seventy years the nation had gone to war against its eastern neighbor. It is not surprising then that following the Liberation the German question completely absorbed French security concerns. De Gaulle reduced the issue to its essentials: "To make France's recovery possible, the German collectivity must lose its capacity for aggression. . . . existence under a threat of war from a neighboring state which had so often demonstrated its taste and its talent for conquest would be incompatible with France's economic recovery, her political stability, and . . . moral equilibrium. . . ."[7] The provisional government mapped out a policy based on the principles of economic dismemberment and political decentralization of the hereditary enemy: detachment of the Ruhr, separation of the Rhineland, annexation of the Saar — this was the essence of France's German policy

[7] De Gaulle, *War Memoirs,* Vol. III p. 57.

in the immediate postwar era. Alliances to the east and the west were to sustain this traditional and reactive policy, but the emergence of the cold war and the division of Germany and the continent ended what little support France had received from her wartime allies in either the east or the west.

The cold war brought the latent bipolar structure of the postwar international system to the surface. It also led France to redefine her security interests: not only was it necessary to reconsider the nature of Franco-German relations; there was also the question of how to deal with the more immediate security threat posed by the Soviet Union. The Fourth Republic's response to these new conditions took two interdependent forms. At the level of East-West relations France declared solidarity with the Anglo-Saxon powers and a reluctant readiness to commit herself to the concept of Atlantic alliance. At the level of Franco-German relations, the French government shifted from a policy based on the assumption of mutual hostility to one based on the principle of reconciliation. This was codified in the policy of integration first manifested by the Schuman plan for a coal and steel community. Unable to control Germany through classic alliances France opted for the creation of a strongly organized West European system in which German recovery could be made compatible with French security interests. Of course it would have been untenable for France to opt for alliance with the Anglo-Saxon powers recognizing their policy of cooperation and reconciliation toward Germany and then take a diametrically opposed stand.

However reluctantly made, these choices represented a departure from the preceding policy and introduced an abiding tension between the values of security and independence. But how much of a departure were these choices? Beyond security and a policy of unmitigated insistence on recognition of French great power status (based on historic right rather than material power), de Gaulle originally charted for France a course of independent diplomacy between the two superpowers. France was to be not a lieutenant of either but a mediator for both. Hopefully she would be the spokesman for a Western Europe so organized as to avoid becoming the object of a political struggle between the two extracontinental powers. Hopefully, Britain would be an active participant in this play. Prior to the deterioration of Franco-British relations over the Middle East, in 1944 de Gaulle tried to attract Britain to the enterprise so that the two could "together create peace, as twice in thirty years they have together confronted war,"[8] but Churchill demurred in favor of reinforcing Anglo-American links. Thus the concept of European organization was not alien to de Gaulle's

[8] *Ibid.*, p. 59.

thinking; the differences between de Gaulle and his domestic opposition came over the question of form — integration versus cooperation. We shall return to this theme below. As for an Atlantic alliance, it was the logical outcome of international polarization. De Gaulle ultimately accepted the principle of the alliance though with some concern about its implications for eventual German entry and rearmament. The structure of the alliance also perturbed him. In 1954 he warned the government to distinguish between a "good alliance and a bad protectorate."

France's European and Atlantic policies between 1950 and 1958 demonstrate the problem of balancing independence, status, and security. In neither case did she have easy relations with her partners. European integration and Atlantic alliance were supported by different groups in France for convergent and occasionally overlapping rather than identical reasons. To some, European integration deserved support because of the implications for French security of a revived and independent Germany. The equation was simple — exchange sovereignty for security. The same reasons applied in the case of NATO — at the time of its debate in the French National Assembly there was no lack of reference to the fact that NATO provided a shield against potential German aggressiveness as well as against the more immediate Soviet threat. For others, European integration was a vehicle to recover the lost status that France, acting on a purely independent basis, could not reestablish. This is the notion of "independence through interdependence," and is one of the more persistent themes of French "Europeans." As one of the most articulate spokesmen of this school of thought, Maurice Faure, stated in 1964:

> France is too small to play the role of full partner with the "greats" on the international scene. She can only find a role comparable to her past . . . if she resumes leadership of the crusade for an egalitarian community of peoples in Europe which would be large enough to meet the demands of this half of the twentieth century.[9]

Central to the thinking of this school is the idea that if France will lead, others will follow; it is a mid-century version of another French theme related to imperial ventures — *la mission civilisatrice.* Still other Frenchmen — the "pure" Europeans — supported the idea of European integration because they believed that the peace and prosperity of Western Europe, hence France, compelled a policy designed to transcend the existing state system and the substitution of reconstruction through integration for reconstruction through the assertion of na-

[9] *Journal Officiel, Débats, Assemblée Nationale,* Nov. 3, 1964, p. 4428.

ional sovereignty. Status and power might be, but were not necessarily, germane to this line of thinking — economic prosperity certainly was.

It is an interesting feature of French "Europeanism" that it often finds its most ardent and uncompromising advocates in the parties out of power. The experience of the Fifth Republic is a case in point. Europeanism, like the crusade against de Gaulle's *force de frappe* is a rallying point for anti-Gaullist forces. It is a modern manifestation of the negative majorities which characterized the Fourth Republic. Whether such a majority could maintain itself as a governing coalition is highly problematical precisely because of the positions taken against the Gaullist European policies have been a consequence of expedience rather than of positive, ordered convictions.

In the Fourth Republic there never was a clear and consistent European majority. The Coal and Steel Community, sectorally limited and politically relatively innocuous, garnered considerable support. Communists and Gaullists formed the main opposition. The European Defense Community was another matter. Gaullists and Communists maintained their negative cohesion but with the exception of the MRP the "European" parties — SFIO, Radicals, and Independents — did not. EDC foundered not on the sensitive issue of German rearmament; it failed because in the last analysis a majority of French politicians were unwilling to trade the inherent loss of sovereignty and independence for the security it would buy. The formula seemed to be "as much integration as necessary, as much independence as possible."

Atlantic alliance politics reveal a similar situation. NATO was initially regarded as essential to French security. It also was seen as a vehicle for augmenting French status: American power would be at the service of common (and French) interests. While France engaged in extracontinental wars to preserve her empire, her traditional continental security interests and those raised by the Soviet threat would be guaranteed by the Atlantic pact. France's colonial policy, however, was a major source of friction between Paris and Washington. These difficulties, which had their origins in the wartime hostility of the United States to the continuation of imperial structures, were a constant source of stress on the Atlantic alliance. The Algerian war was the source of the Suez crisis of 1956 which in turn highlighted the difference of interests among members of the alliance and stimulated French desires for independence and efforts to find means for conducting a more autonomous diplomacy. From this experience came an intensified effort in the direction of becoming a nuclear power and revival of interest in building a European community.

Within the alliance France aspired to equality of status with the Anglo-Saxon powers but this was precluded by the "special relationship" between London and Washington, with the result that France felt increasingly alienated and frustrated by the notion that her opportunities for prior consultation with the United States were inadequate. Because the two "privileged" powers in the alliance possessed nuclear weapons, France came to identify nuclear capability with political influence. Indeed, the French drive for nuclear status was already several years under way when the then prime minister Felix Gaillard stated in 1958 that:

> If in the division of tasks within NATO in research and manufacture, and if, in the precise conditions of use of these arms, France has the feeling of being treated as a subordinate partner, it is evident that this will lead France much more easily to undertake her own (nuclear) effort.[10]

Subordination to the Anglo-Saxon powers was not what France had bargained for when she entered into the North Atlantic alliance. Yet, by the end of the Fourth Republic it seemed that the "good alliance" had indeed turned into a "bad protectorate." Despite these differences, however, the Fourth Republic by and large confined its revisionist efforts to restructuring relationships within the framework of the Atlantic alliance itself. The determination to acquire nuclear weapons, the pursuit of efforts (modified in terms of supranationalism) to create a nucleus of like-minded West European states around France and on behalf of whom France could serve as global spokesman, the further tightening of relations between Paris and Bonn, were all part of this goal. In the context of the themes of independence, status, and security, the following statement by André Fontaine provides a succinct composite judgment:

> The Fourth Republic had turned over the keys of its defense to an American commander-in-chief, dependent on the decisions of the American Government, and was on the way to turning over the keys to its economy to a supranational European community. It had not, however, transferred its sovereignty in any absolute or definitive way. It had loudly proclaimed its adherence to the ideal of European federation, yet it had consistently held that the world-wide responsibilities of France precluded its disappearing into a supranational Europe. It had gotten the production of its own atomic bomb under way, thwarted projects for a European army . . . and, for all its lack of power, had not accepted American terms for the installation of missile launching-sites or American atomic stockpiles on its soil.[11]

[10] *U.S. News and World Report,* Jan. 3, 1958, p. 61.
[11] André Fontaine, "What is French Policy?" *Foreign Affairs,* Oct. 1966, pp. 64–65.

The Pursuit of Independence

If we were to select one concept which most distinguished de Gaulle from his predecessors perhaps it would be "integration."[12] For de Gaulle, the fundamental reality was the nation-state. The state is "an instrument of decision, action and ambition, expressing and serving the national interest alone."[13] The nation is transcendent; ideologies are ephemeral. As Alfred Grosser points out, the international norm in de Gaulle's view was that of "nation-states confronting one another without reference to ideologies" but only in terms of national interests.[14] These considerations were summed up in the September 1960 press conference in which de Gaulle spoke to the question of the unification of Europe:

> To build Europe . . . to unite it is . . . essential. . . . All that is necessary . . . is to proceed, not by following our dreams, but according to realities. Now what are the realities of Europe? What are the pillars on which it can be built? . . . The States . . . are the only entities that have the right to order and the authority to act. To imagine that something can be built that would be effective for action and that would be approved by the peoples outside and above the States – this is a dream.[15]

As for the national reality that is France, de Gaulle asserted that France could not be France without grandeur. Grandeur was not conceived as a particular policy but as a posture, an attitude of dignity and self-respect. Neither of these is possible for a subject people or dependent polity. Hence, *independence* was an essential ingredient in de Gaulle's concept of national interest. Independence could be an end in itself but it also was a necessary precondition to the attainment of "rank" in the hierarchy of nations. For de Gaulle there were two classes of states in that hierarchy — the great powers which had a universal vocation and the others who were confined to more limited arenas of activity. There was no question in de Gaulle's mind to which class of state France must belong.

Certain consequences flowed from the claim of independence. First, it could only be secured if a nation could assure its own defense. De Gaulle did not believe that France could defend itself in the mod-

---

[12] The following discussion is based largely on Lawrence Sheinman, "Nationalism and Politics in Contemporary France," *International Organization,* XXIII, No. 4 (Autumn 1969), pp. 834–858, especially pp. 841–844.

[13] Charles de Gaulle, cited in Alfred Grosser, *French Foreign Policy Under de Gaulle* (Boston: Little, Brown, 1967), p. 15.

[14] *Ibid.*, p. 19.

[15] *Major Addresses,* pp. 92–93.

ern age on the same terms as could the United States or the Soviet Union. But he did think that France's defense could not long be "allowed to remain outside the national framework or to become an integral part of, or mingled with, something else. . . ."[16] The target of this thought, of course, was the integrated structure of the North Atlantic Treaty Organization. On the other hand, this was not a plea for Charles Maurras' "la France seule." "It is obvious," de Gaulle once stated,

> that one country, especially one such as ours, cannot in the present day and age and could not conduct a major modern war all by itself. To have allies goes without saying for us in the historic period we are in.[17]

Alliances, therefore, are normal but an integrated one such as NATO aspired to be was intolerable,

> for alliances have no absolute virtues, whatever may be the sentiments on which they are based.[18]

In saying this de Gaulle was reading a lesson in history to the United States which had wrongly assumed that NATO was inherently different from other and earlier alliances; that the interests of the participants were identical and even transferable from the European to other arenas; and that initial common perceptions of common interests would not change over time.

In view of the Gaullist interpretation of alliances and insistence on national defense, it was axiomatic that independence in the modern age would require a nuclear capability:

> For, however terrifying these means of destruction may be, and precisely because they are so terrifying, a great state that does not possess them while others do is not master of its destiny.[19]

Second, independence must be viewed not only from the perspective of one's present enemies but also of one's present friends and prospective protagonists; the dialogue between states is a dialogue of force. The nuclear dimension of Gaullist diplomacy is not simply a strategic factor; it is a function of the conviction that between states, whether enemies or allies, diplomacy can only be conducted from situations of strength. Third, independence entails monetary policies aimed at en-

---

[16] Charles de Gaulle, Speech at l'Ecole de Guerre, Paris, November 3, 1959, cited in Macridis, *De Gaulle: Implacable Ally*, p. 133.

[17] *Major Addresses*, p. 216.

[18] *Ibid.*

[19] Charles de Gaulle, Speech to officer corps at Strasbourg, November 23, 1961, cited in Macridis, *De Gaulle: Implacable Ally*, p. 137.

suring financial independence which in turn strengthens freedom of political action. The persistent French attack on sterling and the dollar in the mid- and late 1960's dramatized this aspect of the claim for independence: just as the limitation of nuclear weaponry to a single state expresses the strategic hegemony of the nation that possesses it so an international monetary system that treats a particular currency as equivalent to gold raises the potential hegemony of that nation in the monetary sphere.

Independence, again, lies at the heart of Gaullist policy with respect to European and Atlantic questions. His long-range objective was to free Europe from what he called the two hegemonies (Soviet and American) and to assure to France a central role in an eventually re-unified and independent Europe. It was a policy that aimed for an independent France in an independent Europe but a Europe in which some (France) would be more equal than others (Germany) by virtue of certain limitations placed on the latter in such areas as nuclear defense. It was assumed that Germany would agree to do without nuclear arms in order not to jeopardize the possibility of its reunification. From this perspective de Gaulle's policies were those of a liberator: France placed herself at the service of European independence.

The short-term aim of this policy was nothing less than the transformation of the bipolar status quo in which two superpowers dominated the activities of the European states. The United States was thought to pose a particularly serious threat for, through the medium of the Atlantic relationship, it had gained military, political, and economic access to Europe and risked, through the ties of an alliance which tended to share burdens rather than power, committing an unwilling Europe to policies and obligations it would rather not undertake. After the Cuban missile crisis of 1962 de Gaulle went one step further: he came to consider the international power structure more unipolar than bipolar and shifted his policy from tacit support of the United States to an attempt to redress the balance. For a leader who believed ideologies were ephemeral this was not a difficult thing to do. This was not a reversal of alliances but rather a decreasing association of France with American-defined western policies and an increasingly warmer posture toward the Soviet Union. This shift in some measure explains why Paris aligned itself against Israel and the United States in 1967 and also the intensification of France's public protests against American policy in the Far East. Such a posture also enabled de Gaulle to encourage the national self-assertion of East European states vis-à-vis the Soviet Union and added legitimacy to his claims to speak on behalf of an independent international policy.

For de Gaulle resolution of the European and German problems could not be achieved if Europe and the United States were too interdependent or if Europe were too integrated within itself. Hence, a depreciation of the value of NATO and Atlanticism and the pursuit of a policy aimed at increasing detachment of France and its European partners from the United States, while warning against excessive institutionalized action in Western Europe for fear (purely hypothetical) that such integration would preclude chances for a reunification of the two halves of Europe. If, argued de Gaulle, integrated solutions on either the Atlantic or European level were neither feasible nor desirable insofar as they tended to perpetuate rather than to transform the European status quo, then priority had to be given to nationally based solutions. As France was the only continental power with no external claims and no avowed enemies it was free to undertake a dialogue with the East European countries and was thus vaulted into the position of leadership if not of exclusive spokesman. The dissolution of linkages based on ideological confrontation and the reassertion of national personality and national independence was seen by Gaullist France as the great hope for Europe's future. The vision was of a Europe living under a new balance which excluded the United States (though to what degree was never fully clear), rested on the foundation of the nation-state, and in which the western half of Europe was under the guardianship of a France endowed with nuclear power. These considerations explain de Gaulle's rejection of President Kennedy's "Grand Design" for an Atlantic partnership between a united Europe and the United States as well as his rejection of Britain (America's stalking horse) from Europe.

The concept of independence, finally, helps to resolve the contradiction between de Gaulle's ultimate reputation as a great decolonizer (both Algeria and black Africa) and his earlier postwar commitment to the reassertion and consolidation of the French empire from North Africa to Indochina. In 1944, as we have seen, the central concern was the recovery of rank and recognition as a great power. For a country that had very little else of a material nature to offer in support of such claims, and to the extent that the control of territory was identified with power and influence in international affairs, the restitution of the empire was axiomatic. This dimension of de Gaulle's colonial policy is evident from his memoirs where he acknowledged that if the overseas possessions were cut off from France, France's role and claims in the postwar world would be reduced; but if they remained associated with France the latter "would have every opportunity for action on the continent."[20]

The empire has a special significance for de Gaulle beyond its supportive value to claims of great power status. Although, as Denis

[20] De Gaulle, *War Memoirs,* Vol. III, p. 253.

Brogan has noted, de Gaulle "belonged to a school of French soldiers who thought that the empire was a diversion from the realities and interests of French power in Europe,"[21] — i.e. he was a "mainlander" rather than a "colonial" — the collapse of France in 1940 and the availability of colonial territories on which to fall back made a strong impression on the General. The memoirs once again offer evidence: "The war had seen our army fall to pieces . . . the government capitulate, the nation endure occupation. . . . But by virtue of a kind of miracle independence and sovereignty had been maintained in the remotest parts of the Empire."[22] One of those "remote" parts was French Equatorial Africa and it was there, at Brazzaville in 1944, that de Gaulle set down the policy toward empire that was to condition the first postwar decade of French colonial policy — the emancipation of the masses in social and political terms, but not the independence of nations. If the colonies had not existed there would have been no French territory to which to retreat after June 1940!

The constitution of the Fifth Republic created the French Community. Community was a concept that suggested an incomplete metamorphosis of de Gaulle's attitudes toward the importance of colonial possessions for under it France, acting through its president, retained control over the external and defense policies of the membership. When however, the community proved less than viable, de Gaulle swiftly moved to the idea of association between France and fully sovereign ex-colonial states, preferring the maintenance of good relations with the former colonies to formal, but tension-creating, ties between them and the mainland. Independence for France was the key to this orientation: a nation without free hands was not independent. To the extent that there were colonial claims on the political system which prevented freedom of action, those claims had to be satisfied; until then the vision of a fully independent diplomacy could not be fulfilled. Hence, the Algerian settlement and the liquidation of what remained of the French empire in Africa.

A kaleidoscopic diplomacy was put in the service of the Gaullist vision. The apparent discontinuities could be explained partly in terms of the responses the diplomacy elicited, partly in terms of the nature of the international situation at any given time. To a significant degree de Gaulle sought to impose his will on events, but he was not Don Quixote riding against the windmills. Upon his return to power in 1958 de Gaulle faced the national agony of Algeria and incipient crisis over Berlin. His first step was to reiterate in more dramatic and forceful terms the demand which his predecessors had made in muted form —

[21] Denis Brogan, "The Legacy of General de Gaulle," *Interplay*, June–July, 1969, p. 15.
[22] De Gaulle, *War Memoirs*, Vol. III, p. 51.

equality of status with the United States and Great Britain through the creation of a tridirectorate in the Atlantic alliance to coordinate global strategy and the use of nuclear weapons. Acceptance of this policy would have undermined the goal of French independence, but it would have catapulted France into an exalted first-rank status and given her significant influence over the uses of American power. A compelling argument has been made that de Gaulle assumed the bid would be turned down but needed the rejection to lay the groundwork for his undeclared goal of disengaging France from NATO.[23] Starting in February 1959 France took the first of a number of steps toward this end by withdrawing French naval units in the Mediterranean from NATO command.

Failing at the Altantic level, France turned her attention to her partners in the European Community. In 1961 de Gaulle proposed the "Fouchet Plan" for the intergovernmental coordination of foreign and defense policies among the six member states. The plan was rejected partly because of a general sense that this path would lead to the undermining of European integration and the weakening of Europe's Atlantic ties, partly because of Dutch reluctance to accept the Fouchet Plan without British participation. De Gaulle's next move was toward a Franco-German partnership to wean Bonn away from its Atlantic orientation and toward greater reliance on France as its spokesman to the East and its defender in Europe. Once again, however, de Gaulle's plans were thwarted as his principle German supporter, Adenauer, slipped from power and the German Bundestag conditioned its ratification of the 1963 Franco-German Treaty of Friendship on the maintenance of the Atlantic alliance and European integration. The final thrust of Gaullist policy was characterized by efforts 1) to disengage France from NATO which was achieved in March 1966; 2) to create a Europe from the "Atlantic to the Urals" by inaugurating a policy of "detente-entente-cooperation" with the Soviet Union; 3) to make France the spokesman of the Third World against the American policy of intervention, principally in Vietnam. The offensive against American hegemony was carried to America's front line in Asia when at Phnom-Penh, Cambodia in September 1966 de Gaulle spoke dramatically against

a process [escalation] more and more condemned by numerous peoples of Europe, Africa and Latin America, and ultimately more and more threatening to the peace of the world

and called for American withdrawal for

[23] John Newhouse, *De Gaulle and the Anglo-Saxons* (New York: Viking Press, 1970).

there is no likelihood whatsover of the peoples of Asia submitting to the rule of a foreigner who has come from the other side of the Pacific, whatever his intention.[24]

The internal crisis in France in May 1968 revealed the fragility of the French franc and the vulnerability of the economy; the Czechoslovakian crisis in the summer of that year put the concept of a Europe stretching from the Atlantic to the Urals at a very distant remove. These events, coupled with a rapidly developing Soviet presence in the Mediterranean, an area of basic concern to French security, did not force a reversal of French policy, but they did contribute to a Franco-American rapprochement. Foreign Minister Michel Debré referred to the Czechoslovakian invasion as an unfortunate *"accident de route"* thus suggesting that it had not altered the general direction of French foreign policy; and de Gaulle blamed the turn of events on the *"politique des blocs"* which he had unceasingly denounced and for the elimination of which the pan-European policy of détente-entente-cooperation had been created.

Generally, however, the signs pointed toward a moderation in French policy. Thus, the strategic doctrine of *"défense tous azimuts"* (defense directed against all points on the compass and hence a neutralist doctrine) enunciated in December 1967 by the then French chief of staff, General Charles Ailleret gave way, in modified form, to the earlier policy of "directed defense" which distinguished the Soviet Union from the United States. France would not rejoin NATO; nor, however, would she move further away from the Atlantic alliance. The financial crisis of 1968 took its toll on the development of the *force de dissuasion,* setting the program back several years. This in turn meant the continued need for American nuclear protection. The financial crisis also highlighted the strength of West Germany's economy and currency and revealed a growing German disposition toward self-assertion which threatened France's position in the European Economic Community. As a result, de Gaulle in February 1969 raised the possibility of a shift in the French attitude toward British entry into Europe by linking such entry to the transformation of the European Communities into a larger and more amorphous polity, and hence less supranational, but one which would provide an additional counterweight to the political implications of West Germany's burgeoning economic power. For numerous reasons these events failed to materialize. The essential change in de Gaulle's last year in office then seems to be a refocussing of efforts from the pan-European vision of Europe from the Atlantic to the Urals toward the reaffirmation of the need for West European independence and the construction of a Europe based on "realities"

[24] Cited in Alexander Werth, *De Gaulle,* p. 412.

(nation-states) rather than on myths (supranational integration). De Gaulle was never shaken in his conviction that given the conditions of mid-twentieth century a supranational Europe would be nothing more than a valet to the American hegemon.

Independence and Integration

President Pompidou was elected to office on the platform of *continuité* and *ouverture*. The prevailing feature of the early years of the Pompidou *septennat* is the maintenance of a balance between these two themes in the realm of foreign policy. The most striking change undoubtedly has been in the tone and style of foreign policy: monologue has given way to dialogue, bargaining, and compromise; adventurism has yielded to a more conservative and benign policy orientation (evidenced among other things by a relaxing of hostility toward Canada and Israel); visionary politics have been replaced by a more realistic assessment of the relationship between resources, capabilities, and aspirations. Insofar as the distribution of authority among domestic institutions for the control of foreign policy is concerned, however, there is no evidence of the weakening of the presidential role in foreign affairs — the concept of "domaine reservée" persists, although in the context of an expanded participation in the determination and elaboration of policy.

What is evident in the passing of power from de Gaulle to Pompidou is that foreign policy is no longer the predominant concern, and that politics has ceased to prevail over economics in the conduct of foreign policy. The rise of pragmatic politics at the expense of ethereal visions and grand designs is best demonstrated by France's European policy which subsumes policies toward the European Communities, Great Britain, and West Germany. For the current regime European integration is to be judged not from the ideological perspective of nationalism versus supranationalism but in terms of French economic, monetary, and technological interests. The idea of breaking up the Common Market and transforming it into a free trade area (implicit in de Gaulle's overture to Great Britain in February 1969) holds little appeal to de Gaulle's successors who, in defense of French economic interests, have been concerned with tightening and expanding economic arrangements among the EEC members rather than with weakening those ties. Pompidou initiated the summit conference of the EEC states held in December 1969 at The Hague that led to a compromise whereby France, in exchange for terminating opposition on opening negotiations for British entry into the EEC, secured agreements from her partners on completing and strengthening the Common Market. Completing meant reaching final agreement on a definitive financial regulation for the common agricultural policy — a major French interest — while strengthening reflected France's interest in securing closer cooperation and collaboration in the scientific, monetary, and general economic fields. Neither of these economic goals violated Gaullist principles. *Ouverture* was reflected at the domestic level in the distribution of cabinet posts in the government of Chaban-Delmas — the positions most relevant to economic integration (Finance and Economic Affairs, and Agriculture) went to spokesmen for "Europeanism," Valéry Giscard d'Estaing and Jacques Duhamel respectively.

The commitment to *continuité* finds expression in the political realm. Pompidou has defined his view of European union as a "resolute advance toward a union devoid of dreams and surrenders but resting on trust, on realities, on close links between responsible governments ready to impose on themselves common disciplines."[25] The emphasis, as before, is on intergovernmentalism, cooperation, and collaboration, and on the centrality of the nation-states, the "realities." At the Hague summit conference, and subsequently, French spokesmen have emphasized the tangible problems of economic interdependence but, with the complicity of their community partners, circumvented the question of strengthening the central institutions and their supranational powers; no effort has been made to provide the commission with more political weight or legitimacy, and the powers of the European Parliament have been increased only nominally by giving it some enlarged budgetary powers over the resources created by the agreement for financing the common agricultural policy. Furthermore, although the vision of a French dominated pan-Europeanism has slipped from grace, the theme of "European Europe" persists. Thus, in presenting the policy of his government to the National Assembly in June 1969, Chaban-Delmas offered to move "as fast and as far" toward European integration as France's partners desired as long as such a move was "toward a Europe aware of her own destiny."[26] Suitably ambiguous, this Gaullist phrase lurks in the background of negotiations to enlarge the EEC to include Great Britain.

At his press conference of September 1968 de Gaulle remarked that "our desire not to risk an Atlantic absorption is one of the reasons why, much to our regret, we have until now postponed Great Britain's entry into the [European] Community."[27] The changing international situation and the passing of power to Pompidou brought with them the end

[25] Quoted in *The Economist* (London), December 20, 1969.

[26] *Ambassade de France, Service de Presse et d'Information,* Statement by Premier Jacques Chaban-Delmas before the National Assembly on June 20, 1969.

[27] *Ambassade de France, Service de Presse et d'Information,* Press Conference of General de Gaulle, September 9, 1968.

of systematic, doctrinaire opposition to British entry into Europe. The transition does not mean, as we have seen, either an end to the idea of an independent Europe or a return of France to Atlanticism; it does mean, however, that Britain's candidacy will be judged less in terms of *her* Atlanticism and more in terms of the implications of her participation in the EEC for French agricultural, industrial, and commercial interests. In a sense this means a partial return to earlier (pre-Gaullist) French concerns about British entry — concerns that emerged in the 1958 free-trade area negotiations. Then, many non-Gaullist French and many who were sympathetic to the idea of Anglo-French partnership stood firmly against British efforts to change the nature of the EEC or to diminish the agricultural, industrial, and trading advantages that French negotiators had won in the elaboration of the Treaty of Rome. What Britain needs most (concessions on the common agricultural policy) France is least willing and able to give. As far as Britain is concerned, the difference between de Gaulle and his successors may well be only that the latter were willing to negotiate.

French policy toward West Germany also has evolved with the devaluation of grand designs in favor of more orthodox policies. This has in no way impaired the policy of reconciliation initiated under the Fourth Republic and cultivated by de Gaulle; what it has done is to modify the nature of that reconciliation. De Gaulle had sought to mobilize German diplomacy in support of his grand design and had intended the 1963 treaty of friendship between the two countries to be the symbol of a special or privileged relationship. In the view of the current regime, as Chaban-Delmas explained to the National Assembly "[the] treaty of friendship with Germany will continue to occupy an exemplary place. When I say exemplary, I do not mean exclusive."[28] Hence, the close relations between the two countries were to be maintained but generalized. France has dropped earlier efforts to wean Bonn from Washington and to weaken Germany's links with the Atlantic alliance — in fact, France has given support to the *Ostpolitik* of the Brandt government. And there is little evidence that Paris still considers herself the West's special envoy to Eastern Europe and the Soviet Union or a surrogate for German interests.

There is, on the other hand, much speculation that the growing assertiveness of German policy and the evident disparity between the two countries in the economic sector may lead Paris to seek a rapprochement with London and to modify her hard line on economic matters to facilitate British entry into Europe. We noted earlier the inclination

[28] *Ambassade de France, Service de Presse et d'Information,* Statement by Premier Jacques Chaban-Delmas before the National Assembly on June 20, 1969.

of the Pompidou government to stress economic interests in assessing the British candidacy, but it cannot be ruled out that France might be willing to pay something in economic terms to secure a political counter-weight against Germany in the European Communities. Whether this will materialize depends on whether Franco-British political interests are more convergent or identical than are Anglo-German political interests. Currently, Bonn, anxious to secure maximum Western support for her Eastern policy, has tended to support France on most of the issues affecting the European Communities. A complicating but presently muted question is the defense of Western Europe and the matter of control over nuclear decision-making. Neither France nor Britain show any inclination to dispose of their nuclear forces or to create a European structure in which West Germany would gain an influential voice in nuclear strategy and policy-making. For the present the post de Gaulle regime regards French nuclear superiority over Germany as offering Paris a hold over Bonn and a continuing, if diminished, influence over German policy.

In the last analysis, we are too close to the transition from de Gaulle to his successors to reach definitive conclusions on the magnitude of change in the realm of foreign policy. Indeed, if we resort to the categories of continuity and change then we must recognize the very flexibility of de Gaulle's own foreign policy and the adjustments to *les événements* which took place in de Gaulle's last year in office — amelioration of relations with the United States, the overture to Great Britain, the revision of policy on nuclear strategy. The pattern that appears to be emerging under Pompidou is not a reversal of the objective of maximizing France's possibilities at the level of international policy at the least cost to the nation in terms of the continuity of France *qua* France, but rather a greater willingness to give up a limited amount of autonomy or sovereignty in order to secure France's economic interests and development. The main concern of the present French regime, dramatized by the events of May 1968, is to turn France into a modern industrial society and state. The precedence of domestic and economic concerns does not spell the end of aspirations to ensure France an important and perhaps leading role in Europe or the Atlantic world or beyond, but rather a pruning of ambition to a scale more commensurate with French resources and capabilities. France has not, as we have seen, postulated the demise of the nation-state; the thrust remains toward cooperation of national governments, but economic integration no longer appears to be equated with the loss of independence. More profound change may well have to await the arrival in power of a new generation.

10

Legitimacy, Governmental Performance, and Stability

The Legitimacy of the Fifth Republic

The constitution which de Gaulle built has survived the builder's passing, but for how long? How firm are the foundations of what once was described as de Gaulle's Republic?[1] One important indicator is the extent to which the citizenry believes the Fifth Republic to be the legitimate, the proper governmental form for France.

Although the degree of legitimacy which a population attributes to its form of government is difficult to measure directly, the evidence from opinion polls suggests that the Fifth Republic is at least more highly regarded than its predecessor. In April 1962, 59 percent of all respondents in a national survey considered the governmental stability of the Fifth Republic to be a decided advantage, as against 15 percent who thought it a disadvantage.[2] In the fall of the same year, 33 percent of all respondents declared the institutions of the Fifth Republic "better" than those of the Fourth Republic, while 31 percent found them "approximately equal" and 13 percent "worse."[3] In a survey conducted in January 1958, in which respondents were asked to compare the governing of France with that of other countries, 39 percent of the respondents felt that Great Britain was better governed, 58 percent the United States, 52 percent West Germany, and 31 percent the Soviet

---

[1] Two of the early books on the Fifth Republic are entitled *De Gaulle's Republic*, by Philip Williams and Martin Harrison (London: Longman's, 1960), and *The De Gaulle Republic*, by Roy Macridis and Bernard Brown (Homewood, Ill.: Dorsey, 1960).

[2] *Sondages*, 1963, No. 2, "La Vie politique de mai 1961 à septembre 1963," p. 85.

[3] *Ibid.*, p. 86.

Union. When the question was repeated in a survey of January 1965, the numbers who felt that other countries were better governed had dropped to 14 percent for Great Britain, 30 percent for the United States, 21 percent for West Germany, and 15 percent for the Soviet Union.[4]

Popular approval of direct election of the president is much more universal. Since the old parties joined to wage war on de Gaulle over this reform in October 1962, popular approval of the change has increased from 46 percent "yes" votes (out of all registered voters) in the fall of 1962 to 74 percent approval in a poll of May 1964 — including 61 percent of all Communist respondents and 70 percent of Socialist respondents — to 78 percent approval in a poll of November 1965.[5]

Although the old "political class" remains largely aloof from the Fifth Republic, opposition leaders like François Mitterrand, Alain Poher, and Guy Mollet seem prepared to accept the institutions of the Fifth Republic, on condition that the constitutional powers of Parliament be interpreted more generously and those of the president more restrictively. A series of attitude surveys since 1962 indicate that French public opinion also tends to favor a modification of the balance of institutional power in favor of Parliament.[6]

What is the basis for this apparent acceptance of the Fifth Republic? Does acceptance amount to legitimacy in this case? In search of clues to these puzzles, one must examine the means by which governments generally achieve legitimacy. Max Weber, the great German sociologist, suggested three primary bases of political legitimacy: tradition, legality, and charisma.[7] A political leader may be viewed as the legitimate authority because his family has always ruled, because he has been elected in accordance with the law, or because he has powers of personality which inspire belief and obedience. The contemporary social scientist might add at least two more bases of legitimacy: ideology and governmental effectiveness. Let us examine the relative contribu-

[4] *Sondages,* 1966, No. 1, p. 40.

[5] *Sondages,* 1964, No. 3, "La Vie politique d'octobre 1963 à octobre 1964," p. 13; and *Sondages,* 1965, No. 4, Michel Brulé, "Le Français et le mandat présidentiel," p. 44.

[6] For example, in an IFOP survey conducted in November 1968, 36 percent of all respondents favored a more important role for Parliament, as compared to 32 percent who were satisfied with its present role, 4 percent who favored a less important role, and 28 percent who offered no opinion. Comparable responses for the role of the president were 11 percent (more important), 49 percent (same role), 25 percent (less important), and 15 percent (no answer). *Sondages,* 1969, Nos. 1 and 2, p. 32.

[7] Max Weber, "Politics as a Vocation," in Hans Gerth and C. Wright Mills, eds., *From Max Weber: Essays in Sociology* (New York: Oxford University Press Galaxy Book, 1958), especially pp. 78–80.

tion of each of these possible sources to the legitimacy of the Fifth Republic.

As we have noted, political traditions in France tend to be divisive. Apart from the fact that it has the form of a republic, the current government can find little support from tradition, far less, certainly, than can the government of Great Britain. The Fifth Republic's link to the tradition of strong executive leadership may endear it to certain Frenchmen of the Right; but that link is cause for alarm among republicans who view the National Assembly as the only rightful interpreter of popular sovereignty. In any case, the tradition of strong executive leadership in time of crisis is one which may have facilitated acceptance of the Fifth Republic in the early years; it ceases to be relevant once the crisis has ended.

Legality is equally uncertain as a basis for legitimacy in contemporary France. At the outset, by 1958 public opinion had turned so massively against the Fourth Republic that even governments selected in scrupulously legal fashion enjoyed little sense of legitimacy.[8] Among those for whom republican legality is still important, it is difficult to forget that de Gaulle was accepted as prime minister by the National Assembly only because of an army revolt, which certain Gaullists had encouraged.[9]

Once in office, de Gaulle inhibited the development of legitimacy through legality by twisting his own constitution to serve his purposes. His refusal to call Parliament into special session upon its request in March 1960 and his bypass of Parliament in the constitutional amendment of October 1962 are two striking examples. The constitution may yet acquire the kind of sanctity which helps to legitimize political leadership in most stable democracies; but it will take long years of scrupulous adherence to constitutional legality to overcome a legacy of partisan manipulation, which antedates the Fifth Republic.

Charisma cannot be dismissed so easily. Had de Gaulle lacked charismatic appeal there would have been no Gaullist Republic. There is no need to re-examine the nature and sources of de Gaulle's charisma.[10] Suffice it to say that he was a man who inspired trust at a time when the majority of Frenchmen felt a need for firm political leadership. In repeated opinion polls, an average of some 60 percent of the respondents declared themselves satisfied with de Gaulle as president, while some 30 percent felt dissatisfied, and the remainder offered no opinion. When the Republic was threatened by military indiscipline or revolt, as

[8] See above, Ch. 6.

[9] On the role of Gaullists in the May 1958 revolt, see Ambler, *Soldiers Against the State,* pp. 258–261, 264.

[10] See Ch. 5, above.

in the barricades crisis of January 1960 and the attempted putsch of April 1961, his support level rose to over 70 percent — an amazing level for a politically divided society.[11]

Charisma is by nature a personal and usually an ephemeral phenomenon. It has been institutionalized in a limited way in the papacy of the Catholic Church and in the leadership of some Communist societies. Unlike the French presidency, these are cases where there is a creed or doctrine which requires definitive interpretation by someone. Georges Pompidou is respected as an able man, but not revered as was his prophet-predecessor. And yet the authority of the presidency seems unimpaired.

The fourth basis of legitimacy — ideology — is of considerable importance in Communist societies, and in some of the new nations of Africa and Asia, but is of very limited significance in the French Fifth Republic. De Gaulle's vision of French greatness was too vague and his policies too pragmatic to qualify him as a prophet of a systematic ideology. Gaullism's closest approximation to systematic ideology is its appeal to French nationalism. That theme is less stridently proclaimed now that de Gaulle is no longer in command.

With the fading of charisma in French politics, the primary source of legitimacy for the Fifth Republic appears to be governmental effectiveness. The Fifth Republic has produced governmental stability. It has increased respect for France in international affairs. In general the years since 1958 have been prosperous ones for the French economy. This performance is impressive for citizens who recall with dissatisfaction the record of the Fourth Republic. The continued voting strength of the Gaullists undoubtedly reflects widespread approval of their performance. A national attitude survey conducted in 1967 found that, with the exception of the Communists, French respondents of all party persuasions selected the Gaullist UNR (now the UDR) as the party that struggles most for both governmental stability and for economic development. Moreover, these were two of the four issues which the respondents judged to be most important.[12]

Effectiveness in itself is usually inadequate to create legitimacy. A colonial government in the mid-twentieth century, no matter how effective it might have been in the performance of its duties, could not persuade native nationalists that it had a legitimate right to rule. Military dictatorships, even when effective, are likely to have trouble estab-

---

[11] *Sondages,* 1969, Nos. 1 and 2, p. 19.

[12] Pierce and Barnes, "Public Opinion and Political Preferences in France and Italy,", p. 24. The other two issues were educational development and equitable distribution of income, on both of which most respondents felt their own preferred party "struggled most."

lishing their legitimacy unless they are supported as well by ideology or charisma. In the short run, governmental effectiveness creates no more than instrumental loyalties: the population may tolerate a set of leaders, but only so long as these leaders continue to solve the major problems of the nation. A government based upon nothing deeper than respect for effectiveness may go under in the first crisis, whether it be internal violence or economic depression. Governments with deeper roots, like those of Great Britain, the United States, and the smaller democracies of Europe and the Commonwealth, are better able to ride out crises like the Great Depression. In the long run an effective government may inspire more abiding loyalties. A government which is created as a practical response to immediate problems (like the American federal government, for example) eventually may come to be considered the traditional and legitimate political form. Such a development seems to be underway in the Federal Republic of Germany, which has been spared the economic and political crises which destroyed the Weimar Republic.

The transformation of instrumental loyalties into genuine legitimacy is most likely to take place when all the major elements within a society feel that their needs are being understood and at least partially met by the decision-makers. The great majority of citizens must feel that the constitution is not the arm of a single party, class, or religious community, but a servant of all the people. The Fifth Republic, which was created by the Gaullists and which always has been dominated by them, has not yet achieved this kind of constitutional consensus. The IFOP survey of January 1965, referred to above, found that French attitudes toward the present political regime were closely related to attitudes toward de Gaulle. Of those who declared themselves "very satisfied" with de Gaulle's performance as president, 43 percent felt Britain was worse governed than France. Of those who were "very dissatisfied" with de Gaulle as president, only 9 percent felt Britain to be worse governed.[13]

In France, as in most other modern democracies, efficiency and vigor in the management of governmental affairs have been achieved through reliance upon strong executive leadership, at the expense of parliamentary power. If efficiency is to breed legitimacy, it must neither block the access of major groups in society to the organs of government, nor inhibit the responsiveness of government to their demands. When the major channels of communication — Parliament, parties, and interest groups — are shut off, the danger is that discontent will build to crisis proportions. Such was the case in May 1968.

[13] *Sondages*, 1966, No. 1, p. 40.

From the point of view of legitimation of the Fifth Republic, the problem seems to be to increase the responsiveness of the political system to citizen demands without destroying its effectiveness. This would appear to require a more important role for Parliament and for political parties. The Constitution of 1958 does not require presidential domination of the policy-making process. On the contrary, the institutions for which it provides are extremely flexible. Should the president wish, or should he lack Pompidou's political strength, the prime minister might play a more independent role. It is quite possible that a future election will return a Parliament which lacks a stable majority, or whose majority is openly hostile to the president (whose term, it must be remembered, is a long seven years). In such a case, no provision in the constitution, save the article on temporary emergency powers, would allow the president to force through legislation or to maintain an unpopular prime minister in office against Parliament's will. Despite its directly elected president, the Constitution of the Fifth Republic provides no guarantee of stable government. The problem, restated in institutional terms, is a traditional one in French politics: how to balance the powers of the executive and legislative branches without destroying either effective leadership or representative democracy.

Legitimacy and the Party System

If the legitimation of the Fifth Republic is linked to governmental effectiveness, and if effectiveness is dependent upon the continued existence of stable parliamentary majorities, one key to the future of French politics clearly is the party system. Contrary to the impatient predictions of its critics, the Gaullist coalition did not break up after the passing of its creator and arbiter. Despite their factional quarrels based upon personalities and policies, the Gaullists have a number of critical advantages. The direct election of the president provides at least a periodical incentive to form political coalitions, as the presidential election of June 1969 seems to have encouraged the unification of the Gaullists behind Georges Pompidou. As government parties, the Union of Democrats for the Republic and the other Gaullist parties have a natural attraction for ambitious politicians who hope one day to occupy a minister's chair. The restive Gaullist deputy who is tempted to vote against his party on an important bill may be restrained by the recognition that such behavior might weaken his chances for higher office; moreover, if his example is followed, a split in the movement could mean a loss of the Gaullist monopoly over government positions.

Of all the advantages which the Gaullists enjoy, the most important is the inability of the opposition parties to unite. A former Gaullist

Minister of Education, Alain Peyrefitte, told a Gaullist meeting in September 1970 that "we can be in power for thirty years if we don't do anything stupid."[14] A few days later, in a National Assembly by-election in Bordeaux, Prime Minister Jacques Chaban-Delmas captured almost 64 percent of the vote. The remaining votes were dispersed among nine rival candidates, including the would-be leader of the non-Communist Left, Jean-Jacques Servan-Schreiber. So long as the opposition remains factionalized and unable to offer more than the prospect of a flimsy coalition government, the Gaullists will benefit from the citizenry's reluctance to return to the bad old days of Fourth Republican politics.

Beneficial as it may be to the Gaullists in the short run, the absence of an effective opposition poses two problems for democracy in France. First, it deprives the Gaullists and the public of the kind of systematic, constructive criticism which encourages governments to be responsible and responsive in Britain and West Germany. Second, to re-emphasize a point mentioned earlier, where there is no turnover of governing parties, supporters of the opposition tend to look upon the constitution as a partisan instrument. The West German political system took an important step in the direction of greater legitimacy when, in October 1969, Socialist Willy Brandt became Chancellor and the Christian Democratic Party entered the opposition for the first time since the war. When parties alternate in governmental leadership, it is easier for the disgruntled citizen to distinguish between the current administration, which he may detest, and the institutions of government, which he knows can be made to serve other parties and other policies. Should the Gaullists fulfill Peyrefitte's prediction of another three decades of rule, it will be more difficult to achieve the broad popular consensus in support of the constitution which democratic France has always lacked. Lord Balfour, a British Conservative Prime Minister of the first decade of the twentieth century, once remarked that the English were so agreed upon fundamentals that they could afford to bicker about particulars. Until Frenchmen can say the same with respect to their political institutions, political conflict over the particulars of policy will forever risk escalation into a constitutional crisis.

Resistance to Change and Internal Conflict

There is, of course, no pat formula for governmental effectiveness. In a rapidly changing society like modern France, government continually must address itself to new demands and new problems, whether

---

[14] As quoted in the *New York Times,* September 23, 1970.

it be a question of easing the adaptation of French farmers to the Common Market or of satisfying the demand of millions of parents for more education for their children. France is a society caught up in economic "modernization"; yet, as always, it is a society which resists challenges to the habitual way of doing things. "Democratize education? Of course," remark the secondary school teachers; "but don't tamper with the elitist quality of the lycée." "Modernize agriculture? It must be done," add the farmers; "but above all the small family farmer must be protected." "Rationalize the economy? Why not?" the shopkeepers might argue; "but to tax small business at the same rate as chain stores would be an outrageous violation of our rights." And so it goes, with institution after institution battling to defend its traditional privileges. Any government which hopes to satisfy popular expectations of an expanding economy must promote the reform of the old institutions, while at the same time responding as well as possible to the needs of the people who will be affected.

Resistance to change is only one of the barriers to governmental effectiveness and hence to political legitimacy in France. Another, of even greater importance, is the relatively high level of conflict among social and political groups in French society. The higher the level of internal conflict, the more difficult it is for a democratic government to find institutions and policies which will be acceptable to all. If one accepts the "end of ideology" interpretation of contemporary Western European politics, the level of ideological conflict in France ought to be on the decline.[15] In brief, the argument holds that industrialization and urbanization create affluence, greater social mobility, a blurring of class distinctions, a weakening of traditional cleavages, a decline in the importance of dogmatic ideologies, and hence a lessening of political conflict. The result is great political stability and consensus, built upon a common desire to share in the wealth of what the French call the "consumer's society." Conflict will remain, but it will be based upon interests more than upon principles. This interpretation seems to fit postwar German and British politics fairly well. How well does it fit the French case? Let us examine some of the more obvious pieces of evidence.

Despite its reputation, France is a country which has accepted change. For fifty years, economists have bemoaned the backwardness and inefficiency of the French economy. And yet with rapid spurts of energy, the French have managed well enough to keep up with the level

[15] For an introduction to the end of ideology debate, see the exchange between Joseph LaPalombara and Seymour Martin Lipset in the *American Political Science Review,* LX: 1 (March 1966), pp. 5–11, 110–111. On the application of this thesis to France, see Waterman, *Political Change in Contemporary France.*

of prosperity of most other European countries. They have willingly accepted the challenge of tariff-free competition with producers in other Common Market countries. In the political sphere, the rise of the Gaullists is evidence that broad, "catch-all" coalitions are possible in France. In many respects France is closer than ever before to being a consensual society. Religion is less of a political issue than at any time since the creation of the Third Republic. Decolonization is all but complete. Cold war tensions have eased considerably. Student radicals who seek revolutionary change in French society have found few supporters outside the universities. The radical Right has dwindled to insignificance since the end of the Algerian war. In comparison with the 1930's, and even the 1950's, the issues which now divide Frenchmen — particularly the issue of who is to get how much of the national income — are simpler and more susceptible to compromise solutions. In the terminology of Joseph LaPalombara and Myron Weiner, the "load" on the French political system has been reduced.[16] The Fifth Republic drags no albatross comparable to the Fourth Republic's colonial wars.

And yet, this is the Republic which was shaken to its roots by the strikes and demonstrations of May 1968. This is a republic so highly centralized that disorder in Paris may threaten the government of all of France. This is a society which is still capable of rebellion against governmental authority, one in which the alienation of a large proportion of the working class constitutes a permanent threat to any government which appears to be insensitive to the rising expectations of the working man. This is a country in which a communist party, whose commitment to constitutional democracy is by no means certain, retains the loyalty of over a fifth of the French electorate. This is a society in which thousands of students and intellectuals look upon the "consumer's society" as a symbol of materialism and inequality. This is a society in which industrialization is threatening the economic survival of small farmers, small merchants, and workers in depressed areas — building up frustrations which one day could make these citizens recruits for a radical movement.

France's present political institutions are as well established as any she has had since the Revolution. Whether they will continue to perform effectively and accrue legitimacy depends in good part upon the intensity of future political conflict. That, in turn, depends not only upon the behavior of opposition parties and groups, but also upon the skill of governmental leaders in integrating marginal groups — espe-

---

[16] LaPalombara and Weiner, *Political Parties and Political Development,* pp. 3–42.

cially industrial workers — into the decision-making process. Technical efficiency is not enough. The citizen support which a democracy needs in the long run requires also that the major groups in society — workers and farmers among them — feel that they have access to the institutions of government and receive fair treatment from them. In achieving such a goal, the Gaullists must overcome their founder's legacy of disdain for "intermediary groups," as well as his conception of the national interest as a truth visible only to those who hold themselves aloof from the quarrels of selfish interests.[17]

[17] For a cogent and critical commentary upon the Gaullist view of national interest see François Goguel (a Gaullist Secretary General of the Senate as well as an eminent political scientist) and Alfred Grosser, *La Politique en France,* pp. 247–248.

A SELECTED BIBLIOGRAPHY

For the student interested in examining particular aspects of the French political system in greater detail, the footnotes scattered throughout this book will offer guidance. Only a few books of general interest, in English, will be mentioned here.

One of the best of several good general histories is Gordon Wright's *France in Modern Times, 1760 to the Present* (Rand McNally, 1960). David Thomson, in his *Democracy in France since 1870* (5th edition, Oxford University Press, 1969), offers an overview of France in the last one hundred years along with a perceptive analysis of the political and social bases of contemporary French politics. Alexis de Tocqueville's classic *The Old Regime and the Revolution* (Doubleday Anchor, 1955) is still valuable for insights into the origins of some durable features of French society.

The most comprehensive overview of contemporary French society, by a journalist who catches the flavor of modern France, is John Ardagh's *The New French Revolution: A Social and Economic Study of France, 1945–1968* (Harper Colophon, 1968). For some stimulating interpretations of French economic, social, and political behavior, by experts in their fields, see the essays edited by Stanley Hoffmann, *In Search of France* (Harper Torchbook, 1963). The bureaucratic aspects of French society are analyzed and explained by a sociologist, Michel Crozier, whose theories recently have made their way into the speeches of Prime Minister Jacques Chaban-Delmas. See Crozier's *The Bureaucratic Phenomenon* (University of Chicago Press, 1964). The student of French political culture will find much which is still of value in a book written over four decades ago: André Siegfried's *France: A Study in Nationality* (Yale University Press, 1930).

The politics of the Fourth Republic have been discussed masterfully and in detail by Philip Williams in *Crisis and Compromise* (Doubleday Anchor, 1966). Nathan Leites' *On the Game of Politics in France* (Stanford University Press, 1959) analyzes French political opportunism in a portrait of the Fourth Republic which is stimulating but caricatured. For a corrective, see *Parliament, Parties, and Society in France, 1946–1958* (St. Martin's, 1967) by Duncan MacRae, Jr., who draws significant conclusions from a rigorous, statistical analysis of parliamentary roll call votes.

The origins of the Fifth Republic are examined by Roy Macridis and Bernard Brown in *The De Gaulle Republic* (Dorsey, 1960), and by

Philip Williams and Martin Harrison in *De Gaulle's Republic* (Longman's, 1960). De Gaulle himself is best understood through his own writings, notably *The Edge of the Sword* (Criterion Books, 1960) and *The Complete War Memoirs of Charles de Gaulle* (Simon and Schuster, A Clarion Book, 1968). The political style of de Gaulle and the background of his chief lieutenants are described in witty and perceptive fashion by a political commentator for *Le Monde,* Pierre Viansson-Ponté, in *The King and His Court* (Houghton Mifflin, 1964). Henry Ehrmann offers an excellent overview of the Fifth Republic, organizing his material around political functions, in *Politics in France* (Little, Brown, 1968).

Peter Campbell has explored the complex subject of *French Electoral Systems* (2nd edition, Faber, 1966). The political history of recent elections is examined in a collection of articles in Philip Williams' *French Politicians and Elections, 1951–1969* (Cambridge University Press, 1970). Among books in English on French political parties and movements are François Fejtö, *The French Communist Party and the Crisis of International Communism* (M. I. T. Press, 1967); George Lichtheim, *Marxism in Modern France* (Columbia University Press, 1966); René Rémond, *The Right Wing in France* (University of Pennsylvania Press, 1966); Francis de Tarr, *The French Radical Party* (Oxford University Press, 1961); and Harvey G. Simmons, *French Socialists in Search of a Role, 1956–1967* (Cornell University Press, 1970).

The literature in English on the governmental institutions of the Fifth Republic is still very limited. "The French Constitution of 1958" is the subject of two fine articles by Stanley Hoffmann and Nicholas Wahl in the *American Political Science Review of 1959.* Philip Williams' *The French Parliament* (Allen and Unwin, 1968) is sound, but brief. F. Ridley and J. Blondel are authors of a reliable and comprehensive book on *Public Administration in France* (Barnes and Noble, 1964). The politics of French local government, especially in the smaller communes, are analyzed with skill and originality in Mark Kesselman's *The Ambiguous Consensus* (Knopf, 1967).

THE FRENCH CONSTITUTION OF 1958*

Preamble

The French people hereby solemnly proclaims its attachment to the Rights of Man and the principles of national sovereignty as defined by the Declaration of 1789, reaffirmed and complemented by the Preamble of the Constitution of 1946. . . .

Title I: On Sovereignty

Article 2

France is a Republic, indivisible, secular, democratic and social. It shall ensure the equality of all citizens before the law, without distinction of origin, race or religion. It shall respect all beliefs.

The national emblem is the tricolor flag, blue, white and red.

The national anthem is the "Marseillaise."

The motto of the Republic is "Liberty, Equality, Fraternity."

Its principle is government of the people, by the people and for the people.

Article 3

National sovereignty belongs to the people, which shall exercise this sovereignty through its representatives and by means of referendums.

No section of the people, nor any individual, may attribute to themselves or himself the exercise thereof.

Suffrage may be direct or indirect under the conditions stipulated by the Constitution. It shall always be universal, equal and secret.

All French citizens of both sexes who have reached their majority and who enjoy civil and political rights may vote under the conditions to be determined by law.

Article 4

Political parties and groups shall be instrumental in the expression of the suffrage. They shall be formed freely and shall carry on their activi-

* The articles dealing with the French Community as well as others of secondary importance have been deleted in this abridgement.

ties freely. They must respect the principles of national sovereignty and democracy.

Title II: The President of the Republic

Article 5

The President of the Republic shall see that the Constitution is respected. He shall ensure, by his arbitration, the regular functioning of the governmental authorities, as well as the continuance of the State.

He shall be the guarantor of national independence, of the integrity of the territory, and of respect for Community agreements and treaties.

Article 6*

The President of the Republic shall be elected for seven years by direct universal suffrage.

The procedures implementing the present article shall be determined by an organic law.

Article 7*

The President of the Republic shall be elected by an absolute majority of the votes cast. If this is not obtained on the first ballot, there shall be a second ballot on the second Sunday following. Only the two candidates who have received the greatest number of votes on the first ballot shall present themselves, taking into account the possible withdrawal of more favored candidates.

The voting shall begin at the formal summons of the Government.

The election of the new President shall take place twenty days at least and thirty-five days at the most before the expiration of the powers of the President in office.

In the event that the Presidency of the Republic has been vacated, for any cause whatsoever, or impeded in its functioning as officially noted by the Constitutional Council, to which the matter has been referred by the Government, and which shall rule by an absolute majority of its members, the functions of the President of the Republic, with the exception of those provided for by Articles 11 and 12 below, shall be temporarily exercised by the President of the Senate and, if the latter is in his turn impeded in the exercise of these functions, by the Government.

*[Adopted by referendum on October 28, 1962.]

In the case of a vacancy, or when the impediment is declared definitive by the Constitutional Council, the voting for the election of a new President shall take place, except in case of emergency officially noted by the Constitutional Council, twenty days at the least and thirty-five days at the most after the beginning of the vacancy or the declaration of the definitive character of the impediment.

There may be no application of either Articles 49 and 50 or of Articles 89 of the Constitution during the vacancy of the Presidency of the Republic or during the period that elapses between the declaration of the definitive character of the impediment of the President of the Republic and the election of his successor.

Article 8

The President of the Republic shall appoint the Prime Minister. He shall terminate the functions of the Prime Minister when the latter presents the resignation of the Government.

On the proposal of the Prime Minister, he shall appoint the other members of the Government and shall terminate their functions.

Article 9

The President of the Republic shall preside over the Council of Ministers.

Article 10

The President of the Republic shall promulgate the laws within fifteen days following the transmission to the Government of the finally adopted law.

He may, before the expiration of this time limit, ask Parliament for a reconsideration of the law or of certain of its articles. This reconsideration may not be refused.

Article 11

The President of the Republic, on the proposal of the Government during [Parliamentary] sessions, or on joint motion of the two assemblies, published in the *Journal Officiel,* may submit to referendum any bill dealing with the organization of the government authorities, entailing approval of a Community agreement, or providing for authorization to ratify a treaty that, without being contrary to the Constitution, might affect the functioning of [existing] institutions.

When the referendum decides in favor of the bill, the Parliament of the Republic shall promulgate it within the time limit stipulated in the preceding article.

Article 12

The President of the Republic may, after consultation with the Prime Minister and the Presidents of the assemblies, declare the dissolution of the National Assembly.

General elections shall take place twenty days at the least and forty days at the most after the dissolution.

The National Assembly shall convene by right on the second Thursday following its election. If this meeting takes place between the periods provided for ordinary sessions, a session shall, by right, be held for a fifteen-day period.

There may be no further dissolution within a year following these elections. . . .

Article 16

When the institutions of the Republic, the independence of the nation, the integrity of its territory or the fulfillment of its international commitments are threatened in a grave and immediate manner and when the regular functioning of the constitutional governmental authorities is interrupted, the President of the Republic shall take the measures commanded by these circumstances, after official consultation with the Prime Minister, the Presidents of the assemblies and the Constitutional Council.

He shall inform the nation of these measures in a message.

These measures must be prompted by the desire to ensure to the constitutional governmental authorities, in the shortest possible time, the means of fulfilling their assigned functions. The Constitutional Council shall be consulted with regard to such measures.

Parliament shall meet by right.

The National Assembly may not be dissolved during the exercise of emergency powers [by the President]. . . .

Title III: The Government

Article 20

The Government shall determine and direct the policy of the nation.

It shall have at its disposal the administration and the armed forces.

It shall be responsible to Parliament under the conditions and according to the procedures stipulated in Articles 49 and 50.

Article 21

The Prime Minister shall direct the operation of the Government. He shall be responsible for national defense. He shall ensure the execution of the laws. Subject to the provisions of Article 13, he shall have regulatory powers and shall make appointments to civil and military posts.

He may delegate certain of his powers to the ministers.

He shall replace, should the occasion arise, the President of the Republic as chairman of the councils and committees provided for under Article 15.

He may, in exceptional instances, replace him as chairman of a meeting of the Council of Ministers by virtue of an explicit delegation and for a specific agenda.

Article 22

The acts of the Prime Minister shall be countersigned, when circumstances so require, by the ministers responsible for their execution.

Article 23

The office of member of the Government shall be incompatible with the exercise of any Parliamentary mandate, with the holding of any office at the national level in business, professional or labor organizations, and with any public employment or professional activity.

An organic law shall determine the conditions under which the holders of such mandates, functions or employments shall be replaced. . . .

Title IV: The Parliament

Article 24

The Parliament shall comprise the National Assembly and the Senate.

The deputies to the National Assembly shall be elected by direct suffrage.

The Senate shall be elected by indirect suffrage. It shall ensure the representation of the territorial units of the Republic. Frenchmen living outside France shall be represented in the Senate. . . .

Article 28*

Parliament shall convene, by right, in two ordinary sessions a year. The first session shall begin on October 2; it shall last eighty days.

The second session shall open on April 2; it may not last longer than ninety days.

If October 2 or April 2 is a holiday, the session shall begin on the first working day following.

Article 29

Parliament shall convene in extraordinary session at the request of the Prime Minister, or of the majority of the members comprising the National Assembly, to consider a specific agenda.

When an extraordinary session is held at the request of the members of the National Assembly, the closure decree shall take effect as soon as the Parliament has exhausted the agenda for which it was called, and at the latest twelve days from the date of its meeting.

Only the Prime Minister may ask for a new session before the end of the month following the closure decree.

Article 30

Apart from cases in which Parliament meets by right, extraordinary sessions shall be opened and closed by decree of the President of the Republic. . . .

Title V: On Relations Between Parliament and the Government

Article 34

All laws shall be passed by Parliament.

Laws shall establish the regulations concerning:

— civil rights and the fundamental guarantees granted to the citizens for the exercise of their public liberties; the obligations imposed by the national defense upon the persons and property of citizens;

— nationality, status and legal capacity of persons, marriage contracts, inheritance and gifts;

— determination of crimes and misdemeanors as well as the penalties imposed therefor; criminal procedure; amnesty; the creation of new juridical systems and the status of magistrates;

* [Adopted by the two chambers of Parliament, meeting together in congress, December 30, 1963.]

— the basis, the rate and the methods of collecting taxes of all types; the issuance of currency.

Laws shall likewise determine the regulations concerning:

— the electoral system of the Parliamentary assemblies and the local assemblies;

— the establishment of categories of public institutions;

— the fundamental guarantees granted to civil and military personnel employed by the State;

— the nationalization of enterprises and the transfer of the property of enterprises from the public to the private sector.

Laws shall determine the fundamental principles of:

— the general organization of national defense;

— the free administration of local communities, the extent of their jurisdiction and their resources;

— education;

— property rights, civil and commercial obligations;

— legislation pertaining to employment, unions and social security.

The financial laws shall determine the financial resources and obligations of the State under the conditions and with the reservations to be provided by an organic law.

Laws pertaining to national planning shall determine the objectives of the economic and social action of the State.

The provisions of the present article may be developed in detail and amplified by an organic law.

Article 35

Parliament shall authorize the declaration of war.

Article 36

Martial law shall be decreed in a meeting of the Council of Ministers.

Its prorogation beyond twelve days may be authorized only by Parliament.

Article 37

Matters other than those that fall within the domain of law shall be of a regulatory character.

Legislative texts concerning these matters may be modified by decrees issued after consultation with the Council of State. Those legislative texts which may be passed after the present Constitution has become operative shall be modified by decree, only if the Constitutional

Council has stated that they have a regulatory character as defined in the preceding paragraph.

Article 38

The Government may, in order to carry out its program, ask Parliament to authorize it, for a limited period, to take through ordinances measures that are normally within the domain of law.

The ordinances shall be enacted in meetings of the Council of Ministers after consultation with the Council of State. They shall come into force upon their publication, but shall become null and void if the bill for their ratification is not submitted to Parliament before the date set by the enabling act.

At the expiration of the time limit referred to in the first paragraph of the present article, the ordinances may be modified only by law in those matters which are within the legislative domain. . . .

Article 40

Bills and amendments introduced by members of Parliament shall not be considered when their adoption would have as a consequence either a diminution of public financial resources, or the creation or increase of public expenditures.

Article 41

If it appears in the course of the legislative procedure that a Parliamentary bill or an amendment is not within the domain of law or is contrary to a delegation [of authority] granted by virtue of Article 38, the Government may declare its inadmissibility.

In case of disagreement between the Government and the President of the assembly concerned, the Constitutional Council, upon the request of either party, shall rule within a time limit of eight days. . . .

Article 44

Members of Parliament and of the Government shall have the right of amendment.

After the opening of the debate, the Government may oppose the examination of any amendment which has not previously been submitted to committee.

If the Government so requests, the assembly concerned shall decide, by a single vote, on all or part of the text under discussion, retaining only the amendments proposed or accepted by the Government.

Article 45

Every Government or Parliamentary bill shall be examined successively in the two assemblies of Parliament with a view to the adoption of an identical text.

When, as a result of disagreement between the two assemblies, it has become impossible to adopt a Government or Parliamentary bill after two readings by each assembly, or, if the Government has declared the matter urgent, after a single reading by each of them, the Prime Minister shall have the right to have a joint committee meet, composed of an equal number from both assemblies and instructed to offer for consideration a text on the matters still under discussion.

The text prepared by the joint committee may be submitted by the Government for approval of the two assemblies. No amendment shall be admissible except by agreement with the Government.

If the joint committee fails to approve a common text, or if this text is not adopted under the conditions set forth in the preceding paragraph, the Government may, after a new reading by the National Assembly and by the Senate, ask the National Assembly to rule definitively. In this case, the National Assembly may reconsider either the text prepared by the joint committee or the last text adopted [by the National Assembly], modified, when circumstances so require, by one or several of the amendments adopted by the Senate. . . .

Article 47

Parliament shall pass finance bills under the conditions to be stipulated by an organic law.

Should the National Assembly fail to reach a decision on first reading within a time limit of forty days after a bill has been filed, the Government shall refer it to the Senate, which must rule within a time limit of fifteen days. The procedure set forth in Article 45 shall then be followed.

Should Parliament fail to reach a decision within a time limit of seventy days, the provisions of the bill may be enforced by ordinance.

Should the finance bill establishing the resources and expenditures of a fiscal year not be filed in time for it to be promulgated before the beginning of that fiscal year, the Government shall immediately request Parliament for the authorization to collect the taxes and shall make available by decree the funds needed to meet the Government commitments already voted.

The time limits stipulated in the present article shall be suspended when Parliament is not in session.

The Audit Office shall assist Parliament and the Government in supervising the implementation of the finance laws.

Article 48

The discussion of the bills filed or agreed upon by the Government shall have priority on the agenda of the assemblies in the order set by the Government.

One meeting a week shall be reserved, by priority, for questions asked by members of Parliament and for answers by the Government.

Article 49

The Prime Minister, after deliberation by the Council of Ministers, may pledge the responsibility of the Government to the National Assembly with regard to the program of the Government, or with regard to a declaration of general policy, as the case may be.

The National Assembly may question the responsibility of the Government by the vote of a motion of censure. Such a motion shall be admissible only if it is signed by at least one tenth of the members of the National Assembly. The vote may only take place forty-eight hours after the motion has been filed; the only votes counted shall be those favorable to the motion of censure, which may be adopted only by a majority of the members comprising the Assembly. Should the motion of censure be rejected, its signatories may not introduce another motion in the course of the same session, except in the case provided for in the paragraph below.

The Prime Minister may, after deliberation by the Council of Ministers, pledge the Government's responsibility to the National Assembly on the vote of a text. In this case, the text shall be considered as adopted, unless a motion of censure, filed in the succeeding twenty-four hours, is voted under the conditions laid down in the previous paragraph.

The Prime Minister shall be entitled to ask the Senate for approval of a general policy declaration.

Article 50

When the National Assembly adopts a motion of censure, or when it disapproves the program or a declaration of general policy of the Government, the Prime Minister must submit the resignation of the Government to the President of the Republic. . . .

Title VII: The Constitutional Council

Article 56

The Constitutional Council shall consist of nine members, whose term of office shall last nine years and shall not be renewable. One third of the membership of the Constitutional Council shall be renewed every three years. Three of its members shall be appointed by the President of the Republic, three by the President of the National Assembly, three by the President of the Senate.

In addition to the nine members provided for above, former Presidents of the Republic shall be members ex officio for life of the Constitutional Council.

The President shall be appointed by the President of the Republic. He shall have the deciding vote in case of a tie. . . .

Article 58

The Constitutional Council shall ensure the regularity of the election of the President of the Republic.

It shall examine complaints and shall announce the results of the vote.

Article 59

The Constitutional Council shall rule, in the case of disagreement, on the regularity of the election of deputies and senators.

Article 60

The Constitutional Council shall ensure the regularity of referendum procedures and shall announce the results thereof.

Article 61

Organic laws, before their promulgation, and regulations of the Parliamentary assemblies, before they came into application, must be submitted to the Constitutional Council, which shall rule on their constitutionality.

To the same end, laws may be submitted to the Constitutional Council, before their promulgation, by the President of the Republic, the Prime Minister or the President of one or the other assembly.

In the cases provided for by the two preceding paragraphs, the Constitutional Council must make its ruling within a time limit of one month. Nevertheless, at the request of the Government, in case of emergency, this period shall be reduced to eight days.

In these same cases, referral to the Constitutional Council shall suspend the time limit for promulgation.

Article 62

A provision declared unconstitutional may not be promulgated or implemented.

The decisions of the Constitutional Council may not be appealed to any jurisdiction whatsoever. They must be recognized by the governmental authorities and by all administrative and juridical authorities. . . .

Title X: The Economic and Social Council

Article 70

The Economic and Social Council may . . . be consulted by the Government on any problem of an economic or social character of interest to the Republic or to the Community. Any plan, or any bill dealing with a plan, of an economic or social character shall be submitted to it for its advice. . . .

Title XIV: On Amendment

Article 89

The initiative for amending the Constitution shall belong both to the President of the Republic on the proposal of the Premier and to the members of Parliament.

The Government or Parliamentary bill for amendment must be passed by the two assemblies in identical terms. The amendment shall become definitive after approval by a referendum.

Nevertheless, the proposed amendment shall not be submitted to a referendum when the President of the Republic decides to submit it to Parliament convened in Congress; in this case, the proposed amendment shall be approved only if it is accepted by a three-fifths majority of the votes cast. The Secretariat of the Congress shall be that of the National Assembly.

No amendment procedure may be undertaken or followed when the integrity of the territory is in jeopardy.

The republican form of government shall not be subject to amendment.

INDEX